Women Drummers

Women Drummers

A History from Rock and Jazz to Blues and Country

ANGELA SMITH

ROWMAN & LITTLEFIELD
Lanham • Boulder • New York • Toronto • Plymouth, UK

Published by Rowman & Littlefield
4501 Forbes Boulevard, Suite 200, Lanham, Maryland 20706
www.rowman.com

10 Thornbury Road, Plymouth PL6 7PP, United Kingdom

British Library Cataloguing in Publication Information Available

Library of Congress Cataloging-in-Publication Data

Smith, Angela, 1945–, author.
Women drummers : a history from rock and jazz to blues and country / Angela Smith.
pages cm
Includes bibliographical references and index.
ISBN 978-0-8108-8834-0 (cloth : alk. paper) — ISBN 978-0-8108-8835-7 (ebook)
1. Women drummers (Musicians)—United States—Biography. 2. Drummers (Musicians)—United States—Biography. 3. Women musicians—United States—Biography. 4. Musicians—United States—Biography. I. Title.
ML385.S592 2014
786.9'16409252—dc23
[B] 2013043304

∞™ The paper used in this publication meets the minimum requirements of American National Standard for Information Sciences—Permanence of Paper for Printed Library Materials, ANSI/NISO Z39.48-1992.

Printed in the United States of America

To my husband, Charles,
and the original "hep" girl, Viola Smith

Contents

Permissions

A good faith effort was made to obtain permissions from everyone who provided information through interviews and for use of quotes from printed material for this book. Permissions and content approvals were granted by or requested from the following:

Mindy Seegal Abovitz
Meghan Aube
Carla Azar
Alessandra Belloni
Ginger Bianco
Karen Biller
Carla DeSantis Black
Cindy Blackman
Rachel Blumberg
Tanya Bolden
Terri Lyne Carrington
Meytal Cohen
Cora Coleman-Dunham
Linda Dahl
Alice de Buhr
Carol Dierking
Debra Dobkin
Dottie Dodgion
Sheila E.
Wayne Enstice
Stefanie Eulinberg
Rachel Fuhrer
Daniel Glass
Evelyn Glennie
Bobbye Jean Hall
Julie Hill
Jenny Jones
Michelle Josef
Honey Lantree
Jen Ledger
Crissy Lee
Terri Lord
Sara Lund
Samantha Maloney
Sherrie Maricle
Sara McCabe
Linda McDonald
Ikue Mori
Stella Mozgawa
Lisa Pankratz
Debbi Peterson
Roxy Petrucci

Sally Placksin
Dee Plakas
Shauney "Baby" Recke
Layne Redmond
Dawn Richardson
Paloma "Palmolive" Romero
Piero Scaruffi
Patty Schemel
Gina Schock
Poni Silver
Viola Smith
Helene Stapinski
Dena Tauriello
Teresa Taylor
Kopana Terry
Kim Thompson
Linda Tillery
Lynn Perko Truell
Maureen "Moe" Tucker
Sherrie Tucker
Alicia Warrington
Janet Weiss
Meg White
Jyn Yates

Acknowledgments

Women drummers rock! And thanks to a universe full of surprises, I was the lucky one given the chance to write about them. Over the course of this project, I met and interviewed over fifty top women drummers, many of them pioneers from more than eight decades ago who led the way for others. They are featured in this book with some 160 women who have won national and international acclaim for their inroads in the still male-dominated drumming world of popular music. Some are no longer with us or have given up their drum kits for other pursuits. But others are still showing the world—through recordings, live performance, and YouTube videos—the amazing things they can do with four limbs and a pair of drum sticks. My hope is that this book will inspire readers to learn more about them—and maybe even take a shot at becoming rockin' drummers themselves.

The idea for this book was inspired by Bennett Graff, my editor at Scarecrow Press, who reminded me in an e-mail one day of the too often ignored drumming skills of the late Karen Carpenter. Because of him, I was able to pursue this project and meet some of the most outstanding musicians and fascinating personalities in the drumming world. I'm grateful to each of them not only for sharing their stories with me, but for connecting me with others.

My trusted friend and mentor CJ Menge took time from his busy schedule teaching and studying to help me outline the content, read the manuscript, and share resources as well as his extensive knowledge of the drumming and percussion world, in general.

Others lent support by encouraging me and providing names and contacts for women drummers they knew and tips for follow-up. Among these, Andy Narell, Darren Dyke, Matt Ehlers, Phil Hawkins, Tom Berich, Kiya Heartwood, Christa Hillhouse, Donna Hunt, Carolyn McColloch, and Jerry Goodrich deserve special mention. My friend Emily Lemmerman, who teaches music and often sits behind a drum set to encourage her female students, and Carolyn Trowbridge, another good friend who's a talented percussionist and ace steel pan soloist, helped me never lose sight of the importance of this project.

Mindy Abovitz, editor of *Tom Tom* magazine, was with me throughout the research and writing process. If I had a question or needed contact information, she never missed a beat. Her publication was one of my best resources and helped me discover some incredible talent that I otherwise might have overlooked.

I couldn't have completed this book without access to the research of music scholars such as Sally Placksin, Linda Dahl, Sherrie Tucker, Lucy O'Brien, Wayne Enstice and Janice Stockhouse, Tonya Bolden, Layne Redmond, and the late Antoinette Handy. In light of the fact that so little has been written about female drummers, their books and writings were invaluable. I consider them co-authors of sections of this work—particularly the early years. A dissertation written by music educator Meghan Aube was helpful in providing statistics related to women in percussion and also leading me to sources for further research. Works by Daniel Glass and Piero Scaruffi were helpful in providing historical context for later years.

As I gathered information for the book, articles in *Tom Tom*, *Drumhead*, *DRUM!*, and *Modern Drummer*, along with artist pages on commercial percussion sites plus numerous e-zines and blogs, mostly devoted to drums and drumming, were invaluable. Even Wikipedia came through, providing me with references that led to more substantive information as well as additional names for my research list. And thanks to Facebook, I was able to make important initial contacts with the extra bonus of adding some neat rockin' drummers to my "Friends" list.

My husband, Charles, deserves praise for keeping me fed and in clean clothes, and especially for being patient with me when I threw little temper tantrums over having to put away the writing of this book to work on less interesting editing projects. Truth be told, I'm grateful for those projects, because they helped provide the income that allowed me to write about music and other subjects I'm passionate about.

Finally, a big thank you to all the fabulous females who have put stick to skin—professional, amateur, and yet to be. And to those of you out there who I might have missed this time around, there's always hope for another edition. Keep making history!

Contributors

Much of the information in this book was compiled from personal interviews and electronic communication. Other information came from researching material in previously published books; articles in newspapers, magazines, and e-zines; and various websites and blogs devoted to drummers and drumming.

The following is a list of individuals who provided information through face-to-face conversations, telephone and e-mail interviews, and queries conducted between October 2012 and July 2013:

Mindy Abovitz
Carla Azar
Alessandra Belloni
Ginger Bianco
Karen Biller
Carla DeSantis Black
Cindy Blackman
Rachel Blumberg
Meytal Cohen
Helen Cole
Mike Dawson
Alice de Buhr
Carol Dierking
Debra Dobkin
Dottie Dodgion
Sheila E.
Rachel Fuhrer
Evelyn Glennie
Kiya Heartwood
Julie Hill
Christa Hillhouse
Phil Hood
Jenny Jones
Michelle Josef
Crissy Lee
Terri Lord
Sherrie Maricle
Sara McCabe
Linda McDonald
Allison Miller
Paul Moy
Lisa Pankratz
Debbi Peterson
Roxy Petrucci
Shauney "Baby" Recke
Dawn Richardson
Paloma "Palmolive" Romero
Laney Santana
Patty Schemel
Gina Schock
Heather Smith
Viola Smith
Dena Tauriello
Teresa Taylor
Kopana Terry
Lynn Perko Truell
Alicia Warrington
Jyn Yates

Introduction

> Sometimes the best man for the job isn't.
>
> —author unknown

When ninety-nine-year-old Viola Smith walked into a music store in Orange County, California, she was surprised to find an article about her in *Tom Tom* magazine, a publication for and about women drummers. The only problem, she said, was that the picture the magazine used wasn't of her. "The face was OK. I could live with that," she laughed, "but the hair was awful!"

Smith was even more surprised when the owner, overwhelmed at learning who she was, lavishly praised Smith for being one of the pioneer heroes of women drummers. "I can't believe it," the shop owner said. "Viola Smith is in my fucking store!"

Smith, who was 101 years old and still going strong in 2013, was one of the first professional female drummers who rose to popularity in the 1930s and during World War II. She became known as the "female Gene Krupa" and gained a reputation for being the "fastest girl drummer in the country." She and Pauline Braddy, who played with the International Sweethearts of Rhythm, a band that started up in the late 1930s and was composed of African American and racially mixed girls from a school in Mississippi, were considered two of the best women drummers of that era.

Smith put away her vintage 1950s Ludwig drums in the mid-1970s and hasn't played professionally since then, but she and Braddy are still prominent role models for women drummers hoping to break through barriers imposed by a heavily male-dominated field. While more and more women are being recognized as exceptionally talented drummers, the prejudice that Smith, Braddy, and their contemporaries felt as women playing drums is still much in evidence today.

"There weren't many girl drummers before the war," Smith said. "I had the field pretty much to myself. When World War II broke out, female musicians started to be taken more seriously. Before World War II there was great prejudice. The war overcame it to an extent. They could finally see what girl musicians could do. We were finally given a chance."

Exception to the Rule

There was actually a time in history when women were the primary percussionists—around and about 2300 BCE. Today, however, women drummers are the exception to the rule—some estimate one woman to every one hundred men. That holds true not only for popular music but classical music as well. A 2010 survey by percussion educator Meghan Aube found women held only 9 of 176 percussion and timpani chairs in major symphony orchestras. That number had actually dropped since a survey taken thirty-five years previously. Female percussion educators are also a significant minority. And as of 2012, only two of the seven members of the Executive Committee of the Percussive Arts Society, the largest international organization for percussionists, were women.

Why the lack of females? For many years, drumming wasn't considered "feminine" or "ladylike." The notion of musical instruments belonging to a particular sex is as old as music itself and has worked against women for centuries in the Western world. This stereotype, which unfortunately still holds today, was promoted in comments as early as the following from the 1528 Italian diplomat and philosopher Baldassare Castiglione: "Imagine with yourself what an unsightly matter it were to see a woman play upon a tabour or drum, or blow in a flute or trumpet, or any like instrument; and this is because the boisterousness of them doth both cover and take away that sweet mildness which setteth so forth every deed that a woman doeth."

In a 1964 article, *New Yorker* jazz critic Whitney Balliett wrote that women's "peripheral and usually short-lived careers were due to the female's lack of the physical equipment and poise needed to blow, beat, and slap instruments like the trumpet, bass, and drums."

School band directors and parents have often steered girls away from playing drums because of gender stereotyping associated with the instrument. According to a 1978 study by musicologists Harold F. Abeles and Susan Yank Porter and other studies since, the violin, flute, and clarinet are considered the most "female" instruments, while the trumpet, trombone, and drum are considered the most "male." In each of these studies, the drum has taken top honors for most masculine. Such sexist attitudes, gender discrimination, and intimidation by those who feel women drummers will never be as technically adept as their male counterparts have kept more than one girl from picking up a set of drumsticks. When musicians and critics throw around names of top players, the sheer number of male drummers has unfortunately kept many deserving women from making the list.

"To most of us, it is baffling that a woman would want to play drums in the first place," said Helene Stapinski, former drummer with the New York band Stephonic and author of the book *Baby Plays Around*, in a January 29, 2004, *Guardian* interview with Claire Longrigg. "The image of a drummer is of a geeky bloke in shorts with arms like a weightlifter. A 'girly girl' would not want to play the drums."

Not Bad for a Girl

The bias against women is also exhibited in books, magazines, studios, and music stores, where proprietors often dismiss and patronize women drummers or consider them trespassers on male territory. Things haven't changed much since George T. Simon, American jazz writer and occasional drummer, proclaimed in 1967, "Only God can make a tree . . . and only men can play jazz." Consider how many female drummers have heard the remark "Not bad for a girl."

In 2011, *Rolling Stone* magazine asked readers to name the greatest drummers of all time. Not one woman appeared on that list. It's been more than 160 years since women fought for suffrage, but apparently when it comes to drumming, the battle for equality is still on.

A woman drummer is under constant scrutiny and has to prove herself not just on skills but also on looks. As Stapinski states in the January 2004 *Guardian* interview, "When Led Zeppelin were playing, whoever said, 'The drummer's really ugly'?"

Fortunately, the dress code and rules of conduct have changed since Viola Smith's and Pauline Braddy's early days, and women drummers are free to choose what they wear and how they act. Each generation of women drummers has built on the gains of the previous, and perhaps one day drum message boards will be free of wisecracks about drum kits not fitting in kitchens.

While women drummers are still in the minority and will probably remain so for the foreseeable future, the few women who have "made it" and achieved distinction as outstanding musicians deserve credit and more than passing mention. This book is intended to give them that long overdue recognition as well as the historical perspective to understand their achievements. The focus here is not on classical music, drum circles, or drums used in a spiritual or goddess context. Other writers have tackled those subjects. Instead, the emphasis is on women who over the past sixty years have been at the top of their class in popular and contemporary jazz, country, blues, and rock—women such as Karen Carpenter—yes, Karen Carpenter!—Moe Tucker, Sandy West, Meg White, Janet Weiss, Honey Lantree, Gina Schock, Cindy Blackman, Dottie Dodgion, Terri Lyne Carrington, and Sheila E.

In 1942, Viola Smith sent shock waves through the jazz world by claiming in *Down Beat* magazine that "hep girls" could sit in any jam session and hold their own. In short, this book pays tribute to Viola and countless other women who have proven over and over they have the "badass" chops to do just that.

CHAPTER 1

A Few Beats Back in Time

With her gentle waist so slender, and her fingers long and small
She could play upon the rub-a-dub the best of them all.

—"The Pretty Drummer Boy,"
English folksong, author unknown

Women drummers may be the minority today, but there was a time in Western civilization when the lady drummer ruled. In pre-biblical times, women were considered holy, magical beings because of their ability to give birth and be the source for new human life. In matriarchal societies they were the heads of households, and in most ancient cultures they were responsible for the artistic and religious practices of a community. For ceremony and ritual, drumming for them was a primary skill.

Archeological findings and ancient illustrations from Egypt and Mesopotamia provide indisputable evidence that women have been drumming for thousands of years. In numerous cultures—African, South American, and North American Indian, for example—the drum was considered a feminine object, and the beat of a drum for many cultures was representative of the heartbeat of mother earth. Duke Ellington even noted the symbolism in a 1941 recording titled *A Drum Is a Woman.*

In the Western African country of Niger, although drums were the property of males, the primary instrumentalists were women. In neighboring Mali, men were the "professional" or "official" drummers, but women were allowed to drum at their own social events and for recreation. Drummers were often women of high social standing. Women of Guinea and the Congo were also drummers who sometimes performed at initiation ceremonies, funerals, and weddings. In other African cultures, drums were elevated to the status of the human male, and women had to pay the same respect to a drum that they would to a man. In some rare historical cases, women were put to death simply for touching these instruments. In many African tribes, drums were used in fertility ceremonies and were viewed as a sacred medium of communication with the gods. If a woman looked upon a drum during certain rites, her glance was thought to "pollute" the instrument, rendering it impotent and powerless—thus the severe punishment.

Damsels and Their Timbrels

Biblical references in the Old Testament note the use of musical instruments, including the tambourine or timbrel, also known as the "tof," a frame drum that was a circular hoop with skin stretched over it. Sound was produced by striking or rubbing the stretched skin. Among Egyptians the tof was played exclusively by women and eunuchs, and among Jews it was also considered a woman's instrument. A passage from Psalm 68 makes note of women drummers: "The singers went before, the players on instruments followed after; among them were the damsels playing with timbrels." The timbrel was presumably the instrument used by Miriam and her maidens to celebrate Israel's triumph over the Egyptians.

The frame drum is believed to have originated from a grain sieve used by women, and from this association researchers speculate that women were probably the first drummers. Certainly in the ancient Mediterranean world, the drum was played predominantly by women and, like the sieve, was a major symbol for sexuality, fertility, grain, the sun, and the moon.

The oldest known depiction of a drummer can be found in modern Turkey on the wall of a shrine in Catal Huyuk, a well-known Neolithic site in Asia Minor. In the Catal Huyuk culture, which dated back to 7200 to 5500 BCE, men and women were equal but women ruled over religion and art. In excavations, archeologists have uncovered depictions of the hourglass drum, similar to the West African talking drum. Clay figurines unearthed in archeological sites in Israel clearly depict females playing frame drums.

Drumming for the Gods

Move forward a few years to 2380 BCE, and you'll find the first named drummer in history—Lipushiau, the granddaughter of the Sumerian king Naramsin. She was a drumming priestess whose role was to serve as intermediary between divine and human realms. A terracotta figure unearthed in the city of Ur, where the biblical Abraham once lived, depicts her playing a balag-di, a frame drum used in liturgical chanting. Other Sumerian archeological finds provide further evidence of females playing frame drums. A stone document known as a kudurru from the twelfth century BCE depicts a procession of gods carrying weapons and playing lutes, followed by a goddess dancing and playing a tambourine.

Numerous artifacts from the fifth to second century BCE depict women playing frame drums, and players of Greek and Roman drums were almost exclusively women. Drums in those early civilizations were used solely to accompany singing and dancing or in rituals related to fertility or the growing of crops. No evidence has been found that they were ever used for military marches or for any military purpose.

In China during the Tang dynasty (618–907) and Sung dynasty (960–1279), orchestras composed of women who were government slaves performed in royal courts. Illustrations from that time show among the instruments a chieh-ku (side drum), fangxiang (gong/chime), paiban (clapper), and ta-ku (large drum).

Circa 1000 BCE, other illustrations and terracotta figures indicate that women drummers were common in Israel/Palestine and the surrounding region, and that drumming was an essential part of ancient Hebrew worship.

Eventually, drumming became associated with pagan practice, and early Christians abandoned drums and cymbals in worship as "instruments of seduction" and evidence of "the devil's pomposity."

Drumming was, in fact, used in pagan ritual, and some of that history is rather sordid. Early pagans used drums for two purposes: to put worshippers into a euphoric state of mind and to drown out the sounds of sacrifice. Pagan practice often called for the sacrifice of children. When a child was tipped into the fire, drums were used to drown out the noise of the screams. The area of Tophet in Jerusalem was known for the sacrifice of children to the god Moloch. In *Tabernacle of Moses*, author William Mudge writes: "To drown the cries of the poor innocents, large drums were beaten: hence the place became, the valley of Tophet, or a drum, with allusion to its rites of torture and of death."

Even though pagans-turned-Christian converts could handle giving up human sacrifice, they weren't too eager to relinquish their pagan feast days or the music and drumming that went along with those celebrations.

"Instruments of an Insane Cult"

During the second century, a church leader, Clement of Alexandria, attacked musicians, especially those who played cymbals and tambourines, as "instruments of an insane cult." In the sixth century, Pope John III banned playing of the tambourine. It was the perception of many church leaders that rhythm, melody, and meter should be condemned altogether because of connections to "heathenism." In 526 CE, the church decreed: "Christians are not allowed to teach their daughters singing, the playing of instruments or similar things because, according to their religion, it is neither good nor becoming."

According to Layne Redmond in her book *When the Drummers Were Women*, because music was the most "alluring aspect" of pagan worship, the church would not compromise its position regarding the ban. But perhaps to appease music lovers, new rites were instituted to replace pagan practices. These were mostly all-night vigils to honor the dead, and the singing and dancing associated with these rituals were performed primarily by female dancers and musicians. But it wasn't long before all-night prayer vigils and the music associated with them were subject to complaints by church leaders. In Redmond's words, "Clerics across Christendom complained that it led to debauchery in the darkest corners of the sanctuary." The church responded by imposing another ban—no women allowed at vigils!

In ancient religions, women usually led the mourning ritual, and the frame drum was one of the instruments used. In addition to drumming, female mourners lamented the dead with other gestures of grief, such as tearing their hair out, scratching their faces, and ripping their clothes. In the thirteenth century, the church declared that women who "dance in pagan fashion for their dead and go to the grave with drums, dancing the while," were not allowed to attend church services.

No doubt, the church's misogyny seems to have played a significant role in the decline of women pursuing drumming interests. But it's also well to note the church didn't have an easy time convincing its followers that drumming and music were altogether bad. When the church forbade the use of music in Christian worship and replaced it with the singing of psalms a capella, many Christian converts were quick to point out that the Old Testament contained numerous references to the use of music in praise and worship. The frame drum or timbrel had been played by Jewish women for many years in marriage ceremonies and processions. The church argued back that the instruments of the Old Testament were part of the greater evil of idolatry, but that God, perceiving the Israelites were too weak to give up music along with everything else, allowed them to continue it—temporarily—until he perceived they had become stronger and could do without (Redmond 150–51).

During the Middle Ages, priests were the major musicians, and most music was vocal, although paintings, representative of that period, indicate instruments, including drums, were used. Women, however, were relegated to a subservient role and, in accordance with official church decree, weren't allowed to sing in church or play instruments, much less beat time to the music. According to Redmond's book, there was one exception—"women who were asexual virgins were allowed to sing in choirs" (159).

If music was played during a service, it was only to provide "discreet accompaniment." The organ was the primary church instrument, and at that time it was so primitive the organist had to literally pound the keys with heavy blows of the fist, a form of drumming, one might say.

Early Music Outlaws

Fortunately, music had its outlaws even then, including spunky ladies such as Hildegard of Bingen and St. Teresa of Avila who decided making music was more important than any papal order or church decree. The twelfth century mystic Hildegard believed that all music—instrumental as well as vocal—functioned as a bridge between the sacred and profane. Sister Hildegard, who might be considered the first singing nun superstar, is often credited for elevating music in the church with her contributions as an artist and composer. She supported the use of instruments as a way to integrate heart, mind, and body in praise of God. She even gave certain instruments special function and meaning, including the tambourine, which she said "inspired discipline." She compared the skin of a tambourine spread tightly over the frame to that of a fasting body.

In the sixteenth century, another forward-thinking nun, Teresa of Avila, took up the drum, along with the flute, and was known to dance in church to the rhythms of her own tambourine. A zealous leader of church reform, she scandalized more than one person who stumbled upon her teaching the nuns in her convent to dance. She redeemed the drum as an appropriate vehicle for Christian praise and returned it to a respected place in the church as a suitable instrument for worship.

While women were limited in what they could do in church, they were performing frequently in secular settings, mostly as singers and dancers. Little mention is made in historical references to women drummers. During the Renaissance, at least one painting by the Flemish artist Pieter Bruegel shows a young woman playing a pipe and tabor. The pipe and tabor, popular during that period, were a pair of instruments consisting of a three-hole pipe played with one hand and a small drum played with the other. Another late fourteenth century illuminated manuscript shows five women in a procession, all of them playing small drums and handbells.

While women shamans in both Eastern and Western cultures were known to use drumming for healing rituals, in most early Native American cultures, the drum was primarily an instrument played by males. However, Southern Plains Indians claim the first drummer was a woman, chosen by the Great Spirit to instruct other women of native nations in its use.

Silencing the Woman Drummer

Unfortunately, over a period of several hundred years, expansion of military power across Europe and Asia would give rise to a patriarchal society that, like the early Church, virtually silenced the woman drummer and women musicians in general. J. Michele Edwards in *Women in Music* writes: "Throughout the centuries of the Roman Empire and the European Middle Ages, and contemporaneously in China and Japan, music was viewed as a powerful enterprise as well as a source of entertainment and pleasure. The spiritual power and moral suasion ascribed to music gave it special significance and encouraged its regulation. Thus the same institution that proclaimed, 'God established the psalms in order that singing might be both a pleasure and a help,' also suppressed the voices of women."

According to Edwards, middle and upper class women were restricted from public performance, yet their education and leisure gave them the opportunity to cultivate music as a personal accomplishment. In contrast, women musicians who were slaves and servants had "considerable visibility" as professional performers, but suffered the consequences of loss of liberty and treatment as sexual objects (Pendle 49–50).

During the seventeenth and eighteenth centuries more and more women began to make their mark in the music world, but not as drummers. They were mostly active as composers, singers, harpsichordists, pianists, and teachers, according to documentation found in Italy, France, Germany, Austria, and England. Although barriers still existed, some headway was being made, and by the nineteenth century more doors would be opened—alas, not very wide.

During the first half of the 1800s, women in increasing numbers were taking part in musical activities, mostly studying piano and voice to not only provide entertainment in the home but also to improve their possibilities for marriage. Being a serious musician was not encouraged among the fair sex. For the most part, they were content to follow the romantic ethos of the time, which maintained women were primarily around to act the role of domestic and serve as muse for the male artist.

Only a Harp Will Do

Drumming was certainly not on the "acceptable" list of instruments for women at this time. And even if they could play at some type of percussion, the opportunities were limited in a society that even deemed stringed instruments as "unfeminine." Women were discouraged from studying orchestral instruments until late in the century, and orchestras were "men only" clubs. The harp, however, was considered suitable because the movements required to play it were graceful and womanly. The following appeared in a nineteenth century review of a recital by harpist Caroline Longhi: "She played very well, and what is more, looked very well, because she understood how to show off a beautiful figure to its greatest advantage, especially at the harp, where she managed to place herself and deport herself in so many varied and yet still graceful positions that we received a good view of her entire beautiful figure from all sides" (Pendle 169).

In the twentieth and twenty-first centuries, some reviewers would be making similar sexist remarks about female drummers.

But as in every age, the Victorian era also had its share of female musical rebels. Some, being denied the opportunity to play with symphony and opera orchestras, established their own ensembles. Unfortunately, these groups were never given the respect or serious attention enjoyed by all-male musical groups.

One of the first all-female orchestras was the Vienna Ladies Orchestra, which was formed in 1867 and toured the United States in 1871. Despite the fact that all members were talented concert artists, the only places they were welcome to perform were beer halls and restaurants. In 1880, Marion Osgood of Chelsea, Massachusetts, formed a Ladies' Orchestra to perform at private parties and dances. In 1884, Caroline B. Nichols of Boston formed the Fadette Lady Orchestra. By about 1920, more than six hundred women had played in the Fadettes, and many went on to form their own orchestras and ensembles.

All these orchestras obviously used a full range of instruments. Some employed men to play missing parts. Others such as the New York Ladies Orchestra, active in 1888, made do with whatever women instrumentalists they could find. That orchestra, according to historical accounts, had at least one female percussionist who played kettle drum.

Pretty Drummer Boys

Other rebels against the status quo were young girls who cut their hair short and dressed up in male garb to disguise themselves as boys and enlist in the military. They were usually orphans, widows, abused children and wives, and prostitutes. Many became "drummer boys." An English folksong, "The Pretty Drummer Boy," contains the lyrics:

> *I was brought up in Yorkshire and when I was sixteen*
> *I ran away from home, me lads and a soldier I became*
> *With a fine cap and feathers, likewise a rattling drum*
> *They learned me to play upon the rub-a-dub-a-dum.*

Chorus:
With a fine cap and feathers, likewise a rattling drum
They learned her to play upon the rub-a-dub-a dum
With her gentle waist so slender, and her fingers long and small
She could play upon the rub-a-dub the best of them all.

During the Civil War, a twelve-year-old girl, using the alias Charles Martin, ran away from her parents to become a drummer boy for the Confederacy. In 1861, a nineteen-year-old female joined the 112th Indiana Regiment as a "drummer boy" to be with her three orphaned siblings, who sadly all had been killed in battle. At age ten, Annie Glud, then Annie Hudley, donned boy's clothing to serve in the Civil War as drummer boy Tom Hunley. After keeping her secret for sixty-three years, Glud celebrated Memorial Day 1922 by pulling out a battered old drum from an old khaki case, strapping it to her waist, and beating again remembered old battle rhythms.

Change in Status

The status of women began to change dramatically in Western society between 1880 and 1918. Along with the suffrage movement, which was gathering momentum, birth control was now available to expand women's options. Reproductive freedom was possible thanks to the production of cheap rubber for use in condoms and the development of the diaphragm. Birth rates dropped dramatically in the early years of the twentieth century, and women had more time to engage in creative pursuits.

In 1908, there were thirty all-women orchestras active in the United States. During World War I, many of the women who played in those groups were hired and paid union wages to play in hotel orchestras to replace the men who were serving in the military. They gave up those jobs as soon as the men came home.

In the ragtime era of the early 1900s, more women were sporadically appearing in different venues as working musicians. Most were pianists, but others were brass, reed, and rhythm players. They were often part of family bands or side performers in circuses, carnivals, and tent shows. A few more decades would pass before the female drummer would catch up and start to leave her mark on the contemporary and popular music scene.

CHAPTER 2

23 Skidoo

> Not to have danced the two-step to the Hart sisters' drumming was like missing one of life's joys.
>
> —from review in *Indianapolis News*, 1901

Pre-Ragtime to Jazz Age

Although conventional music histories have mostly ignored or neglected mention of the contributions of women musicians, and particularly female drummers in early America, various accounts allude to their participation. For example, the noted U.S. Capitol architect Benjamin Latrobe described the following in a journal entry from February 21, 1819:

> An elderly black man sits astride a large cylindrical drum. Using his fingers and the edge of his hand, he jabs repeatedly at the drum head—which is around a foot in diameter and probably made from an animal skin—evoking a throbbing pulsation with rapid, sharp strokes. A second drummer, holding his instrument between his knees, joins in, playing with the same staccato attack. A third black man, seated on the ground, plucks at a string instrument, the body of which is roughly fashioned from a calabash. Another calabash has been made into a drum, and a woman beats at it with two short sticks.

Latrobe was describing accompaniment to a nineteenth century slave dance that took place in the Congo Square area of New Orleans, today known as Louis Armstrong Park. Along with his vivid written account, Latrobe also made several sketches of the instruments used. The slave dances were held on Sunday afternoons, when plantation owners allowed slaves some time off to get together and socialize.

The anonymous woman cited by Latrobe may have been breaking a taboo by participating in the slave dance as a drummer, but it's just as possible she was performing in accordance with established tradition. Except for an interruption during the Civil War, the Congo Square dances and the purported participation of other women drummers in those events continued until around 1885. Coincidentally, music historians have noted it was around 1885 that the first jazz bands appeared in New Orleans. Some claim Congo Square was, in fact, the birthplace of jazz.

The Minstrel Show

In the mid-nineteenth century, the indigenous American theatrical form known as the minstrel show was at the peak of its popularity. The minstrel show or minstrelsy, which started in about 1840, basically was a comic portrayal of racial stereotypes. White males painted their faces black and lampooned the singing and dancing of slaves in a highly sentimentalized version of plantation life. In an article on the history of musical minstrel shows, John Kenrick describes the typical minstrel show scenario: "Blacks were shown as naïve buffoons who sang and danced the days away, gobbling 'chitlins,' stealing the occasional watermelon, and expressing their inexplicable love for 'ol' massuh.'"

The father of the blackface show was an early African American impersonator, Thomas Dartmouth Rice, who popularized the character of "Jim Crow." The success of his shows gave rise to a number of companies, including the Christy Minstrels who played on Broadway for nearly ten years. Stephen Foster was the company's resident composer.

The Christy Minstrel format was adopted as the standard for these types of shows with little deviation. The usual characters were the formally dressed Interlocutor in whiteface, a group of blackface performers wearing gaudy swallow-tailed coats and striped trousers, and the "end men"—Mr. Tambo, who played the tambourine, and Mr. Bones, who rattled the bones, typically a pair of clappers or castanets.

The end men acted as the show's drummers, providing rhythm for the proceedings—an interchange of jokes interspersed with music—ballads, comic songs, and instrumental numbers often played on the banjo and violin.

Theatre scholar David Carlyon writes in *Dan Rice: The Most Famous Man You've Never Heard Of*:

> America was crazy for blackface. To the twanging thwang of the banjo, and the clatter of tambo and bones—tambourine and bone castanets—white men seared burnt cork on their faces to sing, waggle their legs in imitation of blacks dancing, and tell jokes in "negro" dialect. Between 1750 and 1843, over 5,000 theatre and circus productions included blackface.

Women were not allowed as performers on the minstrel stage, so if there was a female part to be filled, such as a Mammy, a female impersonator took on that role. As they were restricted from performing in the established minstrel companies, women troupes began to form.

In 1870, theatrical manager M.B. Leavitt founded Madame Rentz's Female Minstrels, the first blackface minstrel troupe composed entirely of women, including a woman who played tambourine and another who played the castanets or clappers; in essence they were percussionists who provided the background beat. The women performed the basic minstrel show but added new pieces specifically intended to titillate the audience. Their primary role was not so much to show off their comedic chops or musical talents as to show off their scantily clad bodies.

Bernard Sobel in *A Pictorial History of Burlesque* quotes John E. Henshaw, a former stagehand for Madame Rentz's Female Minstrels:

> In San Francisco, we had advertised that we were going to put on the can-can. Mabel Santley did this number and when the music came to the dum-de-dum, she raised her foot just about twelve inches, whereupon the entire audience hollored [sic] "Whooooo!" It set them crazy.

Madame Rentz's Female Minstrels' show was so successful that at least eleven rival troupes of female minstrels sprang up over the next year, including one that did away with blackface altogether. The movement eventually gave rise to the "girlie show."

Research into these groups is difficult because many groups adopted the same or similar names. For instance, there were at least a half dozen "Minstrel Maids" performing at the turn of the century and in the early years of the 1900s. Most performed in small towns and never achieved the notoriety of mention in various vaudeville histories, but they do turn up in advertisements or reviews in local newspapers. One group by this name toured the West Coast and Northwest. Another group called the American Minstrel Maids toured during approximately the same period and worked primarily in the Midwest and the smaller cities of New York, Ohio, and Pennsylvania. Photographs of that particular group show the women in various poses, but only one instrument appears in the pictures: a tambourine. The tambourine player may have been Flo Rockwell, who autographed photographs with the inscription, "The Syncopated Girl." In photographs, she is shown sitting next to the tambourine.

By the beginning of the twentieth century, more and more women began appearing in minstrel shows in bands and as featured acts. Ma Rainey and Bessie Smith, the great blues singers, both started their careers as minstrel performers.

Life Off the Farm

In the 1880s, the once predominantly rural face of America was being changed by the Industrial Revolution. Half the population had moved off the farm and into cities and towns working at jobs that afforded them a little extra cash and leisure time. They wanted to be entertained, but they were also living in a world where phonographs, film, radio, and television didn't yet exist. Family life was undergoing drastic changes as family size shrank and life expectancy increased. Women not only became part of the labor and work force, they also began taking active roles in politics and social reform.

But full acceptance of women as professional musicians and as drummers was far in the future. That's not to say women were totally excluded from the contemporary music scene. The early history of jazz alludes to participation of African American women in spirituals, gospel, and blues. However, except for singing or playing piano, which was considered "appropriate" and even desirable for women, working as a professional musician was pretty much taboo, especially for middle class Black and White American women. Fortunately, that didn't stop many women from participating in the ragtime craze of the early 1900s and even more so in the vaudeville circuits of the 1920s.

Actually, all-women groups, such as the all-lady orchestras formed in Massachusetts in the early 1880s, had been around for some time. Cornet player Viola Allen led the Colored Female Brass Band, which performed in the Michigan area in the late 1880s. Along with the all-girl groups who performed in vaudeville and minstrelsy, female bands were sometimes house or pit bands or dance orchestras for theatres and venues such as the Hippodrome, Atlantic Gardens, and Lafayette Theatre in New York.

In 1911, Maggie Thompson was playing drums with George Bailey's Female Brass Band in Indiana. Around that same period Lottie Brown and Florence Sturgess were drummers for Marie Lucas' Lafayette Theatre Orchestra. Alice Calloway Thompson played drums for Lucas' Colonial Theatre Orchestra in Baltimore in 1916. She was also drummer for Hallie Anderson's Lady Band at the Lafayette Theatre in 1919.

The Henry Hart Family Orchestra in Indianapolis boasted two women drummers: Hazel Hart on trap, xylophone, and bells, and Clothilde Hart on bass drum. A review that appeared in the April 6, 1901, *Indianapolis News*, waxed eloquent, "Not to have danced the two-step to the Hart sisters' drumming was like missing one of life's joys."

Ragtime

Ragtime, with its music characterized by a syncopated or "ragged" rhythm, came to its peak in popularity between 1897 and 1918. It began as dance music in the red light districts of African American communities in St. Louis and New Orleans years before its publication as popular sheet music for piano. Ragtime was a modification of the march made famous by John Philip Sousa combined with the polyrhythms of African music. It was preceded by its musical cousin, the cakewalk, a pre-ragtime dance form popular until about 1904. The music was usually played at an African American dance contest in which the prize was a cake. Most early rags were cakewalks.

Scott Joplin, considered the "King of Ragtime," became famous in 1899 with the publication of "Maple Leaf Rag." For at least twelve years after its publication, "Maple Leaf Rag" was the major influence on other ragtime composers with its melody lines, harmonic progressions, and metric patterns.

Ragtime, though especially popular with young people, was held in disdain by others. In *Jazz: A History of America's Music* by Geoffrey Ward and Ken Burns, the authors quote what Edward Baxter Perry wrote in *Etude* magazine in 1918:

> Ragtime is syncopation gone mad. Its victims, in my opinion, can be treated successfully only like the dog with rabies, with a dose of lead. Whether it is simply a passing phase of our decadent art culture or an infectious disease, which has come to stay, like leprosy, time alone can tell. It is an evil music that has crept into the homes and hearts of our American people regardless of race, and must be wiped out as other bad and dangerous epidemics have been exterminated.

In a blog entry titled "Ragtime Terror," James Reeves notes hysterical editorials, which appeared in newspapers from 1895 to about 1920, arguing that "maintaining a healthy organism requires a steady pulse," not the "ragged" beat of syncopated music. Doctors, citing Plato, according to Reeves, argued that "ragtime syncopation disrupts normal heart rhythm and interferes with the motor center of the brain and nervous system."

Some opposed the popular music form because of racial issues—it was Black people's music. Others felt the music led to intoxication, unduly infiltrating the population with countless drunken women.

For some reason, women were considered particularly susceptible to the alleged negative influences of popular music. A few years later, a writer for *The American* magazine would predict moral disaster coming to hundreds of young American girls through the "pathological, nerve irritating music of jazz orchestras" (Ward, Burns 79).

Even though ragtime is generally associated with the piano, dance bands and brass bands of that era often performed the music, and chances are a female drummer or two helped on occasion to keep the beat, though rarely in a mixed sex group. History, alas, only alludes to their participation and gives no names.

Cultural Divide

Because female instrumentalists, including drummers, had little opportunity to play in groups with men, they usually formed their own bands or played in family-based groups. They also began to find acceptance in vaudeville, which provided cheap entertainment to the new working class of the Industrial Revolution. Vaudeville not only marked the beginning of popular entertainment as big business, it was also an attempt to bridge a social gap between classes.

This class divide was serious enough that it resulted in a violent clash in New York City that left 25 dead and more than 120 injured. The Astor Place Riot, which occurred on May 10, 1849, illustrated the cultural split and class struggle evident in the entertainment world at that time. The upper classes liked opera and classical theatre. The middle class liked minstrel shows and melodramas. Working class men and immigrants preferred the variety shows and bawdy entertainment found in concert saloons, the American version of English music halls.

The Astor Place Riot was ironically a fight over which of two actors was better at performing Shakespeare, pitting the upper class fans of British actor William Charles Macready against the middle and working class fans of American-born theatrical star Edwin Forrest. Shakespeare at the time was popular with every strata of society: the educated and the barely literate. Many claimed that had Shakespeare been alive at the time, he would have been in his heart, at least, an American.

According to historian Nigel Cliff in his book *The Shakespeare Riots*, the incident further aggravated class alienation and separated the entertainment world into "respectable" and "working class" orbits.

Vaudeville

Tony Pastor was a New York City impresario who is considered one of the major founding forces of American vaudeville in the mid to late nineteenth century. A devout Catholic and devoted father, his major motivation was to provide a variety show that was family friendly and wholesome, as opposed to the risqué and coarse entertainment provided by many venues at that time. Pastor's attempt to produce a "clean" show was an immediate success and drew a diverse and enthusiastic audience, representing all age groups and classes.

Others soon began following Pastor's lead, including Benjamin Franklin Keith and Edward F. Albee. Keith and Albee had become wealthy through staging unauthorized productions of Gilbert and Sullivan operettas. They used their fortune to build a chain of ornate theatres across the northeastern United States and began calling the multiple daily performances staged in these establishments "vaudeville." Keith and Albee were also insistent that acts keep their material clean and posted warnings backstage in all their theatres such as the following, cited by Fred Allen in his book *Much Ado About Me*:

> Don't say "slob" or "son-of-a-gun" or "hully gee" on this stage unless you want to be cancelled peremptorily. Do not address anyone in the audience in any manner. If you have not the ability to entertain Mr. Keith's audience without risk of offending them, do the best you can. Lack of talent will be less open to censure than would be an insult to a patron. If you are in doubt as to the character of your act, consult the local manager before you go on the stage, for if you are guilty of uttering anything sacrilegious or even suggestive, you will be immediately closed and will never again be allowed in a theatre where Mr. Keith is in authority.

Vaudeville spread through the country as more theatre chains and circuits sprang up. The shows offered a wide range of acts and incorporated characteristics of the earlier minstrel shows. Medicine shows and "Wild West" shows popular at the time also provided inspiration. Medicine show troupes traveled through rural areas, offering a mix of comedy, music, jugglers, and other novelty acts along with sales pitches for miracle tonics, salves, and elixirs. "Wild West" shows romanticized life on the vanishing frontier and usually included rodeo trick riding, shooting exhibitions, music, and drama. Circuses that regularly toured the country also provided a source for acts.

Because vaudeville shows were considered "polite" entertainment, inoffensive to men, women, and children, women were welcomed to the vaudeville ranks as entertainers and musicians. If they were willing to tour for forty or more weeks a year and put up with a grueling schedule of multiple performances each day, even those who weren't headliners could make a good wage. In 1919, the average factory worker earned less than one thousand dollars a year. A small-time circuit performer working for forty-two weeks could earn $3,150 a year. It was a rare opportunity for women who had the determination and talent to make a respectable living. Even if travel was uncomfortable, dressing rooms were small and filthy, and theatres were frigidly cold in the winter and hellishly hot in the summer, the money and job stability made any hardships encountered along the way worth it.

Most of the women in the shows were singers and dancers or acrobatic or novelty acts. All-girl bands were also on the roster of several circuits. And mixed groups that included both men and women instrumentalists also made the circuit. Billy Glason, a singer and comedian well known on the vaudeville stage, is quoted in the book *The Vaudevillians*, edited by Bill Smith: "I worked to all kinds of music—from bad to awful. Some bands were really great. For instance, there was the band at the RKO Palace in New Orleans. That band was so good it used to stop the show . . . On the other hand, there was the band at the New York Palace. Owen Jones was the leader. They had some women in the band, and they were so polite they used to let the women finish first—that's how the music sounded. Every act that went on had to stop in the middle and ask Owen Jones to take the tempo over again." Glason's comments leave one wondering whether it was the conductor or the drummer who lost the beat.

Beauty Before Talent

In selecting all-girl bands for vaudeville acts, the attractiveness of individual members of the group was just as important—if not more important—than their musical abilities. The female figure had suddenly become a sexual object. As women began actively pursuing women's rights, fundamental changes in attitudes regarding women's sexuality were taking place. Women began to wear makeup and clothing that accentuated their sexiness. Corsets were out and breasts were in. Psychologist Barbara A. Cohen wrote in an article entitled "The Psychology of Ideal Body Image as an Oppressive Force in the Lives of Women," first published in 1984: "The women's movement of that time period that began as an attempt to liberate the sexuality of women ended with women seeing themselves and being seen by men as sexual objects. To be socially acceptable, to be attractive, to win a husband, to keep a husband, women had to look sexy, free, and available."

Realizing the money to be made from this newfound emphasis on a woman's sexual attributes, vaudeville impresarios began booking more and more acts featuring women, especially beautiful ones. Even a mediocre sister act could bring in more revenue than a good brother act if the ladies possessed the least bit of pulchritude. For ladies of vaudeville, the focus was no so much on talent as on what revealing attire they would wear on stage to show off their curves. The woman who was talented as well as beautiful was usually a surprise.

Ziegfield Follies

No one capitalized on this more than Broadway impresario Florenz "Flo" Ziegfield. He presented the first of his lavish Ziegfield Follies on July 8, 1907, featuring, in his words, "fifty of the most beautiful women ever gathered in one theatre." Ziegfield Follies chorus girls not only danced and sang, they also, according to one account noted in the book *Stormy Weather: The Music and Lives of a Century of Jazzwomen* by Linda Dahl, "played on such diverse instruments as the banjo, flute, xylophone, piccolo, trombone, cornet, and *snare drums*."

In the first of what was a predecessor to the drum and dance shows of today, one act had the chorus showgirls marching up and down the theatre's aisles, beating on drums. The show also featured risqué costumes, comedy, and burlesque. It became the standard for other variety revues and established Ziegfield as the foremost showman of the period. Ziegfield's productions were bold and daring and went from the suggestive to the explicit as time went on.

The Follies gave American music an invaluable showcase. It also gave women a rare opportunity to display their musical skills as drummers, albeit in a showgirl chorus line.

CHAPTER 3

Bee's Knees: The Roaring '20s

> To be sure it is rather hard for membership of the tender sex to play jazz music, but this should not discourage them by any means from the profession of drumming, for there are many other engagements open which are a good deal easier from a physical standpoint.
>
> —George Lawrence Stone, 1921

World War I officially ended with the signing of the Treaty of Versailles in June 1919, and a new era began that tore down prevailing conventions and brought in new social mores. It was a time of anything goes and anything went. The decade that came to be known as "the Roaring '20s" was for the United States a period of unprecedented prosperity. Between 1920 and 1929, the nation's wealth doubled, and a new advertising industry sprang up. People were spending money on cars, refrigerators, washing machines, and vacuum cleaners. For entertainment, they were buying radios, phonograph records, and tickets to movies.

Young people—especially females—took advantage of this new sense of freedom. Women known as "flappers" cut their hair into short bobs and wore skirts that exposed their legs and knees. Many were arrested for indecent exposure for wearing what was considered skimpy beachwear in public.

In politics and in the workplace, the female asserted her independence. Women began to go out alone without male escorts to look after them, reveled at all-night parties, drove motor cars, smoked in public, and held men's hands without wearing gloves. Mothers, indignant over their daughters' scandalous behavior, established an Anti-Flirt League in protest. The younger generation clashed with the older generation and rejected the establishment, preferring to do things their own way.

Linked to this dramatic change in culture was the growth in popularity of a new musical form known as jazz. The new dances created by this music—the Charleston, One Step, and Black Bottom—angered the older generation and caused outrage among many. The *Catholic Telegraph* editorialized: "The music is sensuous, the female is only half dressed, and the motions may not be described in a family newspaper. Suffice it to say that there are certain houses appropriate for such dances, but these houses have been closed by law" ("The Jazz Age," History Learning Site).

New Opportunities for Women Musicians

With the suffrage movement at its peak in the 1920s, more doors were open for women not only in social life, but in the entertainment world as well. The decade known as the jazz age saw the emergence of famous musicians such as Bessie Smith, who became the most popular female singer of that era. All-girl bands such as The Blue Belles, the Parisian Redheads (later the Bricktops), Lil Hardin's All-Girl Band, the Ingenues, the Harlem Playgirls, Phil Spitalny's Musical Sweethearts, the Twelve Vampires, and Helen Lewis and Her All Girl Jazz Syncopators were just a few of the female jazz bands that became popular during the decade. Many of these all-girl bands were offshoots of earlier minstrel groups.

At least one lady drummer started a band that performed regularly during this period. Marian Pankey started her All Female Orchestra in 1916, and they were popular on Chicago's South Side into the '20s. The band, made up exclusively of Black members, was considered one the pioneering female jazz groups.

Helen Lewis and Her All-Girl Jazz Syncopators, formed in 1923, became one of the first widely known bands to demonstrate that women could compete with men as professional musicians. In 1925, the group released a phonofilm, a sound-on-film process developed by inventor Lee DeForest, to show off their indisputable talent. Despite their reputation as pioneers, little documentation exists about them or their music-making peers.

Other all-girl bands, such as Bobbie Howell's American Syncopators and Bobby Grice's Fourteen Bricktops, both popular bands on the vaudeville circuit in the 1920s, created places for other women who were brass, wind, or rhythm players.

The Ingenues

The Ingenues were an all-girl jazz band active in the Chicago area. William Morris started the group in 1925, and they performed frequently on the vaudeville circuit and in variety theatres and picture houses, often billed as the opening stage show before double features. As headliners in the Ziegfield Follies of 1927, "The American Girl," their act featured twelve white baby grand pianos as well as various combinations of brass, strings, and woodwinds. Louise Sorenson, a trumpet player, led the group and, along with her horn, could play every instrument in the band, including drums.

The group specialized in Dixieland, light classics, and Tin Pan Alley. All the musicians in the band, like Sorenson, played multiple instruments. Each was just as adept strumming a banjo or playing an accordion as they were performing on traditional symphonic instruments. They won respect as one of the most versatile groups of their day.

In addition to performing all over the United States, the group also toured Europe, South Africa, Asia, and Australia. The band appeared in several film shorts, including "The Band Beautiful," "Syncopating Sweeties," and "Maids and Music." One of their most interesting performances was in a barn for a research project conducted by the University of Wisconsin. The Ingenues were hired by the university to serenade a group of cows in a test to see if the animals would give more milk to the soothing strains of music.

Redheads Only Need Apply

For the all-girl bands, a member's looks were just as important as ability to play, and band organizers and leaders kept this in mind when choosing personnel.

In a preview of a performance by the all-girl band, the Bricktops, which appeared in the January 29, 1932, *Indiana Evening Gazette* ("Bricktops Play for Dance Tonight"), the writer comments: "The personal appearance of the redheads is as attractive as their stellar music, and they are exceptionally pleasing to rest your eyes on."

A Bricktop claim to fame was the fact that all fourteen members were redheads. Bandleader Bobby Grice started the group as a three-piece orchestra in an Indianapolis high school. The only three girls in the school who had the requisite musical abilities happened to be redheads. As new members were recruited for the orchestra, one requirement was that they also be redheads.

The drummer for the Bricktops was Mitzi Bush, who had previous experience playing in all-girl bands before joining that group. Born Miriam Quackenbush, she was the daughter of Frank and Jane Quackenbush from Elmhurst, Illinois. She took Mitzi Bush as her professional stage name.

Originally, Bush and the band played summer resorts and ballrooms, and toured the vaudeville circuit as the Parisian Redheads. They played the Palace Theatre in New York City's Time Square in 1928 and the next year returned to the Palace, receiving top billing over the Marx Brothers. Their act included, along with music and comedy, "ladder balancing and acrobatic feats." They changed their name to the Fourteen Bricktops after Babe Egan's Hollywood Redheads—another band made up of redheads—brought legal action against them.

The drummer for Hollywood Redheads was Estelle Mae Dilthey, born in 1908 in Fresno County, California. By the time her youngest brother Gene was three years old, her father Edwin formed The Musical Dilthey Family Band. Estelle was the appointed drummer. The father, who worked for the Southern Pacific Railroad, quit his job in 1920 and moved to Los Angeles in hopes of finding opportunity for the family band. Most of their gigs were playing for clubs and fraternal organizations, and to make ends meet, the father was forced to take a second job.

In 1925, Mary Florence Cecilia "Babe" Egan who had been working as a "set" background musician decided to form her own all-girl band. She was a friend of the Dilthey family and recruited Estelle to plays drums and xylophone with her newly formed Hollywood Redheads. In her search for the best young girl musicians in Los Angeles, Babe found no one who could compete with Estelle as a drummer. But Babe wanted the Redheads to be more than just musicians, so she decided Estelle should learn how to tap dance, and she persuaded the famed film and stage dancer Bill "Bojangles" Robinson to give Estelle lessons. Robinson refused to take any money for the lessons, so Babe gave him several silk shirts to express her gratitude for Robinson teaching her drummer to dance.

The Hollywood Redheads' first performance was at the Sacramento Fair. Then bookings started coming from big movie theatres in Los Angeles. The band would play at the beginning of the silent films and then for the newsreel. On November 25, 1925, Estelle and the group set sail for Honolulu, their first booking outside Los Angeles. They played an eight-week engagement there and then moved on to another engagement in Hilo on the Big Island.

In 1926, the band had no shortage of bookings and traveled to play shows in Nevada, Colorado, Wyoming, Nebraska, Illinois, New Jersey, Pennsylvania, Washington, DC, and New York City, where they met President Calvin Coolidge.

Their Palace performance in New York City drew rave reviews. After seeing the act, Broadway impresario Florenz Ziegfield specifically made a point of meeting the band's drummer. However, it was not to praise her drumming talents but to express admiration for Estelle's legs. Estelle, happy to be recognized for whatever reason by the great Ziegfield, said that was "something no girl ever forgets" ("Estelle Mae Dilthy," genealogy.com).

Looks First, Listen Later

The Ziegfield story points out a sad truth as noted by Sherrie Tucker, author of *Swing Shift: All Girl Bands of the 1940s*. Before World War II, most all-girl bands were viewed as "a kind of sex show." Being a good musician wasn't enough. Members of groups were chosen as much for their looks as for their performing skills, and even though many of these women were talented musicians, they've rarely been subjects of serious musical discourse or academic study. When it came to audiences who paid to see these shows, it was looks first, listen later. And the bandleaders and entrepreneurs who organized these bands kept this foremost in mind as they went about their recruiting.

Photographs and videos show women drummers were prominent in other bands of the '20s, but were usually not singled out for recognition unless it was for a novelty role they took as part of the act or, as in Estelle Dilthey's case, a nice set of gams. Except for the bandleader and featured soloists, names of the other members of these groups, including the drummers, rarely appear in historical accounts and whatever information is available is scant.

The Jazz Age

Although the 1920s are known as the jazz age, the musical form called jazz actually was born around 1895 in New Orleans. The first jazz was a mixture of blues and marching band music played by African Americans and Creoles on old U.S. Army instruments such as the cornet or marching drums. The use of improvisation was common because most of the early virtuoso jazz musicians didn't read music. As jazz grew more popular, Whites started to play, melding the European and African music cultures into a new style of music, indigenous to America.

During the jazz age musicians began to experiment and discover new jazz styles. The blues, once the music of poor, itinerant Blacks, was now openly embraced and provided the foundation for these experiments. In a period of growing industrialization, Blacks and musicians from New Orleans began moving to Chicago and New York, and jazz began to spread. With the help of radio, which introduced large-scale national broadcasts in 1922, and phonograph records, as many as one hundred million of them sold in one year, the new jazz sounds rapidly won numerous fans and supporters. Thanks to the new "technology," Americans could now hear the new music without physically being in a venue where jazz was actually being played live. Big name clubs, roadhouses, dance halls, and speakeasies, the illegal pubs that sprang up during prohibition, booked jazz bands and featured their music. As a result, jazz often was linked to alcohol, "intimate dancing," and "other socially questionable activities."

Others from the academic and classical music community found the music equally objectionable. Princeton University professor Henry Van Dyke is quoted in *Jazz: A History of America's Music* by Geoffrey Ward and Ken Burns: "It is not music at all. It is merely an irritation of the nerve of hearing, a sensual teasing of the strings of physical passion. Its fault lies not in syncopation, for that is a legitimate device when sparingly used. But 'jazz' is an unmitigated cacophony, a combination of disagreeable sounds in complicated discords, a willful ugliness and a deliberate vulgarity."

A poll taken by *Musical Courier* magazine revealed that academically trained musicians found "ad libbing" and "jazzing" of a piece "thoroughly objectionable." Many believed this "Bolshevistic smashing of the rules and tenets of decorous music" spelled certain disaster for the future of American music. Even Thomas Edison, the inventor of the phonograph, one of the major reasons jazz had spread and become so popular, didn't care for the musical form. He claimed that he played jazz records backwards because "they sounded better that way" (Ward, Burns 79).

Opponents of jazz blamed it for just about anything, including the death of a celebrated British conductor, who collapsed during a visit to Coney Island. The newspapers blamed the noise of the competing jazz bands on the boardwalk for his untimely death.

Those who believed jazz and the dancing associated with it were morally reprehensible blamed the music for all social ills. *Jazz: A History of America's Music* gives several examples. The Illinois Vigilance Association in 1923 reported the "downfall of one thousand girls could be traced directly to the pernicious influence of jazz music." In Cincinnati, the Salvation Army obtained a court injunction to stop construction of a theatre next to a home of expectant mothers on the grounds that "the enforced proximity of a theatre and jazz palace" would implant dangerous "jazz emotions" in helpless infants.

Others, especially older White Americans, condemned the music for no other reason than its origins: its roots in the Black community. They had decried ragtime for the same reason, and in the future their descendants would use similar arguments to denounce rock 'n' roll. Mrs. Max Obendorfer, the national music chairman of the General Federation of Women's Clubs, declared jazz "the accompaniment of the voodoo dancer, stimulating the half-crazed barbarian to the vilest deeds . . . employed by other barbaric people to stimulate barbarity and sensuality" (79).

Emergence of the School Band

But despite the negative attitudes of many toward the musical form, jazz also played some part in increasing the number of aspiring musicians—including women and female drummers—who would eventually go on to become professionals in the field. Thanks to some clever marketing, jazz was an underlying influence that drove the school band movement of the 1920s.

At the turn of the century, an estimated ten thousand bands were active in the United States. Bands were everywhere—in factories, department stores, churches, amusement parks, prisons, seminaries, and "schools for the feeble minded." Most were small ensembles, but a few boasted over one hundred members. They provided music for parades, civic events and ceremonies, concerts, and dances. Every town had its bandstand, a focal point for concerts and other community gatherings. The large number of bands could be attributed to the great popularity of John Philip Sousa, the American conductor and composer known best for his military and patriotic marches.

By 1920, however, the moving picture, phonograph, and jazz changed everything. The great concert bands stopped touring, and the village bandstand, once the center of a community's social life, stood silent and deserted.

The end of World War I and the new social climate of the 1920s brought about a rapid decline in the number of amateur, professional, and military bands. The band instrument industry was desperate for new customers and decided to target schools as a new market for their sales.

In 1923, one of the first school band contests was held, and representatives of the Conn Company, instrument manufacturer and contest organizer, capitalized on the event by touting the presence of girls in the competition, the extreme youth of some competitors, the participation of an African American band, and the element of jazz. The stated objectives were to promote "music for everyone" and "jazzier jazz bands."

Promoters of the school band movement and others latched onto the idea of mass marketing jazz not only as a specific genre of music but as a category of style. And truth be told, almost anything at that time from music to fashion could be described as jazzy. The wide repertoire of music classified as jazz—everything from the realm of popular music at that time to Gershwin's jazz-based classical compositions—supported this view.

Invading Male Territory

At the peak of bands' popularity from 1870 to 1920, some women found places in various bands. But playing "unfeminine" instruments such as brass and percussion was still considered unacceptable, and if women played in a band it was usually the flute or clarinet. It wasn't until the school band movement was going strong in the 1920s that more female musicians began to participate and play instruments that were once considered exclusive male territory. Drums, however, were still considered "masculine," and, except in all-girl schools, girl drummers would continue to be a rarity.

The predominant instrument for women in early jazz was piano. Some, such as guitarist Danny Barker, speculated the reason women didn't take to the heavier, more masculine instruments went back to the early brass marching bands of New Orleans as evidenced in this quote from his book *Bourbon Street Black: The New Orleans Black Jazzman*: "Marching on the streets, especially with a heavy brass instrument [or drums, he could have just as well added], just wasn't considered appropriate behavior for girls."

A popular percussionist of that time, George Lawrence Stone, wrote in the *Jacobs Orchestra Monthly* in 1923, encouraging women to pursue percussion—but only in certain genres. "To be sure it is rather hard for membership of the tender sex to play jazz music," he wrote, "but this should not discourage them by any means from the profession of drumming, for there are many other engagements open which are a good deal easier from a physical standpoint."

Acceptable Percussion for a Lady

The marimba was one of the "accepted" percussion instruments for a lady, and in 1929 composer/conductor Clair Omar Massur formed one of the first all-women marimba ensembles. The group, comprised of twenty-five players, performed their one and only show at the opening of Paramount Pictures' Oriental Theatre in Chicago.

A year later, Reg Kehoe of Reading, Pennsylvania, formed a group called the Marimba Queens. Over a span of thirty-two years the group would put on over four thousand performances in venues ranging from state fairs to Broadway. In her dissertation on "Women in Percussion," Meghan Aube quotes Kehoe bragging about the Marimba Queens' success, saying they were "smart, good-looking girls who can play real good music and, at the same time, display good figures and bare legs."

In *Black Women in American Bands and Orchestras*, author Antoinette Handy writes that percussion was generally associated with volume and sound reinforcement, and "the gentler sex was deemed devoid of sufficient strength and stamina to meet the challenge." She refers to a male conductor's comments that the "spectacle of a girl engaging in such physical exertion is not attractive."

Despite this reluctance to accept the idea of a woman drummer, the development of jazz did open opportunities for women both as leaders and players.

And it wouldn't be too long before other women would be following the beat of drummers such as Beverly Sexton, who was playing with some of the best jazz combos in St. Louis, Shirley Kennedy of Omaha, Nebraska, and Patty Carter and Leota Hunt of New York City, who in the late '20s had bucked tradition and established careers for themselves as professional drummers.

CHAPTER 4

Swing Cats: The '30s

I got the drums by accident.

—Pauline Braddy

The stock market crash of 1929 brought an abrupt end to the prosperity that Americans had enjoyed during the decade. The United States suddenly found itself in the economic pits. The unemployment rate, which at the beginning of 1929 was 3 percent, by 1933 had risen to 25 percent. Construction virtually came to a halt, crop prices fell, and industry suffered the devastating effects of what would become the nation's longest, most widespread, and deepest depression of the twentieth century.

On top of financial hardships, natural disasters added to the country's misfortunes. Drought transformed the nation's heartland into a giant dust bowl. From South Dakota to Texas, huge dust storms ravaged once fertile land. People abandoned their farms and headed west, seeking a better, more stable way of life.

Criminal activity was rampant, and it was the heyday for outlaws such as Bonnie and Clyde, Pretty Boy Floyd, John Dillinger, and Machine Gun Kelly, all of whom became folk heroes.

During the Great Depression, people did what they could to escape the misery and have a little fun with the limited money they had. They went to the movies, played parlor games, and got up on their feet and danced. While the times may have been depressing, the music of that period most certainly was not.

Birth of Swing

Swing was the term used to describe the new musical form, and the '30s came to be known as the swing era. Like jazz, swing had African American roots. Swing music, also known as "jump" and "jive," abandoned the string orchestra and used arrangements that emphasized horns and wind instruments and improvised tunes.

W.C. Handy, known as the "Father of the Blues," defined swing as "the latest term for ragtime jazz and blues. You white folk just have a new word for our old fashioned hot music." He may have been paraphrasing Louis Armstrong who when asked the definition of swing by Bing Crosby on his radio show said: "Ah, swing, well, we used to call it syncopation—then they called it ragtime, then blues—then jazz. Now it's swing. White folks, yo'all sho is a mess."

Swing gave birth to numerous dances such as the jitterbug, lindy hop, and shag. The musical genre also had its own jargon. A swing musician was a "cat." A female singer was a "canary." "Hep" gave birth to "hip." To "take off" was to solo or improvise. The term "swing" came from the phrase "swing feel" where emphasis is on the off-beat or weaker pulse in the music. Swing bands were usually big bands that featured soloists who would improvise on a melody over the arrangement.

Some jazz historians trace the birth of swing to drummer Chick Webb's band in Harlem in 1931. But the Depression wasn't kind to the nightclub business, especially in poor Black neighborhoods, and the music failed to take off.

Compared to the early jazz of the 1920s, swing was a more sophisticated, "sweet" sound. Benny Goodman, one of the first swing bandleaders to achieve widespread fame, took some of the sweetness out. Young white dancers loved Goodman's "hot" rhythms and his daring arrangements. "Hot swing" became the dominant form of American popular music over the decade.

Women Breaking the Swing Barrier

As in the past two decades, most musicians in the 1930s bands were male. If a woman was to be found, she was either a "canary" or a "fem on the 88s." Other than as vocalists and pianists, women were a rarity in the male-dominated swing world.

A few women took the initiative and formed their own jazz bands in defiance to those who didn't think gals could swing or play jazz. Marian Pankey's Female Orchestra, the all-Black group formed by drummer Pankey in 1916, and Babe Egan's all-White Hollywood Redheads, formed in 1924, have been recognized as two of the pioneering female jazz bands.

Former Ziegfield Follies headliners the Ingenues continued to be a commercial success during the 1930s. Their director Louise Sorenson was praised by *Down Beat* magazine in 1937 for her ability to play every instrument in the band and her exceptional knowledge of harmony and orchestration. The article also singled for recognition the Puerto Rican percussionist Frances Gorton, who played marimba along with all the other instruments of the band (Dahl 51).

Melody Maids, formed in 1933, was another all-girl band that persevered during this period. Original members of the band were sisters Ornie and Mary See Berry. Their mother, Cora Alma Berry, was not happy about the prospect of her daughters being on the road by themselves, so to solve that problem, she learned how to play drums and toured with them.

Ina Ray and Her Melodears

One of the decade's most successful bands of all-female swingers was Ina Ray Hutton and Her Melodears. The group formed in 1934 and was an instant hit. Hutton was a tap dancer turned showgirl. According to music historian Tonya Bolden, Hutton's group had some fine musicians, "but she—aka the 'Blond Bombshell of Swing'—was not one of them. Ina sang OK. The only other instrument she played was her body."

With moves described as similar to those of Mata Hari and a "voice like Betty Boop's big sister," Hutton was known for her "apple pie looks and a jaw-dropping figure." In *American Women in Jazz*, author Sally Placksin wrote: "In some places, policemen had to surround the stage as Hutton danced and gyrated to the music." Hutton herself said, "I'm selling this show as a music program, but if curves attract an audience, so much the better."

Audience members who went to her shows talked about her dancing around and waving her baton more or less in time to the rhythm. With her low-cut strapless gowns and energetic movements, there was always the possibility of a "wardrobe malfunction," which audience members found as enticing as the music itself.

Hutton was born Odessa Cowan in 1916 and grew up with her half-sister June in a Black neighborhood on Chicago's south side. U.S. Census records record her as being "negro" and "mulatto," but Hutton passed as white throughout her career. She was just seven when she won a rave review for her dancing in a Chicago newspaper and made her Broadway debut at age fourteen. When she was eighteen, jazz impresario Irving Mills put together an all-woman band that became the Melodears and made her the leader. She changed her name to Hutton, hoping she might be linked with the notorious Woolworth heiress Barbara Hutton.

The Melodears toured and recorded for five years and appeared in several Paramount film shorts. In 1934 few bands, including the Melodears, could compete with the predominant male groups of that time, but Hutton's band did have some exceptional musicians, including the drummer Lil Singer. Singer is noted in several reviews and articles related to the Melodears, but biographical information on her is hard to find, as it is on so many female musicians of this era. In later years, Virginia Mayers was a drummer for the group. She also played trumpet, saxophone, guitar, and clarinet.

In 1939, Hutton disbanded the group, and, in partnership with tenor sax man George Paxton, formed a new, all-male orchestra. In an April 1940, *Down Beat* magazine article she claimed the reason behind her move was that she was "sick of glamour." The cover photo on that issue might have led some to doubt the complete veracity of that statement (Tucker 267).

Dolly Adams

Another lady with drumming skills, Dolly Adams, who also played piano and other instruments, formed the Dolly Adams Band in New Orleans in 1937. Adams, who was born Dolly Marie Douroux in 1904, grew up in a musical family. The Douroux family band began playing professionally in the 1880s. Dolly's father, Louis Douroux, was a trumpet player with many well known brass bands, and her mother, Olivia Manetta Douroux, played piano, violin, and trumpet.

Dolly began studying piano at age seven and received other musical instruction from her uncle and noted New Orleans bandleader Manuel Manetta. She joined her uncle's band at age thirteen and had the opportunity to play with musicians such as the young Louis Armstrong, Kid Ory, and Joe "King" Oliver, all of whom went on to become some of the most respected bandleaders and jazzmen of the century. In this rich musical environment, she added to her skills by learning to play drums, bass, guitar, and trumpet.

As a pianist, young Dolly found herself much in demand. As most early jazz bands were marching groups made up of brass and reed players, pianos were never used, but once bands started playing in other venues besides the streets, the piano became an instrumental staple. Bands, usually all-male, didn't mind having a woman at the 88s, playing the chords they needed to back up their improvisation.

After two years with the Manetta band, Dolly joined Peter Bocage's Creole Serenaders. She also played with clarinetists Louis "Papa" Tio, Lorenzo Tio, Jr., and Aphonse Picou. At sixteen, she formed and led her own group, which had a regular gig as the pit band at the Othello Theatre on Rampart Street playing backup for vaudeville acts and silent movies.

In 1922, Dolly married, and at her husband Placide Adams' request, gave up life as a musician to stay at home and raise seven children. Using her musical skills, she trained all seven children to play multiple instruments. In 1937, with the family facing a financial crisis, her husband gave in and allowed his wife to resume her career. She formed the Dolly Adams Band, first with her brothers and then with three of her sons. The popular dance band performed well into the late '60s and as musical times changed, so did they, transitioning from Dixieland to rock 'n' roll.

Spitalny's Hour of Charm

In 1934, Phil Spitalny, a Russian immigrant and child clarinet prodigy, entered the scene. He had led an all-male orchestra but disbanded it when the Depression hit. The idea for an all-female orchestra came to him after hearing violinist Evelyn Kaye Klein in a debut recital billed as "Evelyn and Her Magic Violin." Miss Klein impressed him both professionally and personally, the latter so much so he eventually asked her to be his wife.

After securing Miss Klein's services, Spitalny began auditions for other players. To decide who would be part of the group, he reportedly auditioned over 1,500 women. The orchestra, which eventually became "Phil Spitalny's Hour of Charm," was a huge hit and, and as a writer in the August 1938 issue of *Swing* magazine put it, proved that "women could bring to dance music the famous feminine qualities of gentleness, good taste, charm, and romance." The music was cornier than a Kansas cornfield, and, according to most critics of the day, far removed from real jazz musicianship. Linda Dahl in her book *Stormy Weather: The Music and Lives of a Century of Jazzwomen*, states it most succinctly: "A hot band it was not."

Despite any negative connotations, Spitalny's group was so successful that, according to music historian Sherrie Tucker, "its sound and character became synonymous with all-girl bands for years to come. Tucker acknowledges that "the Spitalny creation—the mental image of billowing dresses and cultured white womanhood conjured by the sweeps and flurries of harps and strings and high, 'legitimate' soprano voices—shaped audience expectations on a mass level, for better or for worse, for all other all-girl bands."

This didn't mean there weren't some exceptional musicians in Spitalny's group. They were willing to work in the band, despite its reputation for what was then called "Mickey Mouse" music, because of the good money and great benefits, including paid vacations. Many of the musicians reportedly owned stock in the organization. They also had some prestigious admirers, including the classical conductor Arturo Toscanini, who expressed his amazement at the "precision and skill of these girls."

Because of the generous benefits associated with the gig, women who played in the group were willing to put up with Spitalny's strict rules, which included six hours of practice each day and signing a contract, which prohibited them from marrying without giving six months' notice.

Their network radio show, *Hour of Charm*, introduced thousands of listeners to the concept that women were capable of playing band instruments and inspired more than one girl to take up music as well.

Mary McClanahan

One of the most skillful musicians in the group was drummer Mary McClanahan, who had already established a reputation for herself as a topnotch player before she joined Hour of Charm. She broke new ground for women drummers when the Gretsch drum manufacturing company featured her in a full-page ad in *Metronome* magazine in November 1939. In the ad, the perky Miss McClanahan was shown glammed up in a lavish gown, proudly showing off her femininity as she banged away on a Gretsch-Gladstone drum set.

Below her picture, the ad read: "Vivacious Mary McClanahan, featured drummer of Phil Spitalny's All-Girl Orchestra, in General Electric's 'Hour of Charm' over coast-to-coast N.B.C. network. Mary began playing the drums at the age of five and has been 'going to town' ever since. An artist in both symphony and swing, she now reaches her greatest heights handling her new Gretsch-Gladstone Combination as pictured in action above. . . . When critics lavish their praise on Mary McClanahan's superb performance in the All-Girl Orchestra, she generously honors with the Gretsch-Gladstone Combination that is her constant inspiration" (Falzerano, *DRUM!*).

The Gretsch ad was a milestone because it marked the first time a woman drummer had been endorsed by a major drum company, in fact a company that had built for itself a reputation for making the best drums sets in the jazz world at that particular period. The company obviously considered her more than a novelty, and further affirmed her talent when they pictured her on the cover of their full-line catalog alongside Count Basie's drummer Papa Jo Jones, Artie Shaw's Nick Fatool, Horace Heidt's Barry Mattinson, and Xavier Cugat's Alberto Calderon.

When McClanahan left the Hour of Charm, she was replaced by another outstanding drummer, Viola Smith, who became known as the "female Gene Krupa."

Black All-Girl Bands

One can't ignore the role that race played in the music scene of the 1930s. In fact, women musicians of that decade have even been credited for leadership in paving the way for desegregation. Black all-girl bands were said to have a distinct sound from their White counterparts and won numerous fans for their musicianship. Some White women liked the Black bands' style of jazz so much that they passed for Black so that they could tour with them. These women traveled together, ate together, and shared hotel rooms. But mixing of the races was against the law in most of the South, and more than one woman, trying to pass, ended up spending time in jail.

Of the many African American all-girl bands that became popular in the 1930s, the Harlem Playgirls and the International Sweethearts of Rhythm were among the most critically acclaimed.

The Harlem Playgirls

The Harlem Playgirls were organized in 1935 by Milwaukee-based drummer and bandleader Sylvester Rice. Most of their members, including drummers Henrietta Fontaine and Jennie Byrd, were veterans of earlier bands such as the Dixie Rhythm Girls and Dixie Sweethearts. The group appeared at the Apollo Theatre in 1937 and competed against Johnny Long's big band in 1938 in the prestigious battle of the bands contest sponsored by the Chicago Savoy. Many members went on to perform with the Prairie View Coeds and the International Sweethearts of Rhythm.

International Sweethearts of Rhythm

The International Sweethearts of Rhythm was the first integrated all-girl band in the United States. They became one of the most renowned and respected women bands of the 1940s.

The group started as part of a fundraising effort for the Piney Woods Country Life School in Piney Woods, Mississippi, a boarding school for poor African American children, most of whom were orphans. The school's founder and principal, Dr. Laurence Clifton Jones, had discovered one way to raise money for his struggling institution was by booking the school's musical groups for parties and dances sponsored by local civic and religious organizations. The school had several choirs—the Cotton Blossoms, Magnolia Blossoms, and Orange Blossoms—and an all-male jazz band—the Syncollegians—all performing on a regular basis to raise money for the school.

Inspired by Ina Ray Hutton's Melodears, Jones decided in 1938 to add to Piney Wood's musical groups an all-girl swing band. A former Cotton Blossom turned faculty member, Consuela Carter, was tapped to lead the new band. They were given the name the International Sweethearts of Rhythm because of the multi-ethnic (Asian, Latina, Native American), mixed race backgrounds of some band members.

After an initial successful East Coast tour, the new band went on the road performing in churches and Black venues all over the country, playing as many as twelve engagements in sixteen days. For this group, unlike many of the all-girl groups of the time, there were no gowns or glamour. They lived under strict rules imposed by band manager and chaperone Rae Lee Jones, described as "a big old matron," who like a jail warden would lock up her girls at night.

The Sweethearts won critical accolades everywhere they went. They eventually became professional and severed their ties with the Piney Woods school in 1941.

Pauline Braddy

Drummer Pauline Braddy was one of the original members of the group. She was a student in the Piney Woods school as her mother before her. In a 1985 interview with Sally Placksin, she said, "It was a gorgeous place, and it did so much for so many poor blacks in the South. . . . A kid could go to school and not have to pay anything. You worked your way and they taught you something."

Braddy first played clarinet in the school's brass band. "I got the drums by accident," she said. She recalled her first big band experience was when Jones took a group of girls to Memphis to see Louis Armstrong. She says her heart then was set on playing alto sax. When the drummer they had dropped out, she said everyone was asking, "What are we gonna do for a drummer?" Braddy, despite her resistance to taking the job, was the band's first choice. "They said I had a good sense of rhythm. They said 'Pauline's a natural.' I cried. Who wanted to play the drums? So I was stuck with it, really" (Placksin 135–36).

Braddy readily learned the rudiments of drumming and was rewarded for her efforts by being dubbed "Queen of the Drums." A Chicago newspaper lauded her talent: "This young swing drummer is one of the reasons why the International Sweethearts of Rhythm is by far the most popular girls' orchestra in the country today." Her drumming played a big part in the Sweethearts' third place finish in big band competition sponsored by *Swing* magazine in 1940. Not bad, considering they were the only girl band among the thirty contestants.

In 1938, the band toured Mississippi, playing stock arrangements in dance halls. Rae Lee Jones, no relation to the school's founder, was hired as chaperone. Vivian Crawford traveled with them as tutor, and trumpet player Edna Williams was the music director.

The teenage girls often bucked the restrictions imposed on them. In Placksin's *American Women in Jazz: 1900 to the Present*, Braddy is quoted: "We had records, but we weren't supposed to have them, 'cause it was a religious school. We used to hide them . . . Count Basie and Andy Kirk and all the old black swing bands."

She said the girls would often "sneak off and go places." In Placksin's book, she recalls a time they were caught and run out of an Elks Club by the noted Apollo emcee Willie Bryant. "We had gotten our cigarettes and our rum and Coke—we didn't know anything else to drink. The lights came on and he (Bryant) said: 'Excuse me ladies and gentlemen, I see some of my children.' He put us in a cab . . . tipped the driver, and told him not to leave till we got on the elevator. And we were trying to be grownup! But . . . we were a bunch of little nutty kids."

As a drummer, Braddy said she encountered prejudice from skeptical audiences who often exclaimed, "Oh no, not a girl!" She also said women had to fight the prevailing attitude that women "should stay home and learn to cook and all that kind of stuff." She said letters from the musicians' union always started off "Dear Brother" or "Dear Sir," which she found "kind of insulting" (136).

With women drummers being scarce, Braddy looked to drummers such as Ed Thigpen and Gene Krupa for guidance. She played well enough that she won praise from male drummers such as Sid Catlett who played with Louis Armstrong and Papa Jo Jones who played with Count Basie.

During the 1940s when the Sweethearts were at their peak, a quartet from the band recorded an arrangement of "Blue Skies," and Braddy played a drum solo on her specialty, "Drum Fantasy." "It was fabulous," she said. "You painted your sticks with fluorescent stuff and the cymbals and the rims and then they put on black light. I played with white gloves. It broke up the [audience] all the time" (136).

She continued to play with the Sweethearts of Rhythm until 1955. Braddy also played in the Vi Burnside Combo. Burnside, a tenor sax player, was another musical standout in the Sweethearts of Rhythm. Braddy, who was thirty-three when she left the Sweethearts, performed with numerous jazz ensembles until the late 1960s when she put away her drumsticks and retired. She came out of retirement in 1980 to play in a tribute to the Sweethearts at the Women's Jazz Festival in Kansas City, Missouri.

Braddy died in 1996, leaving a legacy as true pioneer who broke ground for future women drummers. Today she is still considered one of the top female drummers of the twentieth century.

Ivy Benson's All-Girl Band

While drummers like Braddy were making names for themselves in the United States, other female drummers were becoming known in the popular music world overseas. A number of female drummers played in the U.K.-based Ivy Benson all-female swing band. The band formed in 1939 and would continue making music until 1982.

Benson, a child prodigy, was born in Leeds in 1913 and was playing piano professionally—billed as Baby Benson—at the age of eight. Her father, a classical musician who played in the Leeds Symphony, hoped his daughter would become a concert pianist. But after hearing a Benny Goodman record, the young Benson decided jazz was more to her tastes, and she learned how to play clarinet and saxophone. She dropped out of school at age fourteen and took a factory job, saving enough money to buy her first saxophone.

Her first band, Ivy Benson and Her Rhythm Girl Band, was an eight-piece group that rose to fame in the 1940s. They were headliners at prestigious venues such as the London Palladium and eventually became the BBC's resident house band. The group became known as the Ivy Benson All-Girl Band.

Marie Cleve, Betty Thomas, and Jean Pine were drummers for the band during its first decade. In the 1950s, Paula Pyke took over drumming duties, and Crissy Lee was the drummer from 1960 to 1966 and 1970 to 1973. From the mid to late '70s, the drummer was Christine Pierce.

Benson's band was known for its high turnover and over four decades had more than 250 members. During World War II, many of her musicians left to marry GIs they met on tour. English historian Victoria Lowell cited this quote in a November 4, 2008, article in the *Yorkshire Evening Post:* "Only the other week a girl slipped away from the stage. I thought she was going to the lavatory, but she went off with a GI. Nobody's seen her since."

Benson never lacked for female drummers. However, in the book *The New York Times Television Reviews 2000*, a band member recalled she did hire a man in drag for one night only to cover for an ill musician.

CHAPTER 5

Hep Girls: The '40s

> In these times of national emergency, many of the star instrumentalists of the big name bands are being drafted. Instead of replacing them with what may be mediocre talent, why not let some of the great girl musicians of the country take their places?
>
> —Viola Smith, *Down Beat*, 1942

For any woman, much less any female drummer, trying to make it in the male-dominated jazz world, acceptance didn't come easy. An editorial appeared in the February 1938 issue of *Down Beat* under the headline: "Why Women Musicians Are Inferior." The anonymous author wrote: "The woman musician never was born capable of sending anyone further than the nearest exit." The writer had this to say about women drummers: "If more girl drummers had cradle-rocking experience before their musical endeavors, they might come closer to getting on the beat."

The multi-talented Peggy Gilbert who played saxophone, clarinet, violin, and vibes, and directed the Peggy Gilbert All-Girl Orchestra, wrote an article in response, which, much to her chagrin, appeared under the headline: "How Can You Blow A Horn with a Brassiere?" (*Down Beat*, April 1938).

There was also criticism for the number of all-girl bands that sprang up in the 1930s. Catherine Gourley in her book *Rosie and Mrs. America: Perceptions of Women in the 1930s and 1940s* quotes a *Saturday Evening Post* writer who commented: "One more girl band is about all this country needs to send it right back to the depths of the Depression."

Others doubted the competence of any woman in a jazz band. Marvin Freedman wrote in the February 1941 issue of *Down Beat*, "Good jazz is hard, masculine music with a whip to it. Women like violins, and jazz deals with drums and trumpets." That likely ruffled the feathers of more than one woman musician, including drummer Pauline Braddy of the International Sweethearts of Rhythm.

On September 1, 1939, Germany attacked Poland without warning, officially sparking the beginning of World War II. On December 7, 1941, Japan suddenly pushed the United States into the struggle by attacking the American naval base at Pearl Harbor. Four days later, Hitler declared war on the United States, and President Roosevelt called on Congress for immediate and massive expansion of the armed forces.

Call to Duty

World War II brought about drastic changes as nearly sixteen million American men were called on or volunteered to serve in the armed forces overseas and stateside. Women were suddenly in demand to fill gaps created by the depletion of manpower in the labor force. In movies, newspapers, posters, photographs, magazine covers, and articles, a campaign, which pictured the perky, bandanna-clad Rosie the Riveter, stressed the patriotic need for women to enter the work force. In huge numbers, women answered the call.

Suited up in overalls and work boots, women were building aircraft and working in munitions factories. They were laying tracks for railroads and laboring as steelworkers in shipyards.

Women musicians also found themselves in demand. Suddenly newspapers were filled with ads looking for female instrumentalists to replace the men who had gone off to war. All-girl bands began to organize to fill the void. But the prevailing attitude was that these women were just doing their patriotic duty. Being skillful musicians had nothing to do with it.

Some men not eager for combat duty saw all-girl groups as a way to avoid the draft and began to organize such groups for USO tours. Eddie Durham, who led the All Star Girl Orchestra, admits leading an all-girl band was the only way he could stay out of the Army. "So long as I kept the girls' band, I'd be deferred from the army every six months for the duration" (Tucker 50).

Durham's band was female, except for one player: the drummer. In 1943 and 1944, Kid Lips Hackett held that post.

After the war started, many clubs and entertainment venues were closed as America went into a "lights out" mode. Fear of another attack was intense, and if people were listening, it was for the sound of an air raid siren.

All-American Girl Orchestra

Ada Leonard's All-American Girl Orchestra was one of the few bands playing December 7, 1941, when the Japanese attacked. They were performing for the troops at Fort Belvoir, outside Washington, DC. Leonard's orchestra was the first to be signed by the USO when the United States entered the war. Before embarking on her career in music, Leonard had toiled as a stripper in a Chicago nightclub. When her all-girl band started performing in 1940 in that same city, the former stripper had to put up with as many shouts for "Take it off!" as shouts for her musicians to "take off" on solos.

As someone who could convey sex and propriety at the same time, Leonard was the epitome of sexy starlet and girl next door: the All-American girl popularized by Hollywood and the pinup posters that hung over every soldier's bunk.

Leonard had dreamed of heading an all-girl orchestra since being in a 1939 show with Rita Rio and her all-girl band. She was the daughter of vaudevillians and had taken piano and cello lessons, but admitted to being "lousy" on both. Conducting, however, was something she definitely thought she could do (Tucker 262).

When she was recruited to head the new all-girl orchestra organized by saxophonist Bernice Little, trumpet player Jane Sager, and agent Al Borde, Leonard embraced her new role with relish. She loved gliding about the stage in a tight-fitted gown, waving her baton with what historian Sherrie Tucker described as "sophistication and grace of a prima ballerina."

World War II gave the new band their name. The girls wore red and white stripped blouses and blue skirts and were touted as the orchestra of all-American girls.

Playing camp shows for the USO was no glamorous gig, according to Leonard. In an interview, which appeared in the September 10, 1943, issue of the Army weekly, *Yank*, she said, "There's as much glamour in trouping Army camps as there is in digging slit trenches."

The USO schedule was rigorous. For about eighty dollars a week, the musicians would play two shows a night, six and sometimes seven days a week, if they were drafted to do a hospital show on their day off.

When they were not on the USO camp show circuit, the band was playing ballrooms, theatres, and clubs. Their reputation was such that *Down Beat* listed them regularly in their "Where the Bands Are Playing" column.

The band's repertoire was more sweet than swing. Leonard was even quoted in the December 1, 1942, issue of *Down Beat* as saying, "Girl bands should not play too much jazz" and "People don't expect girls to play high powered swing all night long. It looks out of place." Bob Fossum, the writer who interviewed Leonard for that article, went to check out the band at a Wisconsin armory and stated the band "definitely lived up to Leonard's expectations." He gave exceptions to "swing out" performances of "One O'Clock Jump" and "St. Louis Blues," and noted that the drummer Dez Thompson "stole the show with her rock-bound beat and flashy solos."

As time went on, the band took on more swing, winning the respect of critics who had once dismissed them. Bud Kissel wrote in the August 2, 1944, *Columbus Citizen*: "When the band went through a jivey arrangement of 'Seven Nights in Bastille,' they put up a strong argument against those who claim only male musicians can handle fast music."

"Fagel" Liebman

By 1944, the band was "on fire." Those are the words of drummer Florence "Fagel" Liebman who joined the group that year. Fagel, quoted by Sally Placksin in *American Women In Jazz*, said the band's repertoire was "unbelievable. It was a man's book."

Liebman grew up in Brooklyn, New York, and as a child was always tapping out rhythms on anything with a solid surface she could find around her house. She saved her money and bought her first drum set for twenty-five dollars. The young drummer, who had never taken music lessons and who couldn't read music, taught herself to play by listening to the big bands on radio, records on her family's wind-up phonograph, and finally by watching some of the best bands live. In uptown Manhattan, she heard Duke Ellington at the Apollo Theatre. In Times Square, she caught Benny Goodman's band at the Paramount. But for her, the life changing experience was seeing Gene Krupa. She told Placksin: "When I saw Gene Krupa, something just happened to my insides. I was never the same after that."

As a teenager, Liebman played in an all-girl quartet booked for summers at Jewish resorts. She later played with an Hour of Charm style band led by Al D'Artega. Liebman said D'Artega was a "great arranger," but he "didn't feel jazz at all." She left the band because jazz was really what she wanted to do. Joining Leonard's All-Girl Orchestra finally gave her that opportunity. She describes her days with the band as "the first really thrilling musical time of my life because that was all jazz" (Placksin 158).

But she admits the grueling time on the road was difficult as evidenced by this quote from Placksin's book:

> I would have to say there were times when we were so tired that we literally thought we were gonna die. Once on a train we were so

> tired—we hadn't laid our bodies down on a bed in I don't know how long—that we put newspapers on the floor and lay on the floor of the train. And we would dream of baths and showers. And, of course, a week in a theatre or something was like heaven. One-nighters, it was very rough. But if you wanted to play, that's what you had to do at that time. For me, there was never any question, ever. If it came with the package, then I bought the package. I had to play to breathe, and that was it.

Viola Smith

Spunky drummer Viola Smith, who made a name for herself as "America's fastest girl drummer," was in her heyday during the war years. She was called the "Female Gene Krupa" for the way she would hurl her drumstick in the air, then jump up in the air and catch it as it bounced. "Women musicians came out of the woodwork during the War," Smith said. "Bands knew I was available, and I had a lot of offers. I had the field pretty much to myself. There weren't many girl drummers."

Smith said that before World War II there was great prejudice against women as professional musicians. "The war overcame it to an extent. Female musicians started to be taken more seriously. [People] could finally see what girl musicians could do. They were finally given a chance."

Smith, a strong advocate for women musicians, deserves much credit for women being given that chance. In a 1942 editorial she wrote for *Down Beat* titled "Give Girl Musicians a Break," she stated: "In these times of national emergency, many of the star instrumentalists of the big name bands are being drafted. Instead of replacing them with what may be mediocre talent, why not let some of the great girl musicians of the country take their places?" Smith says she was standing up for women musicians not just as temporary wartime substitutes but for women to become permanent fixtures on the music scene, acknowledged for their skills and capabilities.

In the editorial, she argued that "girls have as much stamina as men" and "can stand the grind of long tours and exacting one-night stands." To those who maintained girls were able "to play only legitimately" as Western classical musicians, she countered that "hep girls" could "sit in any jam session and hold their own."

As for the "long on looks and short on talent" barbs against female musicians, Smith posed that women could be good musicians, good looks notwithstanding, and the fact they were visually attractive might even provide a little bonus showmanship. "Think it over, boys," she wrote.

Smith's editorial opened a floodgate of heated letters to the editor and debates between readers that lasted for months. Responses such as this from William Peri of Stockton, California, were common: "I'll tell you right now that I don't like girl musicians. Girls should leave this kind of business to persons who know what it's all about. And I mean men." Anne Hudee of Fredonia, New York, responding to Peri's comments, wrote: "I am a girl musician and I'm sorry but I'll have to say that most men musicians aren't as terrific as you think! I've heard girls play and brothers, some of them give out with the righteous jive!"

Surprisingly, the sides taken in this debate didn't always take gender lines. For example one woman from Cincinnati, Ohio, wrote: "Through no fault of my own, I happen to be a girl and I definitely agree with William Peri that girls do not make good swing musicians. When it comes to playing good music, girls, how about leaving it to the boys? We ought to be proud to be able to dance to such bands as Tommy Dorsey, Count Basie, etc. Our place is listening and dancing to music, not sitting in with the band and blowing our brains out."

And a man from Yuma, Arizona, had this response: "Who is William Peri to state dogmatically that girl musicians are inept? I have run across girl musicians who could blow some men off the stand" (Tucker 45–46).

As music historian Sherrie Tucker states in her book *Swing Shift*, this certainly wasn't the first time persons had debated over jazz musicianship and with whom or in what form it was most authentic. Throughout the 1930s and 1940s, people had argued not only about who the best jazz musicians were, but over issues such as the racial integration of bands and whether vocalists featured with a band added or detracted from the jazz experience. But Smith's editorial to "give girl musicians a break" was "historically specific," and, according to Tucker, addressed the question looming in the minds of many, especially the musicians' union: "What will happen to the jobs of drafted men musicians at a time when big band jazz and swing looms as the most popular American music and the biggest morale booster of U.S. citizens as the country enters the war?"

A month after Smith's editorial appeared, the following appeared in *International Musician* magazine: "building up of an army of 3,600,000 men is making drastic change indeed in orchestral line-up . . . top flight band membership is going to depend more and more on youngsters eager to show their mettle or older men who have previously stepped out in favor of youth, and on girls. All-girl orchestras, in fact, are notably successful in supplying those necessary build-ups to any swing ensemble: gayety [sic], comeliness, and ability" (47).

Born to Drum

Who was this rockin' drummer who started a firestorm by suggesting bandleaders replace drafted men musicians with "hep girls"? Viola Smith was born on

November 29, 1912, in Mount Calvary, Wisconsin. The sixth of ten children, eight girls and two boys, she was eleven years old when she took up her first drumsticks. She started performing and touring in the early 1920s with the Schmitz Sisters, a family band started by her father, a cornet player who owned a theatre/dance hall in Mount Calvary. Her father was adamant that each of his children should play the piano and at least one other instrument, and by the time Viola came along, "all the other instruments had been taken," so she was the appointed drummer.

Her parents set a mandatory two hours of practice each day during summer months and vacations and at least a half hour daily during school months. "It was hard work for everyone else but me," she said. She compared playing drums to playing tennis. "It was never tiresome—I loved it."

Smith, who celebrated her one hundredth birthday in 2012, said she had taken great pleasure in playing drums and felt it was a major reason for her longevity. "If I had been a trumpet player, it would have killed me," she joked, referring to her sister who died at age thirty-two. "I attribute her death to her trumpet playing." Along with her drumming, Smith says she's kept herself in shape by exercising, taking her vitamins, and drinking one large glass of red wine a day. She adds, "White wine is not quite as beneficial. There is a community in the southwestern part of France where the longevity rate is a hundred years. That's higher than in France in general."

At the time the author interviewed her for this book just before her one hundredth birthday, she was working three afternoons a week pricing articles at a quilting store in Costa Mesa, California. She hasn't played professionally since age sixty-two, but she was giving a few lessons in drum rolls to a lady drummer in an Orange County band, the Piecemakers. "There's a difference in how a drummer does single stick rolls for rock 'n' roll and legitimate drum rolls, and I'm teaching her the difference," she said with all the authority of a ninety-nine-year-old experienced drummer.

"I came here from New York to visit my cousins for two days and extended the stay to one and one half years," Smith said. She said the Piecemakers band was actually the "house band" for the store where she works. The store, which also goes by the name "Piecemakers," sells patchwork quilts to twenty-two countries and has a school that teaches quilting and other grassroots arts.

Smith admits that being part of a family band gave her a definite advantage. "Other girl musicians had a tough time getting started." Her father's connections also helped. The theatre was a stop for many first-rate ragtime and jazz musicians, such as Bix Beiderbecke, "one of the greatest trumpet players of all time," said Smith, and she and her siblings had a front row seat in learning from the best. In addition to playing between movie reels at the theatre, she and her sisters played gigs during weekends and school vacations.

By the time Smith was twelve, her dad acquired permission from the local musicians' union for the girls to travel the vaudeville circuit. The Schmitz Sisters, who later became the Smith Sisters, fast became a favorite on the RKO vaudeville circuit. Viola and her sisters performed with Jack Fine's Chicago Band Revue, engaging in battles of the bands in theatres throughout the Midwest on the Keith-Orpheum Circuit and sharing the bill for one year with another sister act, the Andrews Sisters. Smith's sister, Sally Ehlenbeck, replaced LaVerne Andrews at the piano at rehearsals when LaVerne joined Patty and Maxene in trio dancing numbers. Smith recalled that she and Maxene double-dated male ushers at the Oriental Theatre in Chicago. Lake Michigan was nearby and they would ride bicycles along the shore.

In 1936 Major Bowes, the host of a radio talent show, *The Major Bowes Amateur Hour*, a precursor to the later *Gong Show*, sent scouts across the country in search of an all-girl band to accompany winners of the competition in a nationwide tour. "Television announcers Ted Mack and Lloyd Marx came to Wisconsin to audition us," Smith said. Their orchestra was chosen for the gig and augmented to eighteen members.

The Schmitz Sisters disbanded in 1938, and Smith and her sister Mildred formed the Coquettes, a twelve-piece band that was frequently cited as the only rival to the very popular Phil Spitalny's Hour of Charm. Mildred played saxophone, violin, banjo, and clarinet, and Viola played drums, vibes, and tympani. The Coquettes played theatres and ballrooms throughout the East and Midwest.

Reviews often cited Smith's drumming talent. A critic for the *Schenectady Times* wrote: "She is full of tricky and subtle licks and puts her heart into it." Another reviewer in Hartford, Connecticut, wrote: "It is a real treat to watch this drummer beat and brush those drums." And from a review in the *San Antonio Express*: "pulchritudinous miss who so adeptly maneuvers the drums and cymbals" (Collins, "Viola Smith: High Heels and High Hats").

The Coquettes' drummer made such an impression that Smith and her drums made the cover of *Billboard* magazine in February 1940. She also attracted the attention of fellow Wisconsonite and jazzman Woody Herman, who offered her an opportunity to join his show. She turned him down because she was more interested in working as a drummer than being featured as a novelty act.

The Coquettes as a group also got their fair share of praise such as this rave from a Houston fan: "A swing band that gets hotter than a stump fire in a thicket gives a forty-five-minute performance that not only knows what it is all about at all times but winds up exactly at the right moment to prevent a feeling that you are getting a little too much for your money. I salute the young ladies and recommend them to anybody in search of a spoonful of sassafras tea for his spirit. The band has a very professional polish" (Collins).

An End and a Beginning

When Mildred married in 1941 and several other girls left the band for personal reasons—to go to college or to avoid divorce—that was the end of the Coquettes and the start of a colorful and extraordinary career for the drummer. As soon as people knew she was available, Smith started receiving offers from big bands, but they all required travel. "I was tired of the travel, and I wanted to be in New York," she said. "I had always wanted to be a New Yorker. I couldn't wait to get there and get my union card. I was ready to go."

At that time, the place to be was 52nd Street, also known as Swing Street, where some of the best small jazz bands of the time were playing every night. Smith says the clubs there were "jammed with sailors and army boys," and she wanted to be part of that scene. "Jiggs' Place was one of the Swing Street clubs, and they asked me to play drums," Smith said. "I didn't have my union card, but they wanted me to audition anyway. I ended up getting permission from the local union president to play without a card." He waived union rules that required a two-month wait before a card could be issued.

She said one of the best parts of her experience playing 52nd Street was the opportunity during intermissions to visit the other clubs and see great performers up close.

The young drummer also attracted her share of attention. Celebrities such as the renowned drummer Billy Gladstone, who was playing Radio City Music Hall, came to see her when she performed at Jiggs' Place. "I took lessons from him as did Gene Krupa and Buddy Rich when they were in New York," she proudly boasts. "Tommy Dorsey's drummer, Louie Bellson, came to see me three times mainly to see what I was doing with all those drums."

Other drummers checked her out for her unusual drum placement. "I was the only one at the time who had drums on top. I noticed others started copying my beats up high style."

She said there wasn't much jealousy among women drummers "because there wasn't anything to be jealous of. We were all doing our own thing. No one was trying to get my job."

While Smith was still playing with the Coquettes, she contacted Phil Spitalny about an audition for the Hour of Charm. As a courtesy to her fellow band members, she informed them of her action. Her audition, however, turned out to be a disaster. One of her fellow Coquettes, Rose Gilmartin, "a terrific musician," Smith said, "who could play two clarinets at once," sabotaged the audition by unhooking the legs of her drum. As she started playing her snare drum began to go down and then turn sideways. "It was all chaos!" She laughed, recalling the experience. "Everything went wrong." Nevertheless, she joined the orchestra and was part of the group for thirteen and a half years after the Coquettes disbanded.

She recalled another incident that wasn't so amusing: "On June 6, 1942, my father died, my fiancé was crossing the English Channel, and I was doing five shows a day at the Paramount Theatre in New York, plus the weekly TV show. While Phil Spitalny was introducing me, I fainted, but remained upright on the chair. Spitalny told the bass player to check me out. She shook me and I swung into action like a robot and played the solo like a robot. However, I did miss catching a stick that I had thrown on a drum," she said. "It bounced up high and landed with a thud on the bass drum—and instead of applause, gasps from the audience."

She said she had learned about her father's death from a nearby relative, but had told a friend in the orchestra not to tell the others. "It was easier to carry on pretending I had not received the news," she said.

Charm-Filled Life

Her "lovely life" as an Hour of Charm musician was further enhanced because she was a soloist and paid above union scale. She said she and her fellow musicians worked hard and played hard. Spitalny was generous with benefits, including some summers off.

She also said Spitalny could be difficult and wouldn't put up with any backtalk from his musicians. "Any girl that made him unhappy—that was the end," Smith said. She recalled one such instance of Spitalny's rage. "A fiddle player was taking her makeup off after a show, and I was packing up my drums. Spitalny called to her, 'They're waiting. Get on the bus!' She answered, 'But Viola is still packing up.' Spitalny yelled, 'Get the hell out of here!' She yelled back at him, 'Don't you swear at me!' That was the end of her."

While working as drummer for the Hour of Charm, Smith also was featured in films such as Abbott and Costello's *Here Come the Co-eds* in 1945 and *When Johnny Comes Marching Home* in 1942 with Allan Jones and Jane Frazee.

"While I was in Hollywood filming the Abbott and Costello movie, Charles Boyer held the door of the commissary open for what he could see were a few Spitalny girls entering. He didn't know there were twenty-two more musicians and ten dancers waiting to enter. As they continued to march endlessly into the room, the diners started to applaud Boyer. He took a very gracious bow in acknowledgement."

An attractive woman, working with high-profile celebrities, Smith was also at no loss for social invitations. She revealed in one article that she had no trouble turning down Frank Sinatra for a date—not once, but twice throughout her drumming career!

One of her most interesting dates was with an Algerian general who she met and dined with at the Excelsior Hotel in Rome, Italy. "It was during the French/

Algerian War, and I waited in the lobby while the general received messages about war activity in Algeria. After the general was briefed, he and I went for a carriage ride. He was one of the most interesting people I've ever met."

Smith also was an avid student and completed numerous extension courses in psychology and esthetics through Columbia University in 1946 and 1947 and in 1949 and 1950, philosophy and English composition at Hunter College in New York. In the summer of 1948, she received a scholarship to Julliard School of Music and was a member of the Julliard Symphony Orchestra under conductor Walter Handle. Later she studied with Karl Glassman, tympanist with the NBC Orchestra under Arturo Toscanini. In 1949 and 1950, she was a percussionist with the National Symphony Orchestra under Leon Barzin.

Smith honed her drum set skills, studying with swing drummers Cozy Cole and Ted Reed and getting tips from Buddy Rich and Gene Krupa. She, Reed, Krupa, and Rich were all students of Billy Gladstone. Smith considered Gladstone one of her major mentors and was the proud owner of one of his renowned snare drums.

Viola Smith's successful career and legendary stage presence were celebrated in review after review:

"Viola Smith does a Krupaesque smash solo at the traps, including an electric bit with radium-painted drumsticks" (*Variety*).

"We could just let down our hair and really do some raving. Such a mood hit us the other night—perhaps it was the savage beat of Viola Smith's drumming" (*Hollywood Radio Daily*).

"It takes a lot of skin beating to stop the show, but Viola Smith, dynamic drummer does just that! You should hear her play her own 'Drum Concerto'—a sensational exhibition of stick work that leaves audiences gasping" (*Los Angeles Daily News*).

In the 1950s, producer David Merrick retained Smith as a contractor to put together an eight-piece all-girl orchestra for his Broadway production of "Some Like It Hot." Smith said he specified that all girls had to be of equal height and weight. "That was a tall order," she said, "as the girls also had to be young and excellent musicians."

In the mid-1940s, she was "courted" by another top Broadway producer, the Tony award winner Jules J. Leventhal. "One of the perks of that courtship was accompanying Jules on many of his visits backstage and meeting famous Broadway stars. Another perk was that he gave my friend Audrey Swensen, from the Spitalny orchestra, a part in one of his plays."

After she left Hour of Charm, Smith joined the Broadway production of *Cabaret* with original cast members Joel Grey, Jill Haworth, Lotte Lenya, Anita Gillette, Bert Conway, and Jack Gilford as the on-stage drummer for the Kit Kat Club's all-girl band. After three years on Broadway, she traveled with the

Cabaret show, spending six weeks at Papermill Playhouse Theatre in New Jersey and a month in Boston. She played a month at Michael's Club in New York and did one-week stands in numerous cities throughout the United States. In the spring of 1974, she appeared with Liza Minnelli in Bob Fosse's TV concert special "*Liza with a 'Z'*." Later that year, Viola put her sticks away and retired.

Still "Hep" Today

Her reputation as a pioneer among women drummers is undisputed. In a 2002 article in *Not So Modern Drummer* on female drummers of the swing era, Beverly C. Collins writes:

> Viola Smith made an indelible mark on the drumming community. The evidence of her far reaching inspiration and influence are readily apparent today. . . . In 1942, Viola Smith declared to the American music community that "hep" female drummers might just be here to stay—and it was the rim-shot heard 'round the world!

On September 12, 2000, Smith was among eight musicians honored at New York's Lincoln Center in a tribute to women legends of jazz. She has been featured in the International Who's Who in Music (Mid-Century Edition) and the National Who's Who in Music.

As of 2013, when this book went to press, 101-year-old drummer Viola Smith was still going strong and hadn't missed a beat.

CHAPTER 6

Called to Duty: War Years

> Sometimes the guys were a little leery of girls playing drums. But I think they kind of respected me a little bit because they would let me sit in.
>
> —Helen Cole

The International Sweethearts of Rhythm, thanks to the musicianship of members such as drummer Pauline Braddy, came to be known during the war years as one of the most popular all-girl bands in the country.

Music scholar Sherry Tucker's vivid description of a wartime performance of "Lady Be Good" in her book *Swing Shift* demonstrates why they were so popular:

> The entire band in unison plays a rapid descending five-note sequence, which is answered by Pauline Braddy's cut-time drums, as if to signal just how fast this rendition is going to be. Again, the sequence, and again, the drums. The reeds take the first chorus in swift, close harmonies, full of swirling figures and elaborations around the melody. In the short spaces between phrases, the brass respond with a flurry of notes at the same breakneck tempo. . . . While the crowd whistles and cheers, the entire band punches out a few lines, then halts suddenly. It's time for a show-stopping drum solo by Braddy. Chorus after chorus, Braddy's drums draw shouts of applause at every new configuration of paradiddles. As the crowd rises, clapping and yelling, the ensemble rejoins the drums to start guiding this piece to a close . . . the band hits the finale. The soldiers respond with wave after wave of thunderous applause.

Members of the International Sweethearts of Rhythm, who had toured for three years under the sponsorship of the Piney Woods School in Mississippi, suddenly severed their ties with the school in April 1941. A headline in the Washington, DC, *Afro-American* newspaper read: "Girls Band Flees Dixie After Tiff with School" (Patterson 63).

The newspaper article reported that the band had returned thousands of dollars to the school but themselves only received two dollars a week in wages and fifty cents a day for "traveling expenses." In a follow-up article that appeared in the May 3, 1941, *Afro-American*, the band's getaway was described. According to the article, the seventeen members of the Sweethearts who made their escape were "pursued by highway police . . . through seven states to Washington and freedom" (Placksin 132).

Hardly missing a beat, the Piney Woods school took no time replacing them with the understudy band, the Swinging Rays of Rhythm.

The Sweethearts' chaperone Rae Lee Jones, who some speculated had instigated the break with the Piney Woods school, became the Sweethearts' manager, and Arlington, Virginia, became the band's new home base.

By August 1941, the new group made its debut at New York's Howard Theatre as part of an all-female revue headlined by Billie Holiday. By 1944, a *Down Beat* poll ranked the Sweethearts "America's #1 All-Girl Orchestra."

In 1945, the Sweethearts were off for a six-month tour through France and Germany to entertain the troops.

White and black players in the racially mixed Sweethearts band often found themselves living together as roommates. For example, black drummer Mattie Watson, who joined the Sweethearts in the mid 1940s, was a roommate to white trumpet player Maxine Fields. Fields, in Tucker's *Swing Shift*, recalls a conversation between her and the drummer. "One night we were sitting there making up. And she started yelling, 'Isn't this a damn shame?' And I said, 'What's a damn shame?' She said, 'Look at you. You're putting darker makeup on. And I'm sitting here putting lighter makeup on. You're curling your hair, and I'm straightening mine.' And we both started cracking up."

Another drummer, Ruth Raymer, who played with the California Sweethearts of Rhythm, a ten-piece offshoot of the original group, was black, blue-eyed, and fair. She was constantly threatened with arrest during a tour of the South because police thought she was white. "It was a mixed band, she said, and there were white girls, and they wore very dark makeup at that time, very, very dark makeup" (157).

The experiences of these two black drummers dramatically illustrate the discrepancies of the rigid Jim Crow laws governing the South at that time. If a white woman was "passing" for black or vice versa, it meant the races were co-mingling—that is, working, traveling, and eating together. Under Jim Crow laws, that was a crime.

Prairie View Co-Eds

The International Sweethearts of Rhythm weren't the only all-girls band of color making an impression during the war years. An article in the March 11, 1944, *Pittsburgh Courier*, headlined "PV Co-Eds Keep Music Alive While Boys Battle Axis," declared: "The absence of millions of men have [sic] left vacancies in many fields, which are rapidly being filled by the fairer sex. At PV (Prairie View) in order that music may still be kept alive, the co-eds have taken over . . . with tremendous success."

Prairie View College, an all-black school in southeast Texas, became home to the Prairie View Co-Eds when in 1943 the music director Will Bennett decided to create a "draft-proof" band. When war depleted the school's all-male dance band, the Collegians, Bennett began to recruit girls from the school's music department and its concert and marching bands. He also looked to high schools for possible recruits. Colleagues at Terrell High School in Denison responded that they not only had three outstanding women players, but all three were members of a local co-ed swing band performing regularly with their teachers for dances and other events.

One of the three talented musicians was drummer Helen Cole. The other two were trumpeters Clora Bryant and Elizabeth Thomas. Bennett had already recruited another Terrell High School alum, trombone player Margaret Bradshaw.

Helen Cole

Helen Cole said drumming for the Co-Eds was "the only way that I had of trying to put myself through school." Cole played French horn in high school but switched to drums "on a dare." As president of the senior class, Cole came up with the idea of putting together a jazz band featuring class members. She had a pianist, bass player, and trumpet player, but needed a drummer. The drummer for the school band was in another class, but his brother was a senior so she figured since the two lived together, the drummer brother could teach his older brother how to play. When her classmate refused, she said, "All you have to do is get behind the drums. Let me show you how. Now I had never been close to a drum, but, somehow, I knew what to do. I just sat down and started playing. Then the teacher said, 'I don't want to butt in, but I think you should play.' And I said, 'Oh no, no, no, I can't do that.' And he said, 'Well, maybe you better do it anyway.'"

Cole said the teacher invited her to stay after school because he wanted to try her out on some different rhythms. "He played the piano, and I kept up with him. I ended up being the drummer in the school band."

It didn't take long for Cole to discover she really enjoyed playing, and when the opportunity came to play drums with the Prairie View Co-Eds, she grabbed it. However, she needed a drum set. "My mother was a single parent and a domestic, and we didn't have a whole lot of money. But she and the people she worked for were determined that I would have my own drums, and they got them for me."

When she arrived at Prairie View, it soon became evident to Bennett, the music director, that she was an experienced dance band drummer and better than the drummer who was then playing with the Collegians. Cole had spent the previous summer before entering college playing in a swing band with her teachers. The band had a regular gig at a club in Denison. Because of that experience, Cole found herself not only playing with the Co-Eds but with the boys' band as well.

At first the Prairie View Co-Eds stuck close to campus performing for school dances and events. They soon started playing clubs, theatres, dance halls, and military bases in neighboring Texas towns. Because they were students, gigs were confined to weekends. During the summer of 1944, the Co-Eds, most of them aged seventeen, went on tour. They were represented by Moe Gale, a New York–based booking agent. Traveling in three station wagons, the group performed in Texas, Louisiana, Florida, Virginia, West Virginia, the Carolinas, Tennessee, Alabama, Mississippi, and New York.

Cole says soldiers were their most enthusiastic audiences. Tucker quotes her in *Swing Shift:* "Oh yes, boy, I'll tell you they were very good. They were real appreciative because, I guess, you know how that would be, where you don't see a bunch of girls. They were just thrilled. They made noises and everything."

At a base where the Co-Eds played for Black soldiers, another band member Margaret Grigsby recalled in an interview with Tucker seeing the men up in trees. "And when we started playing, they turned loose and fell out of the trees. They yelled, '*That's* what I'm fighting for!'" (122).

Cole said while some of the members of the Co-Eds had stories of racial prejudice, she herself never had those experiences. She also admits it was probably because she avoided "going to places where I knew I wasn't wanted. I knew where the boundaries were. Why would I go where I wasn't welcome?"

She said later when she left the Prairie View Co-Eds and had her own band, she did experience a racial incident while working in a club in Peoria, Illinois. "We were playing in a black club across the street from a white club. Our club got most of the business, so the owner of the white club would come over to hear us. He was always inviting us to come to his club. One day a white guy who had money came to our club and invited us to the white club for drinks. We accepted the invitation, knowing the owner would welcome us. When we finished our drinks, the bartender took every glass and broke them in front of us. Suddenly, everyone else in the club started breaking glasses. I got up and said, 'I'm leaving. You don't have to break any more glasses for me.'"

Cole said she and the band members later encountered the bartender, and he apologized for the incident. "He blamed it on his boss man. We knew that wasn't true because it was his boss who had invited us to the club in the first place."

When they were in New York playing at the Apollo, the Prairie View girls snuck out at night to catch music at the local clubs. They dropped in on jam sessions and sometimes did more than just listen.

Cole recalled: "Sometimes the guys were a little leery of girls playing drums. But I think they kind of respected me a little bit because they would let me sit in." In fact, Cole says one of her biggest thrills came when she sat in with Duke Ellington's orchestra.

At the end of the 1946 tour when the Co-Eds disbanded, Cole played with a smaller combo, a sextet that kept the name Prairie View Co-Eds for a short time. She gave up on pursuing a business degree and decided to stay with the combo. "It could have been the wrong decision for some people, but it was the right decision for me," Cole said. She said her main intent was to help her widowed mother, and as she was making good money as a drummer, she felt that was the way she could help her the most.

Over the next twenty-five years, Cole would work with various combos, touring fourteen countries and hauling her drum set throughout the United States, Canada, and the Caribbean Islands. In addition to working with Tiny Davis and her Hell-Divers, she and pianist Maurine Smith worked as a duo, and Cole also shared a few double bills with movie star Van Johnson, who became a good friend.

"I never had any problems finding bookings," Cole said. "I worked all the time." She credits her agent Joe Gayle for the steady work. Although based in Chicago, Cole was constantly on the road, traveling "all over the place." She said she still keeps in touch with many of the club owners who used to book her and her band regularly.

As to repertoire, Cole says her bands always played what the people wanted—not necessarily what she wanted. That meant along with jazz, her band played waltzes, polkas, and sing-alongs—"I played it whether I liked it or not."

She also recalls one time before getting a gig being asked, "Can you sing?" Even though she had never sung, she answered, "Oh, yes, we all sing," speaking as well for the rest of her non-singing band members. "When you're looking for a job, and they ask if you sing, you sing," she said. "The minute he booked us we started singing."

She said her efforts at vocalizing were less than stellar, and she was amazed when people would walk up and say to her, "You've got a nice voice."

"The more I sang, it got a little better—but not that much better. Today I can't hold a tune for the life of me."

She said one of the worst experiences on the road came when the pianist in a trio she was leading collapsed and died of a cerebral hemorrhage during an intermission. "I was a mess after that." She said the pianist's stepmother who lived in New York wouldn't take any responsibility, so Cole ended up taking the body back to her hometown in Denison to be buried.

Cole retired and returned to Denison in 1976 to care for her mother. She also enrolled in business school, earned her certificate, and then got a job in a local hospital. Aged eighty-six at the time of this interview, she said her "bad legs" wouldn't allow her to play drums anymore, but she keeps up with the latest music and frequently downloads tunes from the Internet.

In 2007 Cole received the Commander's Award for outstanding civilian service to the U.S. Army during World War II. The award was presented at a concert by the Jazz Ambassadors, the Army's field band at the Eisenhower Auditorium in Denison.

Entertaining the Troops

Symphony and pop percussionist Virgil Whyte formed another all-girl swing band, the Musical Sweethearts, in Racine, Wisconsin, in the early 1940s. The group, made up mostly of young blondes of Scandinavian background, performed up-tempo jazz in contrast to the sweeter, cornier style of some all-girl groups at the time. Whyte's intent was to take Phil Spitalny's all-girl concept into the swing and be-bop era. Known for their hot musical style and cited in reviews for their "sock and punch," the Musical Sweethearts entertained thousands of troops at some four hundred military bases between 1944 and 1948. In one year from 1945 to 1946, it played USO concerts in forty-seven states. When Virgil was drafted—much to his surprise, as USO service was supposedly exempt—his sister, drummer Alice Whyte, took over as bandleader. Virgil and Alice often ended their shows with a drum battle of the siblings. Alice, who drew her inspiration from Gene Krupa, later went on with four other women to form the Vadel Quintette, playing "lite" jazz in Chicago clubs into the 1950s.

Some all-girl bands doing USO tours overseas saw the war close up and personal. Drummer Marjorie Kiewatt played with D'Artega's All-Girl Orchestra, and on the way to a show in Italy, their ship was attacked by a German submarine in the Strait of Gibraltar. Fortunately, the ship, its crew, and passengers survived. Kiewitt says that in the weeks leading to VE Day, the band followed the troops north and played near the front lines. She recalls at one of the sites being warned, "Don't hit those drums too hard." An unexploded bomb was later found under the stage. In still another incident, she said a bomb dropped on a concert site just fifteen minutes after the band and troops dispersed on seeing a German spotter plane circling overhead (Tucker 257).

Black drummer Rae Scott also led an all-girl band that saw action overseas in what was called the "Foxhole Circuit."

The War Ends

When the war ended in 1945, the millions of men who had served in the military were anxious to return to their previous jobs. Many women who had become part of the war labor force were just as eager to go back to what they thought was their "rightful place" in the home.

Women musicians who had filled the void created by men who had been drafted suddenly found themselves without work because "patriotic" bosses who ran clubs and other entertainment venues thought guys returning from the war should get first shot at jobs and gigs. After all, the returning veterans needed income to support their families and children. No consideration was given to the women who also had family and financial responsibilities.

Tonya Bolden writes in *Take-Off*: "There were Joans, Sharons, Connies, Jeans, and Ediths who hung up their neck straps, packed away their drum kits, and stashed trams and trumpets in trunks because they were simply road-weary, discrimination-weary. Others wanted to marry and have children, and couldn't see a way to make band and family mix."

In *Swing Shift*, Sherrie Tucker tells of a returning soldier who torched his wife's musical memorabilia. "Also a musician, and jealous that his wife had occupied the bandstand while he was in combat, he destroyed the objects that would remind her of her career."

It was also a time when musical tastes were starting to change. Big bands were on the way out and jazz combos were in. Lady drummers were now looking for work with duos, trios, quartets, quintets, and sextets.

Margie Hyams

At least one female percussionist jumped on the small combo bandwagon as soon as the war ended. Marjorie "Margie" Hyams was a jazz vibraphonist, pianist, and arranger who had begun her career in the 1940s, playing with Woody Herman from 1944 to 1945 and the Hip Chicks in 1945. After the war ended she led her own group, a trio, which performed on 52nd Street in Manhattan.

In one account, Hyams was introduced to Herman by mutual friend Jack Siefert. Another account says Herman discovered her when he heard her playing in an Atlantic City nightclub. He tried to talk her into starting her own band, but she opted to play with his band instead. Herman had already broken convention by hiring a female instrumentalist in 1941: Billie Rogers, who played trumpet with Herman until 1943. When Hyams joined the group, she became part of a distinguished Who's Who of vibraphonists who played with Herman's band: Terry Gibbs, Red Norvo, and Milt Jackson.

In *Stormy Weather* by Linda Dahl, Hyams describes her experience working with the band: "In a sense, you weren't really looked upon as a musician, especially in clubs. There was more interest in what you were going to wear or how your hair was fixed—they just wanted you to look attractive, ultra feminine, largely because you were doing something they didn't consider feminine. Most of the time I fought it and didn't listen to them. Only in retrospect, when you start looking back and analyzing, you can see the obstacles that were put in front of you. I just thought at the time that I was too young to handle it, but now I see that was really rampant chauvinism."

One of the ways Hyams fought the rampant chauvinism was by refusing to wear a dress and insisting on wearing a band uniform instead.

As a member of Herman's band, Hyams won numerous fans, and critics favorably compared her to other popular vibes players of the swing era. But she was frustrated by the inability to "stretch out and really play" in that large band context (Dahl 87).

In 1945, she left Herman and formed her own trio, which stayed together until 1948. In 1947, she played a critically acclaimed Carnegie Hall concert with pianist Mary Lou Williams and June Rotenberg on bass. In 1949, she joined George Shearing's popular combo and remained there until 1950, when she gave up her mallets for marriage.

Changing Times

With music trends changing, bands such as the Prairie View Co-Eds and the International Sweethearts of Rhythm disbanded by 1946. Phil Spitalny's Hour of Charm lasted a few more years until 1954. His drummer Viola Smith went on for about twenty years as a solo act, billed as "Viola Smith and Her Seventeen Drums." Helen Cole, the drummer with Prairie View Co-Eds, joined fellow Prairie View Co-Ed Bert Etta Davis, as part of the sextet that morphed into the Hell-Divers headed by Tiny Davis. Davis also played drums along with several other instruments. The Hell-Divers toured internationally and recorded some singles for the Decca label. Another drummer, Fagel Liebman, played in combos led by trumpeter Flo Dryer.

Unfortunately for those of us who would later write about the drummers of these all-girl bands, little has been recorded about them or their fellow musicians. Seldom have they been subjects of biographies or oral histories, and information about them is scarce in most books written about the music of that era. Books on post-war jazz either ignore them or give them cursory or even condescending mention. Is it a surprise that most of these books are written by men?

Typical were comments such as this from George Simon, former *Metronome* editor, who wrote in his book *The Big Bands*: "The early part of her [Ina Ray Hutton, former head of the Melodears] career had been spent fronting an all-girl orchestra, one that most of us have forgotten and that she has probably been trying to forget ever since she gave it up to surround herself with men. For her an all-girl orchestra was like all all-girl orchestras. 'Only God can make a tree,' I remember having written in a review of some other such outfit, 'and only men can play good jazz.'"

Viola Smith, Helen Cole, Fagel Liebman, Pauline Braddy, Margie Hyams, and countless others who would come later would beg to differ with him.

CHAPTER 7

Hip and Diggin' It: Post-War to the '50s

> There are only five girls in the whole U.S. who are capable of playing first-chair trumpet . . . only three girl drummers, and only three girl altos who could handle their parts in a band such as I have now.
>
> —Ada Leonard

While many women drummers who had backed bands during World War II put away their sticks and gave up paradiddles to pursue other interests such as marriage and school, many stuck it out and continued to be active as musicians through the '40s and into the '50s.

In post-war America, the "nuclear family" with its "father knows best" mentality came into vogue. Specified gender roles called for the husband to be the breadwinner and head of the household and his wife to be a content June Cleaver apron-wearing homemaker. They had a couple of well-behaved children and lived in a suburban white picket–fenced utopia.

With the beginning of the Cold War between the United States and the Soviet Union, marriage, home, and children were all important. How better to ensure domestic security and protect the American way of life from nuclear threat and a Communist takeover. But some women didn't buy it. Given the choice between marriage and music, here's what one gal had to say: "The guy wanted to marry me. He said, 'It's me or the horn.' I said, 'Well it ain't you, babe'" (Tucker 317).

In her book *Swing Shift*, historian Sherrie Tucker describes how the nuclear family marginalized working women, single women, women whose primary relationships were with other women, and women who lived with friends or relatives. The female musician had to scramble to find work, and the opportunities available to her were now mostly limited to teaching, accompanying, performing in novelty acts, and working in cocktail lounges and churches. Many women musicians took day jobs to supplement their dwindling income.

The new social structure and changing economy of post-war years also had an impact on the music scene in general. The reckless spending of the war years had come to an end. Instead of going out to hear live music, people saved their money and stayed home. Once profitable and thriving ballrooms, hotels, and nightclubs, unable to cover expenses, went bankrupt and closed their doors. The primary source of entertainment now was black-and-white television, which by the early 1950s had made its way into almost every American home.

Post-War Chauvinism

For any woman struggling to be a professional musician, the post-war chauvinistic stance taken by booking agents, managers, commercial studios, and the American Federation of Musicians (AFM) was no help. AFM, eager to help the returning vets, issued lapel labels for them to wear, urging civilians to hire them in return for their courageous service and sacrifice. Meanwhile, women AFM members who had done duty during the war entertaining troops and providing music for studios, ballrooms, and orchestras were being asked to "bow out gracefully and let the returning GIs claim the jobs that were rightfully theirs." Any woman who didn't do so was considered a greedy, unpatriotic opportunist (Tucker 320).

In the rally to make certain male vet musicians were employed, little consideration was given the musician who was a discharged military woman. One company, however, has to be credited with making an effort to remedy the imbalance. In 1947, Hormel, best known as the makers of Spam—the canned meat kind—decided to organize a women's drum and bugle corps composed entirely of GI Janes who had served in the WAVES, WAACS, SPARS, and the Marines.

Admittedly, Jay C. Hormel, son of the Hormel founder, wasn't completely altruistic in coming up with the idea. He saw the female musicians as a flashy addition to an advertising campaign to promote his product. During the war, the United States had shipped Spam to American troops and allies abroad, and because of tin conservation at home, Americans had missed out on several years of this canned meat "delicacy." The Hormel company saw this as an opportunity to not only show their patriotism and support for women who had served their country but also as a way to jump-start sales for their signature canned meat product.

The "Spamettes"

To be a part of Hormel's troupe, a woman didn't necessary have to play drums, bugles, or any other instrument; the only requirement was that she be an ex GI. Hormel figured once the girls got involved, they could be trained as musicians as well as in sales. By August 1947, some sixty girls had been recruited, and instruments and uniforms were ordered for the Hormel Girls Drum and Bugle Corps, which would later come to be known by the somewhat apt nickname, "the Spamettes."

In August, the ladies began drilling and practicing in preparation for entering the American Legion National Drum and Bugle Corps Championship competition just a month away in New York City. They would be the first all-female corps to compete in that contest. For five weeks, the girls drilled their routine in ninety degree temperatures. According to an article in the August 24, 1947, *New York Times* ("It's a Lot of Noise . . ."), their hours of marching and the noise they made caused neighbors to unite in an attempt to file a temporary injunction against them. To avoid the legal suit, they moved their practice to a nearby baseball field. Over the duration of their few weeks of practice, the girls were reported to have gone through five hundred pairs of nylons.

In the contest, the women placed thirteenth, and as one clever Spamette put it, "failed to bring home the bacon." Despite their ranking, the Hormel girls were a crowd favorite. Following the competition, the women, decked out in their green, flight-attendant–like uniforms, marched up Fifth Avenue with the other bands, waving to an enormous and enthusiastic crowd.

After the contest, many of the troupe members gave up their drums and bugles and went home. Twenty-one remained and became part of a special sales force for Hormel. With fewer women veterans around, the stipulation that members had to be former military was dropped, and Hormel began to hire only professional musicians for the group. Many former members of civilian all-girl bands of the 1940s jumped at the opportunity, including drummer Marjorie Kiewatt who had played in the Al D'Artega All-Girl Orchestra. Carolyn Wilson Eklin, who joined the troupe, said she was a singer and flutist but learned to beat a drum like many of the other girls so that she could perform in the show's trademark drum-and-bugle finale and march in parades. One can only speculate how many of these women who learned to "beat a drum" for the sake of Spam went on to pursue that interest later.

In 1951, the Hormel Girls' Orchestra consisted of six violins, five saxophones, four trombones, five trumpets, one harp, four rhythm section players, and one marimba. Two smaller ensembles were also developed: a Dixieland band and a group that performed Latin-style music. The group traveled caravan style, about thirty thousand miles each year, in thirty-five white Chevrolets, performing in concerts, parades, radio broadcasts, and in-store campaigns, making music and beating drums for the purpose of selling Hormel meat products. When they weren't making music, they might be going door to door handing out coupons or in a grocery store passing out samples of the forty-odd canned products sold by the company at the time.

The Hormel girls received generous benefits—ten paid vacation days every three months along with free trips home—in return for respecting the company's authoritative rules, which made them subject to weight checks and forbade them from marrying and getting pregnant.

Deciding the expense of maintaining the troupe was too much, Jay Hormel finally disbanded the group in 1953. While Hormel had more than doubled their sales in the five years the group had been in existence, the drummers and other musicians who had played a major role in that effort would largely be forgotten.

Worth the Hassle

Despite the obstacles presented by post-war America for women in music, a number of talented women drummers bucked the prevailing sentiment and decided making music was worth whatever hassle they had to go through.

Pauline Braddy continued her stint on traps with the International Sweethearts of Rhythm and then with Vi Burnside's Combo until the 1950s when she decided to retire. Her five-year "retirement" ended when she joined a trio with Edna Smith and Carlene Ray in New York.

Drummer Elaine Leighton took a job backing duo vocalists Jackie and Roy from 1945 to 1950. Later she joined an all-woman trio headed by Beryl Booker, a self-taught Black pianist active on the New York jazz scene in the late '40s. The trio recorded and toured Europe in 1954 as part of a historic show called Jazz Club USA and opened nightly for Billie Holiday and other jazz legends.

In 1947, Ernestine "Tiny" Davis, known as "Tiny" because she was short and rather wide, formed a group called the Hell-Divers. Davis had played with the Harlem Playgirls in the mid-1930s and then moved to the International Sweethearts of Rhythm in 1939. She was with that group for eight years. When she left to form her six-piece combo, she recruited members of the former Prairie View Co-Eds, including drummer Helen Cole.

Davis, a multi-talented musician who played trumpet and several other instruments, often brought out her inner percussionist by pounding conga drums and thumping a tambourine. Her longtime partner was another drummer, Ruby Lucas. Lucas, a pianist as well, also played in the Hell-Divers.

When the war ended, Davis and Lucas realized women musicians were no longer in demand. They decided the best way to tackle that dilemma was to establish a "permanent gig" for themselves. In the early 1950s, they opened a club, Tiny and Ruby's Gay Spot, on South Wentworth Avenue in Chicago. The city eventually took over the property, and the two women went back to playing in other clubs. They performed regularly in nightspots in and around Chicago until Davis' arthritis forced them out of the music business. Davis and Lucas were featured in a 1988 short film produced by Andrea Weiss and Grete Schiller. Titled *Tiny and Ruby—Hell Divin' Women*, the film won numerous awards, including the Audience Favorite Award at the 1989 San Francisco Gay and Lesbian Festival.

Survival

During the early 1950s, some of the all-girl bands and their drummers continued to survive, thanks to radio and television. At least two groups—those led by Ina Ray Hutton and Ada Leonard—had already performed in short subject musical films and Hollywood feature length musicals. Their transition to television was an easy one, and they took advantage especially of the locally produced variety shows programmed by Los Angeles stations KTLA and KTTV. Unfortunately, the African American all-girl bands weren't so lucky in that regard. Because the 1950s were so culturally segregated, advertisers weren't keen on supporting a television show featuring Black artists. The variety all-girl programs also were limited to the West Coast, which was obviously more open to female-centric entertainment than the Midwest, East Coast, and the South.

Alas, the all-girl band variety format on television was short-lived. In 1952, Ina Ray Hutton's contract was not renewed, and Ada Leonard's show was dropped after just a year. The music trade magazines attributed their failure to the female bands being unable to compete with their male counterparts. Kristin McGee in her book *Some Liked It Hot: Jazz Women in Film and Television* quotes a review from *Down Beat*: "Ina and Ada made every effort to assemble bands in which musicianship was placed ahead of glamour (though there are some real cover kids in both outfits and the overall line-up that could supply plenty of cheesecake) but neither was able to produce a band that any honest critic could compare favorably with the average male ork."

Leonard, who gave up on girl bands and switched to leading a group of male musicians, proclaimed that girl musicians were too hard to find: "There are only five girls in the whole U.S. who are capable of playing first-chair trumpet . . . only three girl drummers, and only three girl altos who could handle their parts in a band such as I have now." In another interview, she said: "Top-notch girl musicians don't like to work in all-girl bands. They like to feel that they've been hired not because of their looks or their sex appeal, but because they are good musicians" (McGee 216–17).

Hutton's all-girl band returned to the television scene in 1955 for a program on NBC. Despite that show's initial high ratings, the program was dropped after only six weeks.

Sheelagh Pearson

Sheelagh Pearson had just completed a two-year (1950–1952) gig at a Gibraltar nightclub when she returned to London to find two offers awaiting her: one from Ivy Benson and the other from Gracie Cole, a trumpet player who had been working with Benson's band and who had decided to form her own orchestra. She played a few times with both groups and decided to go with Cole.

Pearson was born in Westminster, London, in 1928 and grew up in Kent. According to her bio ("A Modernist at Heart"), "I quickly showed an interest in music, learned how to play the accordion, and when I was eighteen, started playing in a local dance band. I was more interested in playing the drums, though, started playing them, and two years later I turned professional."

Her new career as a drummer began at the Mecca Ballroom in Edinburgh, where she stayed for a year, then a summer season in Devon, where she had her first experience playing in a pit orchestra for a pantomime show.

Pearson felt she was very lucky to be in a great band like Cole's after only a few years in the business. "Many of the arrangements we played had been written by Johnny Dankworth, and the band was hot!" The all-girls band was a sensation, and Pearson was voted "best girl drummer in the UK" in the 1954 *Melody Maker* Poll.

In 1956, Pearson joined the Lena Kidd Quartet, formed by tenor sax player Eleanor "Lena" Kidd, a former member of both Benson's and Cole's bands. A year later, she joined the Dinah Dee All Girls' Band and stayed with that group until 1960. In 1963, she decided to retire after twelve years of touring to set up her own business. She worked for twenty-five years in the Netherlands as office manager for a Dutch charity and then in 1993 moved back to Devon where she joined the Sidmouth Town Band as percussionist. She finally retired from music in 2004.

Kay Carlson

Katherine "Kay" Carlson was another drummer who successfully beat the odds in the male-dominated drumming world of the 1950s. Carlson, born in

Cleveland, Ohio, in 1931, started playing drums at age nine and by age eighteen was playing professionally.

In an interview with Los Angeles talk show host Sharon Dale before her death in 2010, Carlson told about growing up poor, living in an apartment with her parents and grandparents. There was a piano in the apartment, and her sister decided she wanted to take piano lessons. "As soon as I heard that, I wanted to take piano lessons, too," Carlson said. Unfortunately, there was money only for lessons for one, and the sister got them. Carlson said in the interview she was "crying all the time" when her mother told her about a friend who was a drummer for a theatre in downtown Cleveland. "He offered to give me drum lessons for free. So, I tried out the drums and I loved it!"

Two weeks after that drumming lesson, her sister quit the piano and never touched it again. However, Carlson had decided by then drumming was her passion. Her teacher gave her an old drum set. "You wouldn't believe how old it was, but it was my pride and joy," she said.

In high school, Carlson became known as "the girl drummer" in the band. "Because I was taking lessons and learning how to read music, I was able to play better than most of the boys and became head of the drum section," she said.

But she says at school dances, the boys always got to play the drum set, and that made her jealous. "They were playing without any idea of what they were playing."

By the time she graduated from high school in 1949, Carlson was already getting gigs around town. In the Dale interview she said, "I got lots of jobs, not because I was a girl, but because they needed a drummer and I was schooled." She also started teaching drums to some of the boys in the high school band. "I made them pay me fifty cents a lesson!"

The Cleveland Symphony at that time was all male, so Carlson joined the Cleveland Women's Symphony and became a member of the musicians' union.

Carlson said she had planned to go to college to study music, but her mother had a son late in life and decided he would be the one to go to college. She told Dale, "My music was important, but his future was more important."

Throughout the '50s, she played in various bands and orchestras touring the United States and internationally. She was part of a female big band that entertained U.S. troops in Japan and Korea for the USO. She was also drummer for an overseas show starring radio personality Johnny Grant. In the United States, Carlson was the drummer for the Spade Cooley Show on television and freelanced with various jazz combos and big bands. She eventually formed her own nineteen-piece big band, which performed regularly in the Los Angeles area.

Carlson told Dale that the standard uniform for women musicians playing at that time was a long gown, "because that's what the men expected." She recalls one day sitting at the drum set and straddling the snare drum. A very upset woman came up to her at intermission and said, "We can see all the way up to your undies." Carlson said she immediately bought a pair of evening slacks and wore slacks or pants from then on.

As a drummer she also found it difficult wearing high heels, especially when it came to dealing with the foot pedal. She revealed in the interview that during intermission she would secretly change to flat, evening-type shoes, and eventually began wearing flats all the time. She also had to wear cowboy boots when playing with a Western band on TV. "They had a heel, which was very uncomfortable, but I got accustomed to working the pedals," she said. "You do what you have to do."

One of the first women to be endorsed by the Ludwig Drum Company, Carlson was also one of the first female drum set teachers. For fifty years, she would teach over two thousand drum set and percussion students at Loyola Marymount University and in her private studio.

Carlson won national recognition when the REMO Drum Company presented her with its "Excellence in the Profession of Percussion Instruction" award in 1989. In 1993, the Pro Mark Drum Stick Company recognized her for exceptional dedication to percussive music education. She was also among the select group of women interviewed for the documentary *Lady Be Good: Instrumental Women in Jazz.*

Carlson died April 5, 2010. In her obituary, which appeared in the *Los Angeles Times*, she was recognized for "a remarkable trailblazing career" that "helped open doors for female musicians everywhere."

CHAPTER 8

Rock 'n' Roll, Baby! The '50s and '60s

> How can it be a gimmick just because we have a girl, Honey, on drums? Honey plays with us purely and simply because she is the right drummer for the job. If she wasn't any good, she wouldn't hold down the job.
>
> —Dennis D'Ell, Honeycombs lead singer

In the late 1940s and early 1950s, America found itself reaping the benefits of a post-war economic boom. With money being spent freely, the music scene thrived, albeit in a segregated world. Rhythm and blues was considered "race" music and was found almost exclusively in Black communities. According to music historian Daniel Glass, major record labels rejected it because they felt it was "too rough, raw and vulgar for 'mainstream' (a.k.a. white) listeners." Except for musicians such as Duke Ellington and Nat King Cole, most black musicians were forced to exist in a separate and not equal world. Their recordings were released on small independent labels, and Black neighborhood hangouts such as barbershops, grocery stores, and mom and pop outfits served as their sales outlets and distribution centers.

Because of this segregation, White America knew little about the music known as rhythm and blues, or R&B. And then cultural phenomena occurred: a new baby boomer generation of adolescents caused an explosion that completely changed the direction of the music industry. The teenager with leisure time and a weekly allowance became the new ruler in the realm of popular music. Savvy advertisers wasted no time in targeting this new "youth market," realizing its viability as a potentially lucrative demographic.

White disc jockeys on mainstream radio stations such as Hunter Hancock and Dick "Huggy Boy" Hugg began adding rhythm and blues records to their playlists. They did live broadcasts at high school "record hops" and started promoting mixed race R&B shows. Teenagers loved the pounding rhythms and beat. The new music was easy to dance to, and even better, they could identify with and own it.

Birth of Rock 'n' Roll

In 1951, a popular Cleveland disc jockey, Alan Freed, began playing rhythm and blues records on his nationally syndicated radio show. In 1954, Freed renamed his radio program *The Big Rock 'n' Roll Show*. (Drum rollllllll. . . .) Rock 'n' roll was "officially" born!

Although music historians say rock 'n' roll derived most directly from the rhythm and blues music of the 1940s, which developed from earlier blues, boogie woogie, jazz, and swing music, it was also influenced by gospel, country western, and traditional folk music.

To throw in a bit of trivia, sailors originally used the phrase "rocking and rolling" to describe the movement of a ship on the ocean. In the early twentieth century, the phrase was used to describe spiritual fervor; other times it was a metaphor for sex.

The teenager's love affair with this new musical form was demonstrated in the records they bought, the music they played on jukeboxes, the radio stations they listened to, and television shows they watched, especially *American Bandstand*, where they could hear the latest new music and learn the steps to the hottest dance crazes. It extended to films they saw that celebrated the rebel rocker and influenced a lifestyle that included leather jackets and pedal pushers, ducktail haircuts and cuffed jeans, hot rods and motorbikes, and a new rock 'n' roll jargon.

The older generation, for the most part, was not pleased with this new youth obsession. They were concerned that the music's influence could lead to juvenile delinquency and social rebellion. The realization that rock 'n' roll culture was shared by different racial and social groups was especially troubling to some. Daniel Glass in his book *The Ultimate History of Rock 'n' Roll Drumming 1948–2000* writes: "Something with so much power to affect an entire generation was sure to be viewed as a dangerous threat. Religious and community leaders lashed out against rock 'n' roll, claiming that it was leading their children into a life of juvenile delinquency. Many radio stations, vowing never to play the 'devil's music,' sponsored 'record breakings' at which hundreds of rock discs were publicly destroyed. For some, no doubt, the fact that rock music had its roots in African American culture was reason enough to condemn it."

As for performers in early rock 'n' roll, it was pretty much an exclusively male venture. Very few references are made to women and especially to women drummers until the 1960s. In fact, in researching the literature, most music historians neglect mention of any women during this period, and some say it wasn't until the 1980s that women really began to lay claims to the rock 'n' roll stage.

Women in the first decade of rock 'n' roll were still under the confines of a post-war America, which pressured them to stay in traditional roles—that is, find a husband, have children, and settle into life as a happy homemaker. Author Lucy O'Brien in her book *She Bop: The Definitive History of Women in Rock, Pop and Soul* proposes that perhaps rock was "too rigorously male-defined for a woman to find a comfortable place." This might have been especially true for women drummers who had to fight not only the gender bias of their instrument but the condescension of those who felt they weren't brash, ballsy, or masculine enough to handle the music.

Fortunately, with each decade, more women drummers took the risk and picked up drumsticks to take a rightful place in this male-dominated field.

Three of the first female drummers to receive any kind of mention in historical references were Claire Lane of the American instrumental pop group the Ramrods, Tina Ambrose of the British pop group The Ravens, and Honey Lantree of the London band The Honeycombs. Both Ambrose and Lantree were the only females in their bands and as a rarity naturally stood out based on that factor alone.

Lane and her brother Rich Litke formed the Ramrods in Connecticut in 1956. "Ghost Riders in the Sky" was their one big hit. Lane left the Ramrods in the late '60s to pursue a solo career as a singer.

Ambrose, a London native, was sixteen years old when she joined The Ravens in 1964. They made one recording, "I Just Wanna Hear You Say I Love You." Other than a YouTube video of their recording and a photograph of the band in which Ambrose is behind her drum set wearing a spiffy white leather suit, research turned up little else.

Other lesser known bands with female drummers included the Liverbirds, an all-girl Liverpool group that was active between 1962 and 1967. Silvia Sanders was the band's drummer. The Liverbirds never achieved much success in the United Kingdom, but they were a big hit in Germany.

The Mission Bells started out as the Intruders in 1963. The drummer for the East London band was Laraine Hall, who was later replaced by Laurie Brown.

Faith Orem was drummer for the Tremelons formed in 1963 in Niles, Michigan. In 1966, they changed their name to The Luv'd Ones and recorded for Dunwich before disbanding in 1969.

Honey Lantree

Anne Margot "Honey" Lantree was born in London in 1943. Before joining the Honeycombs, she was a hairdresser working in a North London salon owned by Martin Murray, the Honeycombs' founder. After a day filled with cuts and perms, Lantree took guitar lessons from Martin. The drummer in Martin's band often left his drum kit in the rehearsal space, and Lantree would try her hand at a few licks. She was good, and it wasn't long before Martin asked her to join his band. The band, originally called the Sheratons, played gigs in London's West End and at a North London pub. The group was later rechristened The Honeycombs as a pun on the drummer's name and her job as a hairdresser.

Lantree soon became the focal point of the group, which performed from 1963 to 1966. Her drumming skills—plus the fact she was extremely attractive—drew the attention of reviewers and fans. She was also an excellent singer. At age twenty-one she became the first woman drummer to play on a number one chart topper, "Have I the Right," released in June 1964. Their hit was distinctive for the prominence of the drums, whose effect was enhanced by group members stomping their feet on wooden stairs. "Have I the Right" reached number one not only in the United Kingdom but also in Australia and Canada.

Following the success of that recording, the Honeycombs went on tour to the Far East and Australia, and were consequently not able to promote their new records at home. Interest in the group waned as U.K. newspapers dismissed the band as a one hit wonder. Others called it a gimmick band with a pretty girl behind the drum kit who couldn't really play. To these charges, lead singer Dennis D'Ell responded in an October 17, 1965, article written by Peter Jones in the *Record Mirror*: "How can it be a gimmick just because we have a girl, Honey, on drums? Honey plays with us purely and simply because she is the right drummer for the job. If she wasn't any good, she wouldn't hold down the job."

After the Honeycombs disbanded in 1966, an attempt was made to form another all-female band featuring Lantree, but it was shelved when the organizers couldn't find enough "talented" female musicians. Even though female vocalists were becoming more plentiful, lady pop musicians were still a rarity in the '60s.

Lantree with her brother John, Dennis D'Ell, and Peter Pye later recorded a cover of "Live and Let Die." In recent years, she has been actively involved with the Joe Meek Society, an organization promoting the legacy of the man considered to be the British equivalent of the American record producer Phil Spector.

Moe Tucker

In the mid-1960s, another female drummer came on the scene, ready to leave her mark in music history. Long Island native Maureen Ann "Moe" Tucker, born August 26, 1944, started playing drums at age nineteen. She was asked to join the fledging rock band Velvet Underground in 1965.

An Ithaca College dropout, Tucker was working as an IBM keypunch operator when she replaced the band's original percussionist, Angus MacLise, who quit because he felt the band had sold out by taking a paying gig. A member of the band, guitarist Sterling Thompson, remembered her as a college friend's younger sister who played the drums and convinced the group to draft her. Her bio on the Velvet Underground website states: "Famed for her hatred of tree-hugging hippy bullshit and high hats, her cymbal free drumming style became the band's anchor." Daniel Glass in his book, *The Ultimate History of Rock 'n' Roll Drumming: 1948–2000*, said Tucker "kept the Velvets' music rooted in traditional rock rhythms, while the band's other members overlaid abstract (and often disturbing) lyrical images, feedback and other sound textures." The Velvet's manager, avant garde artist Andy Warhol, according to drummer/drum historian Glass, also encouraged the group to explore androgyny and other "gender-bending" ideas, "that would soon become commonplace among rock acts, ranging from David Bowie to the New York Dolls."

Tucker, herself, was noted for her androgynous appearance and massive attitude. She was also distinctive for her unconventional style of playing. She played standing up rather than seated. She said this gave her easier access to the pedals of the bass drum. Her kit included tom toms, a snare drum, and an upturned bass drum, which she played with a mallet rather than drumsticks. She had no use for cymbals, deeming them unnecessary, redundant, and overwhelming in their tendency to drown out other instruments of the band. Completely self-taught and faithful to a philosophy of keeping it simple, she believed the purpose of a drummer was solely to "keep time."

Tucker, acclaimed for her "primal, mesmerizing backbeats," counted rhythm and blues artist Bo Diddley and Nigerian drummer Babatunde Olatunji as her major musical influences. Apart from her drumming, Tucker sometimes sang vocals with the Velvet Underground and occasionally played the bass guitar during live gigs. After a two-year tour through North America and Europe, Tucker left the group in 1971 and moved to Phoenix, Arizona. After six years with the band, she was frustrated with the group's lack of success and decided to seek her fortune elsewhere.

While in Phoenix, she played drums in the short-lived band Paris 1942, and in the early 1980s divorced her husband and moved with her five children to Douglas, Georgia, where she took a job at a Walmart Distribution Center. She quit that job in 1989 when she was asked to join the band Half Japanese for a European tour.

Tucker is prominently featured in the Half Japanese mock-documentary *The Band That Would Be King*, which humorously chronicles the career of a band made up of Velvet Underground disciples. In the film, Tucker discusses the adverse effect of MTV on children. Then she and fellow band members rip into a frenzied version of the Velvet's "I Heard Her Call My Name."

In the 1990s, Tucker fronted her own band and started recording and touring again, releasing five solo albums on small independent labels that mostly feature her singing and playing guitar. Her guest musicians included the late Sterling Morrison, John Cale, and Lou Reed of the Velvet Underground; Jad Fair, Don Fleming, and John Sluggett of Half Japanese; guitarist and punk rocker Sonny Vincent; and drummer Victor DeLorenzo from the Violent Femmes. When the Velvet Underground got together for a 1992–1993 reunion and European tour, Tucker participated and is featured on the VU double album *LIVE MCMXCIII.*

In later years, Tucker continued to perform with various members of Velvet Underground in addition to Half Japanese, Magnet, and the New York/ Memphis punk rock-delta blues fusion group, The Kropotkins. She also played drums on and produced the 1999 album *The Lives of Charles Douglas* by the indie rocker and author of that name, also known as Alex McAuley.

By 2005, Tucker was back in Douglas, Georgia, and no longer performing but spending her time taking care of an eight-year-old grandson.

However, in 2009 she achieved notoriety again: not for her drumming, but for her political activity in the conservative U.S. Tea Party movement. In an interview that appeared in the October 18, 2010, St. Louis *Riverfront Times* she stated: "To be honest, I never paid attention to what the hell was going on. My always voting Democratic was the result of that. My philosophy was and is all politicians are liars, bums, and cheats."

Despite her political leanings, Tucker has never lost respect for her artistry as the driving force in one of the most important bands in the history of rock 'n' roll. To quote the Velvet Underground official website: "Anyone listening to such gems as 'Venus in Furs' or 'Ocean' can immediately appreciate just how vital Moe was to the Velvets. Without her they wouldn't have been the same band."

Some say her greatest contribution was inspiring the idea of female-as-instrumentalist into the collective rock 'n' roll consciousness. As biographer Michael Sandlin noted: "Rrrriot Grrlrs, Schmmrriot Grrrls. If it wasn't for Moe, they'd still be playing with Barbie dolls and filling high school detention halls."

Ginger Bianco

According to Ginger Bianco's website, it all started for her when her kindergarten teacher wanted to know who was making that great rhythm on the blocks. "I was so proud," she said, "when I realized she was talking about me."

Ginger, who played with the iconic 1960s all-female band Goldie and the Gingerbreads, said she was always drawn to the sound of drums and at age seventeen got her first professional drumming gig with the rock 'n' roll band Devlin and the Premiers. "We had a great opportunity to audition for Sid Bernstein's office. (Bernstein was famous for having promoted the Beatles' first U.S. tour.) They loved the idea of a female drummer and booked us into the Eden Rock Hotel in Miami, Florida."

Excited at the prospect of the Miami gig, she rushed home to tell her parents, only to have them tell her, "You're only seventeen and you're not going to Miami with four boys!" Ginger was devastated. So she did what any rebellious girl from an Italian Catholic family from Long Island would do. She wrote a good-bye note, packed a bag, jumped into her '62 Ford XL 500, and drove away into the night.

The young drummer never made it to Miami. Instead she wound up playing at the Cinderella Club in Greenwich Village with bass player Mickey Lee Lane. "As fate would have it, his drummer went south with Devlin and the Premiers while I stayed in cold, damp New York City, unaware of the events to come that would change my life forever."

One night between sets, Ginger said Lane suggested they go to Trudy Heller's club on Sixth to hear the Escorts and their singer Goldie. "I thought to myself: what's a Goldie? So, off we went."

Walking into the club she heard an unusual singing voice. As they got closer and closer, Lane kept saying, "Isn't she great, that Goldie Zelkowitz? Isn't she great?!" Ginger said the only thought in her mind was "What kind of name is Goldie Zelkowitz?"

As soon as the set ended, Lane introduced his new drummer, Ginger Panebianco, to Goldie. "I could see it in her face," Ginger said. "She was thinking, what kind of name is Panebianco?'"

Ginger describes that first encounter: "Goldie seemed so tough with her Brooklyn accent and that cigarette hanging out of her mouth. Then there was me, meek and shy, thinking God was going to punish me for something I didn't even do yet."

Ginger said she knew then her life would never be the same. "She was Goldie the singer, and I was Ginger the drummer. When we put it together, we became Goldie and the Gingerbreads."

Ginger said they then began their search for "more breads." It was difficult, she said, because female rock musicians were "few and far between."

The first organist and guitar player were good, Ginger said, but lacked that "FAMILY, die for the band attitude." They finally found the organ player and "third bread" they were looking for in Margo Crocitto. After a tour of Germany with Chubby Checker, they found their "fourth bread" in singer/guitar player

Carol MacDonald who at the time was playing at The Page Three club with the controversial Tiny Tim.

Ginger said to convince her to join the group, they told her "she too could have leather pants!" She said the reluctant MacDonald came to hear them play, and that was it: "Leather pants or not, she was in. We had our fourth bread."

Goldie and the Gingerbreads was officially born.

"We were bigger than life," Ginger said, "rocketeers, ready to play where no band—all-girl band, that is—had ever played before. And it was just the 1960s."

Goldie and the Gingerbreads would become the first all-girl rock band to receive a recording contact in the United States and Europe. They topped the charts in the United Kingdom, toured with the biggest groups of the era, and were at the center of London's music and social scene at the time of the British Invasion.

The first big break for the all-female band came when they were booked to play at a party thrown by fashion photographer Jerry Schatberg for Andy Warhol superstar Baby Jane Holzer. The Rolling Stones' Mick Jagger and Ahmet Ertegun, chairman of Atlantic Records, were there, and Goldie and the Gingerbreads soon found themselves signed to a record deal with Atlantic and off on a tour of Europe where they opened not only for the Rolling Stones, but also for The Animals, The Beatles, The Yardbirds, The Hollies, and The Kinks, just to name a few.

Throughout the mid-'60s, when the band was touring extensively through North America, club and venue promoters weren't nearly so interested in the band's music as in the novelty of an all-female musical group. Goldie and the Gingerbreads did have one single, "Can't You Hear My Heartbeat" that reached number twenty-five on the charts in the United Kingdom in 1965. The single was also released in the United States, but a recording of the same song by Herman's Hermits released two weeks prior to the Gingerbreads' release doomed the Gingerbreads' chances for a hit single in the United States.

During the time she played with band, Ginger won acclaim and endorsements from Ringo Starr and other top British drummers of the day.

By 1968, the band broke up, but Ginger and Carol MacDonald went on to form the acclaimed all-female, horn band Isis. According to Ginger, Isis was literally born "out of the ashes of an explosion." She recalls that after the Gingerbreads broke up, she, Margo, and Carol formed a group called Blithe Spirit. "We were playing in a club in Huntington, Long Island, and were into our first set during a big thunderstorm. There was a gas leak and the club blew up. I was thrown off my drum seat from the building into a parking lot." She said the keyboard player, Tracy Robbins, was badly injured and while they were waiting for her to recover she and MacDonald took some gigs in Florida and discovered a book about the Egyptian goddess Isis. Ginger thought it would be an incredible name for a band, and Isis was born.

Isis was signed to Buddah Records and in the '70s toured with ZZ Top, Three Dog Night, Leon Russell, Aerosmith, the Beach Boys, and Kiss. Their first album released in fall 1974 drew comparisons to Chicago; Blood, Sweat & Tears; Earth, Wind & Fire; and Santana. The LP made the Billboard Top 100, and the album cover created a stir with its photograph of the band members in nothing but metallic body paint.

Ginger said her experiences with both the Gingerbreads and Isis were "intense and complicated." She said being in any band was like being in a dysfunctional family and she had learned from those experiences. "You have to have patience," she said, "I don't think you grow out of your pain. You just learn to understand it and put it in a different place. You just learn how to handle it better, and by holding on to your dreams, you continue to go forward," she said.

"My biggest dream," she said, "is to see Goldie and the Gingerbreads inducted into the Rock and Roll Hall of Fame as pioneers, even though we never got that hit record. Although I have to say it was such a great honor to be a part of the 'Women Who Rock: Vision Passion Power' exhibit at the Rock and Roll Hall of Fame a couple of summers ago."

At the time of this interview, Ginger was working on a documentary she had entitled *Walk With the Drum* to tell her story. "'Walk With the Drum' was the last song that Carol MacDonald and I wrote together some time ago," she said. "I never realized it would become the anthem for this project today. Goldie and the Gingerbreads and Isis still live in my heart. We were so original in our ideas and so brave to come together as a female band and play in a domain dominated by men. In other words, thank God for your vision, trust in your heart, and follow your dreams. That is what I hope we all will do when we 'walk with the drum.'"

"As a little girl, I never studied drumming," Ginger said. "Maybe if I did, I wouldn't be working in a Home Depot, but teaching. It's easy to think about what you could have done better instead of simply giving thanks for what you have. We all have our selfish moments when we think what we have is not enough." She says her occasional bouts with low esteem fade away when she hears great drummers say to her, "You nailed it, Ginger," or "Your backbeat is amazing."

"The dragons and fears are always there," she said, "but you have to have the vision and faith to walk through the fire and accept yourself as you are."

The Quatro Band Drummers

Goldie and the Gingerbreads were the first all-girl band to sign with a major record label. The second was The Pleasure Seekers who later morphed into

Cradle. The garage rock band from Detroit, Michigan, was formed in 1964 by singer and bass player Suzi Quatro and her sisters. Nancy Ball played drums with the group until late 1965. Drummer Darline Arnone then joined the band and was with them until 1969. In 1968, the group was signed to Mercury Records.

When the group morphed into Cradle and changed musical direction, another Quatro sister, Nancy, joined the group as vocalist and percussionist.

Jenny Jones

Talk show host Jenny Jones started her performing career as a drummer in the '60s. The daughter of Polish immigrant parents, Jones, born in 1946, grew up in London, Ontario, Canada. After her parents divorced, she and her mother moved to Montreal. Unhappy with her life living with an alcoholic mother, Jones ran away from home with an older girlfriend at the age of eleven. Passing for a sixteen-year-old, she got a job waitressing for about a month before the police found her. Her mother, unable to deal with her daughter's rebellious attitude, sent her back to London to live with her father and his new wife. Jones ran away again, but a friend alerted her father and she was taken back to London.

The unhappy teen saw show business as her only way out so she signed up with a modeling agency and started learning to play drums. Her father told her she would no longer be welcome at home if she joined a band. Despite her father's threat, she dropped out of school at age seventeen and went on the road as a drummer with a rock 'n' roll band. After touring Canada and the United States for two years, Jones took off in her Corvair convertible with one suitcase and her drums and headed for Los Angeles. To make ends meet, she sold movie tickets and worked as a hostess in a strip club. She finally found a regular gig as a drummer in a Santa Monica beer bar and then another one in Las Vegas.

At age twenty-two, she formed her own all-girl band, The Cover Girls. The group toured for two years, and after her father came to a show in her hometown, he finally accepted her career in music. Jones was twenty-four when the band split; she settled in Las Vegas with her musician husband. It was there she was discovered by Wayne Newton who signed her up as a back-up vocalist and arranger. When she formed her band Jenny Jones and Company three years later, she had given up drums to focus on being a lead vocalist.

Her popular television talk show, which first aired in September 1991, set a new standard for daytime television by becoming the first talk show to feature hip music acts and outdoor concerts.

Jones said she was drawn to the drums "because playing them came naturally to me. I think I was born with a good sense of rhythm. It was really fun to play—doesn't everyone want to sit behind a kit and try out playing the drums?—and I still miss playing even today. There were very few female drummers in the '60s when I started out, and no one expected me to become a successful, working musician, but I taught myself to play and had my first job in three months. It never occurred to me that I might not succeed—I just had to do my homework and ignore the naysayers. That lesson has guided me through everything else I've accomplished in life."

Crissy Lee

The early years of rock were also memorable ones for Crissy Lee, considered one of the pioneer female drummers in the United Kingdom and Europe. Lee started her auspicious career in the 1940s as a four-year-old drummer in a Salvation Army Band.

In an interview with music journalist Mike Dolbear, Lee said her interest in playing drums "sort of just happened." Her father brought home some drumsticks and "started doing a little tapping on the side of the chair, much to my mother's dislike, because they had wooden arms in those days." She said she was a "very excitable little girl" and immediately "wanted a go" with the sticks. Her father was amazed when instead of doing straight single sticking, she began to play drum rudiments and rhythms far more complicated than any he could show her. "It took me over from that moment. I couldn't put those sticks down."

Lee said her dad and members of her family were brass players with a Salvation Army background, and as a result she was no stranger to Salvation Army bands. "I loved the music. It was jolly."

She began playing side drum in the Colchester, Essex Salvation Army Band and played in other Salvation Army bands as well as local youth orchestras until the age of sixteen. "There's a lovely picture of me at about eight years old standing next to my drum with my little Salvation Army beret on. I was absolutely enthralled because it was quite a big band with trombones, trumpets, horns and things. I loved it and I just naturally did all the 2/4 and the 6/8 march rhythms because I was brought up on that. It was a wonderful start for a drummer because all I had was a snare so you have to work it all. I wasn't shown or told or had lessons. I just made my own way, but that's never let me down."

At age seventeen, Lee joined Ivy Benson's All Girl Dance Band, touring Europe and other parts of the world. During that time she performed with artists such as Dinah Washington, Frank Sinatra, Jr., Fats Domino, Freddie Cole (Nat King Cole's brother), Al Jarreau, Maynard Ferguson, and Tom Jones.

When she left Ivy's band, the young drummer went on to create her own group, The Beat Chics. They worked with Lulu and Eartha Kitt and were so good that the Beatles asked them to join them on their first tour of Spain.

In the interview with Dolbear, Lee says, "I went all jelly like 'cause at the time I thought Paul was the best thing since sliced bread. I thought he was gorgeous! We did four gigs, and they had to do the concerts in the Spanish bullrings because there were no other venues big enough for the capacity of people. We flew with them in their private jet, and we would be driven in a chauffeur driven car following them in another chauffeur driven car with all the fans screaming and them and us because we were big out there, too."

Lee said it "was an absolute honor to share the stage with such a huge band. And it was so exciting to play to such massive audiences."

As a result of the exposure they received touring with the Beatles, the Beat Chics' first EP "Skinny Mini" hit the top of the charts in Spain, Italy, and Brazil and numerous other Latin American countries as well as the Billboard 100 in the United States.

After the Beatles tour, Lee's band did some shows, traveling with English pop singer Cilla Black. She said when the group returned to England, "Nobody knew us!" She said the band "pottered about . . . doing this and that." Lee said the group went on tour throughout Europe and then a couple of the girls left so the group disbanded. Ivy Benson was getting ready to embark on a big tour and desperate for Lee to return to the orchestra. She said, "Crissy, we're going to need you on this. We're going to be playing with some big stars." For the next two years, Lee was part of Ivy's band.

In the late 1960s, Lee joined the Mike Holly Big Band while working on her next project, the Christine Lee Set, a seven-piece band influenced by the music of Blood, Sweat & Tears. They became the resident band at the Sheraton in Cairo, Egypt, and had a weekly spot on Egyptian television. After playing other venues throughout Europe and the Middle East, they opened the Top of the Carlton Hotel in Johannesburg, South Africa. She later augmented the band to a twelve-piece group, which was in residence at many hotel ballrooms throughout the country, including the famous Lyceum in London.

With her own series of projects, ranging in size from the renowned thirteen-piece Crissy Lee Jazz Orchestra down to the Crissy Lee Trio, she has performed at numerous jazz festivals throughout the United Kingdom, Europe, South Africa, Egypt, and Australia.

Lee has also worked closely with Paul Stevenson. The two collaborated on a CD performed by the Crissy Lee Jazz Orchestra and Stevenson and featuring Lee as the central, driving force of the band.

Having never considered herself a "purist" in the true jazz sense, Lee loves to highlight the other musical influences that also play a huge part in her musical make-up. This has led to her working more recently with artists such as Clare Teal.

Lee was also drummer for The Skinnerettes, the resident band on the ITV Frank Skinner Show. While there she had a reunion with Ringo Starr who was a guest on the show. When Ringo said he didn't recognize her, Skinner told him, "Take your mind back to Spain . . . you had a support band called The Beat Chics." When Ringo said he didn't remember them, the audience began booing, and Skinner put up a picture showing Lee standing next to Starr watching John Lennon playing the guitar in the dressing room.

Lee is heavily involved in sharing her experience with young musicians by leading drum clinics—an activity that has taken her around the globe. Also, by teaching both in schools and privately at her percussion studio called, rather appropriately named "Fiddlesticks," she takes great pride in the fact that many of her pupils have gone on to become professional drummers in their own right.

"I love being able to pass on my talent and experience to young drummers/ musicians," Lee said. She has taught at Felsted School in Essex for almost three decades.

Felsted School held a seventieth birthday celebratory concert for Lee on June 26, 2013. "I was humbled," she said, "to receive a video message on that evening from the renowned Dame Evelyn Glennie—an honor indeed!"

Lee said through music she "discovered a sensitivity, emotion, and connectedness with other people—initially other musicians—that has moved into all other areas of my life. Music is a language that all can understand and resonate with. I feel blessed that I have been able to contribute in this way. I get the biggest 'buzz' with not necessarily any financial gain—by getting together with others to play and 'jam.'"

Over the years Lee has won the praise of many drummers, including Buddy Rich who once said she was the most talented female drummer he'd ever seen. "I know he had to put in the female bit," Lee said, "but it didn't matter." She says she's not a feminist and is the first to admit her favorite drummers are all male. However, she's also quick to add that her opinion is only based on her experience. She hasn't met or heard all the girl drummers.

CHAPTER 9

Trippin' and Groovin': The '70s

> Even the rough times were good. How many teenage girls get to do what we did in a lifetime?
>
> —Sandy West

The 1970s brought us Watergate, Vietnam, women's lib, drugs, free love, and vinyl records. The feminist movement started to gain momentum during the late '60s, but it wasn't until the beginning of the '70s that women began to get serious about improving their status in the workplace, politics, and family life. Membership in the National Organization for Women, one of the largest mainstream organizations of the women's movement, dramatically increased from 1,200 in 1967 to more than 48,000 in 1970. Formation of subgroups such as Redstockings and the Women's International Terrorist Conspiracy from Hell added a radical impetus to what was happening.

Feminist musician Helen Reddy expressed the sentiments of many when she said the women's rights movement was something that profoundly altered how she felt about herself and about life. Reddy, like so many others, saw the movement as an opportunity to end sexist oppression and finally break through cultural confines and gender stereotypes imposed on females by society and tradition.

Unfortunately, many men and some conservative women like Phyllis Schlafly, best known for her aggressive campaign in successfully defeating the Equal Rights Amendment, saw women who were active in the movement as angry "man-hating freaks" and "bra-less bubbleheads."

While women were fighting for their rights, the rock scene during this period continued to be dominated by males. Although women gained some prominence as singers and songwriters, when it came to playing instruments—especially drums—they were rarely heard or seen. Nor were they encouraged to do so. The prevailing opinion was that the guys did it better; they were more aggressive and more skillful musicians.

But during the decade, a few all-female rock bands started to buck the trend, and the number of bands fronted by women grew, especially with the emergence of punk rock. The late film critic Roger Ebert in a commentary on the movie *Beyond the Valley of the Dolls* credited the fictional band "Carrie Nations," created for that film, with inspiring the girls' band movement. He noted that prior to the film such bands were rare, but their number dramatically increased after the film's release.

Alice de Buhr and Fanny

Many credited the rise in interest to bands like Fanny, a group formed in California in the late 1960s. Called the "first honest to goodness 'real' girl rock band," Fanny is widely regarded as a pioneer among rock groups composed entirely of women.

Drummer Brie Brandt, known as Brie Berry at the time, was in high school when she joined sisters June Millington on guitar and Jean Millington on bass to form the all-girl band The Svelts, the forerunner to Fanny. In the late 1960s, the Svelts played in clubs all along the West Coast and in Nevada. Brie dropped out of the band to have a baby and was replaced by Alice de Buhr from Mason City, Iowa. De Buhr was described as a "slamming drummer with hair that almost touched the floor when she sat behind her drums" (Iowa Rock 'n' Roll Music Association).

Born in 1949, de Buhr was the youngest in a family of four children. She got hooked playing drums in the second grade and claimed her life changed direction from that point on. She said she had no idea what drew her to the drums at that early age, but when asked by her mother if she wanted to learn to play drums, she said "Yes!" "I was in school band and orchestra from second grade through high school, but self-taught on a full drum kit," she said. Her family was supportive throughout. "My eldest sister 'made' my father buy me my first kit . . . for fifty dollars."

At age seventeen, after her parents divorced, she moved to California. The Svelts, who had just lost their drummer, recruited her. When the Svelts disbanded, de Buhr formed another all-female group, Wild Honey, with the Millington sisters.

"Most of my Wild Honey memories are painful, but if we hadn't broken away from the Svelts, we wouldn't have gained the maturity to 'bury the hatchets' and regroup."

In the male-dominated rock world, the women of Wild Honey were frustrated by the lack of success and respect and decided to disband after one final open-mike performance at the Troubadour Club in Los Angeles in 1969. Producer Richard Perry's secretary happened to be at that last gig and got them an audition with Perry, who was so impressed he went to Warner Brothers and asked them to sign the band. Before recording their first album, the band was renamed Fanny.

They became the third all-female band, following Goldie and the Gingerbreads and The Pleasure Seekers, to sign with a major label and the first to actually release an album on a major label. During the years they were active, they made the Top 40 on Billboard's Hot 100 twice and released five albums, all of which achieved critical acclaim.

In a December 1999 interview with *Rolling Stone*, Fanny fan David Bowie said, "One of the most important female bands in American rock has been buried without a trace. And that is Fanny. They were one of the finest . . . rock bands of their time. They were extraordinary . . . . they were colossal and wonderful . . . they're as important as anybody else who's ever been, ever; it just wasn't their time" (Fanny, fannyrocks.com). Bonnie Raitt praised the group, saying, "It was so great having a real rock band full of smart tough and talented women who could really play" (Iowa Rock 'n' Roll Assoc.).

Perry, who "discovered" the group, produced Fanny's first three albums. The band also worked as session musicians, most notably on Barbra Streisand's 1971 album *Barbra Joan Streisand*. Their fourth album was produced by Todd Rundgren. They toured worldwide and opened for artists such as Slade, Jethro Tull, and Humble Pie.

After the fourth album, de Buhr and June Millington left the band and Brie Brandt returned on drums. They signed with Casablanca Records and released their final album, *Rock and Roll Survivor* in 1974.

Brandt went on to an active post-Fanny career, touring and recording with Carole King, Jimmy Buffett, Elton John, Robbie Nevil, and Jack Wagner. She fronted American Girls, a band that released an album in 1986, and Boxing Gandhis, which has released four albums since the mid-1990s.

De Buhr returned to play with the band in a reunion concert held at Berklee College of Music in April 2007, where she and the other band members received the *Rockrgrl* Women of Valor award for their achievements.

She says she no longer plays gigs, but adds, "I have a terrific time in my living room."

De Buhr said as a female drummer, she was "oblivious" to any particular challenges. "I just played." She also feels attitudes toward drummers of her gender haven't changed much through the years. "I think female musicians are still looked at as oddities or gimmicks, never getting real appreciation for being musicians."

De Buhr said she was very proud of what Fanny accomplished. "It was a critical time of my growing up and definitely shaped who I am today."

To aspiring female drummers, she offers this advice: "Don't give up and find a good roadie!" She also shares this lesson: "The KISS principle still works today. Keep It Simple, Stupid."

Liver Favela and Birtha

In the early 1970s, when Fanny was breaking through as the first female rock band recording on a major label, drummer Olivia "Liver" Favela joined the new all-female band Birtha. The other members were bassist Rosemary Butler who played with The Ladybirds, an all-female band who toured, opening for The Rolling Stones; guitarist Shele Pinizzotto, who was in the Los Angeles psychedelic band The Daisy Chain; and keyboardist Shelly Hagler.

Dunhill Records paired up the group with producer Gabriel Mekler of Steppenwolf fame. Favela was the drummer and leader of the group. The Wizard of Roz in "Female Drummer Newsletter" called her "without a doubt, the wildest singing drummer of all time. . . . Just picture Janis Joplin behind the drums and singing at the same time."

Fanny's label Reprise Records had decided to brand their girls with the ad slogan "Get Behind Fanny." Dunhill, not to be outdone, went one better with "Birtha Has Balls." The editors of *Playboy* magazine were so shocked and offended by the questionable tastefulness of the slogan, they refused to print the ad or reproduce the slogan on matchbox covers when Birtha played the Chicago Playboy Club. However, the t-shirts that became part of the campaign were big sellers, so much so that members of Alice Cooper, Fleetwood Mac, and the James Gang all wore them while playing their sets at the 1972 Rockingham Festival.

Although never as popular as Fanny, Birtha won raves from music critics for their ability to match and even exceed the power and drive of most male groups. Wizard of Roz in "Female Drummer Newsletter" called their album *BIRTHA*, released in 1972, "probably the most exciting record ever made by a female band. It's a shame this record was virtually ignored by everyone in the '70s in this business of rock 'n' roll. This is the record that should have been and still should be played along the classic rock stations and books and files of all time." Citing a killer drum solo by Favela in one track, she says, "This drumming is unlike any you will hear from any other drummer."

Comparing Favela's drumming to Thor wielding his hammer, another critic dubbed her "Liv, the tornado," and wrote, "Opening with a 4/4 high hat, I can just picture Liver sitting behind that kit bouncing up and down and beating the shit out of those skins, her long air whipping and flying all over the place sticking to her sweaty body, while she hollers and oozes sex appeal" (Mrs. Ahab, headheritage.co.uk).

Favela and Birtha made two albums, but despite critical praise, they never quite made it and broke apart. Some say success never came because they were too aggressive in taking on the male-centric rock ethic. Men didn't really want to hear rock chicks singing about freedom and sexuality. They wanted music that made them feel in control. And unfortunately for Birtha, some women felt the same way, too. As one reviewer said, "Maybe they were ahead of their time . . . Birtha equaled everything the boys did because they had balls, but maybe . . . it was simply the balls that ruined them" (Mrs. Ahab).

Sandy West and The Runaways

Just as Birtha was disbanding, a fifteen-year-old drummer, driven by ambition to play professionally, was seeking out fellow musicians to form a band. That band, the Runaways, eventually would go down in history as the first teenage all-girl hard rock band to achieve international notoriety. And the young drummer Sandy West would come to be known by some as "the greatest female drummer in the history of rock and roll."

West (Sandy Pesavento) was born in Long Beach, California, in 1959. Her early passions were the beach, animals, and rock 'n' roll. She's quoted on The Runaways' official website, "When I first heard The Monkees, that's when I had to learn how to play drums," she said. On her ninth birthday, her grandfather gave her a drum kit. She took to it immediately and in no time became proficient. At age thirteen, she was the only girl in local bands, playing at teenage parties. After hearing Led Zeppelin and Aerosmith, she traded in The Monkees for heavy metal.

At age fifteen, she met producer Kim Fowley, who had by then earned a reputation as a notorious hustler. Fowley put West in touch with another young talented musician, fifteen-year-old guitarist Joan Jett. When Joan and Sandy met at Sandy's home to jam, the two clicked, and some say the inception of The Runaways came about that day. The two teen rockers, aware they had something, called Fowley and asked for a hearing. Fowley was impressed with what he heard and began to seek other girls who could be members of the band.

Twenty years later, Fowley remarked in the documentary *Edgeplay: A Film About the Runaways*, "I didn't put The Runaways together. I had an idea, they had ideas, we all met, there was combustion, and out of five different versions of that group came the five girls who were the ones that people liked."

Fowley's interest in the girls made some nervous, especially Sandy West's mother. In the documentary she recalls her first meeting with him. "Here was this big enormous man in an orange suit. When Kim walked in he was bad news. I didn't know whether I should throw him out or laugh at him." She went on to say, "As I look back, I should have tied her to the bed and said you can't do this . . . but you can't take your children's dreams away."

Despite her mother's worries, West and The Runaways were soon on the Los Angeles party and club circuit as a power rock trio with singer and bassist Micki Steele, who would later join the Bangles. They soon added lead guitarist Lita Ford, who originally auditioned for the bass spot. Steele was fired and local bassist Peggy Foster took over on bass but left after only a month. Lead singer Cherie Currie was recruited for the band. At the time she was working in a local teen nightclub called the Sugar Shack. She was followed by Jackie Fox on bass, who had originally auditioned for the lead guitar spot.

The band was signed to Mercury Records in 1976, and their debut album, *The Runaways*, was released soon after. Unfortunately, many in the music industry dismissed the album, in part because Fowley was known for hyping gimmicky acts and suspicion that the band was being marketed as "jailbait on the run."

In West's obituary, which appeared in the London *Guardian*, Garth Cartwright described The Runaways' music as "hard rocking, melodic and memorably direct." He wrote: "Young women singing of adolescent desire and alienation, getting high and casual sex, shocked many, and U.S. radio stations refused to play them. Male critics dismissed the band with misogynistic loathing. 'These bitches suck,' declared the rock 'n' roll magazine *CREEM*, while the liberal *Village Voice* dismissed them as 'bimbos.'"

On tour—especially outside the United States—their performances were usually sell-outs, and if they weren't headlining, they were opening for bands and artists such as Cheap Trick, Tom Petty and the Heartbreakers, and Van Halen.

Each girl patterned her look after her rock idol. For Currie it was David Bowie; for Jett, Suzi Quatro and Keith Richards; for Ford, Jeff Beck and Deep Purple guitarist Ritchie Blackmore; and for West, Queen drummer Roger Taylor.

On the release of their second album, *Queens of Noise*, they were being categorized as a punk band because of their alliances with mostly male punk bands such as Blondie, The Ramones, and the Dead Boys as well as the British punk bands The Damned, Generation X, and the Sex Pistols. In Europe, music critics called them "pioneers of girl power."

In the summer of 1977, after the release of their second album, the group toured Japan. In that country, only ABBA, Kiss, and Led Zeppelin were ahead of them in terms of album sales and popularity. They were superstars there with number one hits, every album hitting gold, and sold-out stadiums with screaming, devoted fans.

West said the Japanese fans were the best and next were the Europeans. She felt parts of the United States and especially the U.S. press never took the band seriously.

Along with her drumming skills, West also co-penned some of The Runaways' biggest hits, including "Born to Be Bad" and "California Paradise." Her self-written "Right Now" was the debut single of the band's last album.

Jealousy and Drugs

After four years of recording and world tours, The Runaways disbanded in 1979. The pressures of living a rock lifestyle proved too much for some of the young women. They were extremely competitive and jealous and constantly fighting among themselves. Fowley described them as "twisted, tormented teenage goddesses" (*Edgeplay*).

West felt the band was torn apart not by the girls themselves but by others who were trying to manipulate and control them. "Greed, power, jealousy, they're very ugly things." Plus, she added, "We were on drugs and that never helps any situation" (*Edgeplay*).

The band was also split artistically over whether to present themselves as hard rockers or go the glitter glam route.

Once The Runaways disbanded and the money ran out, each of the musicians, including West, made varied attempts to continue their careers. West was especially brokenhearted when the band split. In *Edgeplay*, she said: "I went crazy. I was very upset and sad. . . . It was pretty mind boggling. I had watched these girls grow up, and when I saw them ripping and tearing apart, my heart was ripping and tearing apart, too. You feel lost. Where do I go? Where do I fit in?"

West, who was nineteen when The Runaways broke up, went on to play with other Southern California bands before forming The Sandy West Band and released a solo album, *The Beat Is Back*. West also did some session work with John Entwistle of The Who and taught drumming. None of these ventures proved profitable, so she was forced to spend most of her time earning what she could outside the music field, mostly in construction, along with a little bartending and work as a veterinary assistant.

West and other band members later accused Kim Fowley of not paying them what they were entitled to. West felt she owed Fowley for introducing her to the music business, but she also blamed him for being without work and broke.

To make ends meet, West alluded in various interviews that she engaged in not so ladylike activity. In *Edgeplay*, she describes how she broke someone's arm and shoved a gun down someone's throat.

In the 2005 documentary, made more than fourteen years after The Runaways disbanded, West was still expressing anger over the band's splitting. "People say that's my past, but I'm still broken up. I'm an angry person inside. We were the most awesome band, and that band should have kept going."

In 2005, West, who had always been a heavy smoker, was diagnosed with lung cancer. She died October 21, 2006, at the age of forty-seven. On The Runaways' website, former bandmate Cherie Currie said: "Sandy West was by far the greatest female drummer in the history of rock and roll. No one could compete or even come close to her, but most important was her heart. Sandy West loved her fans, her friends and family almost to a fault. She would do absolutely anything for the people she loved. It will never be the same for me again to step on a stage, because Sandy West was the best and I will miss her forever."

Joan Jett, in a eulogy to West, which also appeared on the website, said: "We shared the dream of girls playing rock and roll. Sandy was an exuberant and powerful drummer. I am overcome from the loss of my friend. I always told her we changed the world."

To this day, West continues to inspire women musicians to rock as hard as the boys. All-female groups such as L7, Shonen Knife, and Bikini Kill have credited West and The Runaways for paving the way for their success. As for West, she said all she wanted of life was "to be a drummer in a rock band—having fun."

Palmolive

Paloma Romero, who would take the stage name Palmolive, was born in Spain on December 26, 1954, and grew up there under the dictatorship of Francisco Franco. She was one of nine children, sometimes sharing a room with four sisters in her family's apartment. By age thirteen, the young Catholic school student was already starting to rebel. According to her website, she became "fascinated with anarchy, hitchhiking, and anything dangerous."

Unhappy with her life in Spain, she moved to West London in 1972 and eased into a hippie lifestyle. "I had no money and I really didn't know anybody, but I was full of excitement and expectations," she said. She described the government-owned housing where they lived as the "perfect breeding ground for dropouts and lovers of the counterculture revolution, a place to explore our dreams without the inconvenience of paying rent or utility bills."

After two years, Paloma found the "utopian" life getting a little stale, so she decided she'd learn how to play the drums. After a "whole week" of learning, she was ready to be part of a street performance act.

Punk was exploding in London at the time, and Paloma's boyfriend John Graham Mellor, who changed his name to Joe Strummer and who had previously been with the pub rock band the 101'ers, had just joined The Clash.

When Clash bassist Paul Simonon met Romero for the first time, he found it difficult to pronounce her name "Paloma" so he gave her the name "Palmolive." Romero liked it and adopted it as her stage name.

Through her boyfriend's connections, Palmolive met Sex Pistols bassist Sid Vicious and for a time she played with him in the band The Flowers of Romance with guitarist Viv Albertine. After meeting fourteen-year-old Ari Up at a Patti Smith concert, Palmolive decided they should form an all-female punk band, The Slits. It didn't take long before The Slits were playing gigs with The Clash, the Sex Pistols, Buzzcocks, and other top bands in London's early punk scene.

The band was described as "threatening" and "dangerous" and became notorious for their fights on stage and provoking their audiences and anyone else who got in their way.

Palmolive not only played drums, she also wrote several of The Slits' songs, which appeared on their records, even after she left the group in 1978. The Slits' debut album, which came out after Palmolive's departure, features studio drummer Budgie, who played with Siouxsie and the Banshees.

Paloma said her break from the group resulted from shared concerns about Malcolm McLaren being their manager. "He had said in our meeting with him that he hated women and music and 'I thrive on hate.' When the idea came up of the LP cover in which band members were to be shown naked and slathered in mud, I refused to do it and soon after I was dismissed from the group." Budgie also opted to sit out for the photo session,

After leaving The Slits because of tension within the group, Palmolive joined another female punk band, The Raincoats, in 1979. During the six months she was with that group, The Raincoats recorded one single and an album and toured the United Kingdom with the Swiss band Kleenex. There were no fights on stage, she said, but the band shared The Slits' "experimental attitude to push limits," which won fans such as Kurt Cobain, Courtney Love, and Sonic Youth.

Dissatisfied with the music scene in general, Palmolive left The Raincoats and took off for India where she spent the next six months on a spiritual quest with her boyfriend and future husband Dave McLardy. In 1981, the couple moved back to Spain, and Palmolive gave birth to the first of three children. She and her family left Spain and moved to London and then in 1989 came to the United States, where they settled in Cape Cod, Massachusetts. While in the United Kingdom, the former punk drummer became a "born-again" Christian and began active involvement in church work. She and her husband also started a cover band Hi-Fi with a repertoire that includes songs that reflect their religious beliefs.

Palmolive says, "Following Jesus has not stifled me." On her website Palmolive2day.com, she is quoted: "The excitement and the dynamics that I liked in punk music, which was so shallow, I can now experience in a deeper way."

Olivia Records

Thanks to Olivia Records, the first woman-owned women's music label, numerous female drummers found work and were able to establish reputations as top session musicians, among them Janet "Jake" Lampert of the electric rock band BeBe K'Roche. Olivia Records, the brainchild of a group of lesbian-feminists, was a collective founded in 1973 to record and promote women's music. Olivia produced about forty albums and sold over a million records. Although their recordings mostly focused on solo acoustic acts, they sometimes took risks such as signing electric rock band BeBe K'Roche, featuring drummer Lampert. The band's exotic French name was inspired by the sight of a baby cockroach in a cup of coffee. Lampert had been the original drummer for the Berkeley Women's Music Collective, which was also signed to the Olivia label.

In addition to Lampert, Olivia's impressive cadre of musicians included session drummers M.L. Orth, Cam Davis, Linda Geiger, Christine Hanson, and Linda Tillery aka Tui.

Josie and the Pussycats

Another all-girl band—though not a real one, but a cartoon—also made an indelible mark on the music scene of the 1970s and probably inspired more than one young girl to become a drummer. *Josie and the Pussycats* was an animated television series based on the *Archie* comic book series created by Dan DeCarlo.

The Hanna-Barbera television series, which aired on CBS in the early '70s, featured fictional lead singer and guitarist Josie McCoy, tambourinist Valerie Brown, and drummer Melody Valentine. The fictional band toured the world, getting mixed up in strange adventures, spy capers, and mysteries. Each episode featured a Josie and the Pussycats song, usually played over a chase scene.

An actual real-life band was put together to provide the singing voices for the girls in the cartoon, and session musicians, likely all males, provided the instrumental tracks. The singer chosen for the voice of the drummer Melody was Cherie Moore, who later became known as Cheryl Ladd, the actress who replaced Farrah Fawcett in *Charlie's Angels*. In publicity shots, Ladd is shown playing the drums.

A movie, loosely based on the cartoon, was released in 2001, and Tara Reid who played the drummer in the film actually took drum lessons to prepare for the role.

In both the cartoon and movie, Melody was depicted as a blonde, slightly lacking in intellect, but making up for it in heart, wit, and optimism. To the present day, many still consider her the "quintessential queen" of drums, sweetness, and laughter.

CHAPTER 10

Bad to the Bone: The '80s

> Ultimately they will find me slumped over my drum kit still grasping my sticks in my cold dead hands . . . but I'm not dead yet!
>
> —Roxy Petrucci

The decade of the 1980s opened with a big change in U.S. politics—the election of Ronald Reagan—and a musical milestone—the advent of MTV. The women's movement entered a new phase, characterized by both advancement and backlash. While women had made substantial progress in changing social attitudes toward gender roles, their attempt to add the Equal Rights Amendment to the U.S. Constitution failed in 1982, three states short of ratification.

MTV, which would revolutionize the music industry and become a worldwide influence on pop culture, launched on August 1, 1981, with the words spoken by an MTV creator John Lack: "Ladies and gentlemen, rock and roll." The first music video to air on the new cable channel was the Bugles' rather prophetic "Video Killed the Radio Star." And while MTV provided plenty of evidence that more and more women were making their mark in popular music, especially as singers, the female drummer was still an anomaly.

Gina Schock

Gina Schock was one lady who bucked the current with determination and success, landing herself a well-deserved place in music history. Schock was born August 31, 1957, in Baltimore, Maryland. In an interview with Erin Amar of *Rocker* magazine, she tells how at age eleven she had an epiphany when she attended her first rock concert, featuring The Who with Led Zeppelin opening. It was then she knew what she wanted to do the rest of her life. It didn't matter whether it was singing or playing an instrument: the all-important thing was to be on a stage performing and making music.

After taking a few lessons on different instruments, she started saving her allowance to buy a drum kit, purchasing it piece by piece. As soon as she got home from school, she would begin practicing and found playing drums was so easy she knew she'd never have to take a lesson.

At age thirteen, she was playing with several different bands. In the *Rocker* interview, she said, "Being a girl drummer was certainly a novelty at that time; there weren't many girls doing that, so it was easy for me to get into bands, and, of course, it would always be with all guys who loved having a thirteen-, fourteen-, fifteen-, sixteen-year-old drummer girl."

Schock's professional career began to take off when she became drummer for Edie and the Eggs, a punk band featuring Edith Massey, a star in director John Water's cult films. At the time, Massey owned a small thrift shop in Baltimore and Schock would visit her there.

"One day I went in and she said, 'Hey, I want to be in a punk band, do you want to be in my punk band?' and I was like, 'Sure, Edie, I'd love to,'" Schock said.

The band, made up of two other girls, played in Philadelphia, New York, Kansas City, Los Angeles, and at the San Francisco Warfield. Schock, who was twenty at the time, suddenly realized she had made the "big time."

On returning to Baltimore she decided she was going to move to New York, Los Angeles, or San Francisco because those were the places music was happening. She spent three weeks in New York, a month in San Francisco, and decided to move to LA, which, she said, was "just an easier place for me to settle in."

As soon as she got to Los Angeles, she put her name up in all the music stores and started playing with two or three bands. Then a friend told her she should check out a band that had been around for about six months, The Go-Go's.

"I saw them play, and they were really kind of crappy, but fun, and they had something . . . something about them that made them special and made me take notice." She said she met two of the band members at a party, and they asked her if she'd be interested in joining the band. After rehearsing with them the next day, Schock was told they were firing their drummer, and she was in.

Schock felt her decision to join the band represented a big commitment, and she was determined to do all she could to make the band successful. She said the other members of the band were mostly in it for fun, but because of her experience, she came in with a different work ethic. When she was told the band rehearsed once every couple of weeks, she said, "No, you guys, we have to rehearse five nights a week. You work during the day, and then at night, you rehearse."

All that rehearsal paid off because The Go-Go's came to be known as one of the most commercially successful all-female bands in history. Moreover, they weren't controlled by male producers or managers. They wrote their own songs and played their own instruments on singles and albums that rose to the top of record charts.

Their debut album, *Beauty and the Beat*, which reached number one on the Billboard 200 and stayed there for six weeks, is considered one of the cornerstone albums of the New Wave explosion of the late '70s and early '80s. New Wave incorporated much of the original punk rock sound but was more complex in its music and lyrics, along with use of synthesizers and electronic production. The music was quirky and eccentric but melodic and catchy, making it ideal for the pop music scene and MTV, with its programming devoted to music videos introduced by VJs.

Beauty and the Beat sold more than three million copies and reached triple platinum status, making it one of the most successful debut albums by any artist ever.

When The Go-Go's formed in 1978, originally as the Misfits, it included Belinda Carlisle on vocals, Charlotte Caffey on guitar, Jane Wiedlin on vocals, Margot Olavarria on bass, and Elissa Bello on drums. The band had changed its name to The Go-Go's by the time Schock replaced Bello in the summer of 1979.

In 1979, the band recorded a demo and spent half of 1980 touring England where they gained a sizable following. While there they recorded a single, "We Got the Beat," on Stiff Records, which became an underground club hit in the United States.

In December 1980, bassist Olavarria fell ill with hepatitis A and was replaced with Kathy Valentine, a guitarist who had never played before. Then in early 1981 The Go-Go's signed with IRS Records and their debut album became one of the surprise hits of the year.

In 1982, The Go-Go's released *Vacation*, but while the album went gold, it lacked the momentum of the first album. In 1983, Caffey broke her wrist and the band was unable to perform, and then the next year the band released *Talk Show*, considered their most musically ambitious undertaking. The album had two Top 40 hits, but failed to go gold.

In their heyday as America's rock darlings, The Go-Go's were known for their wild lifestyle, popping pills, trashing hotel rooms, and living up to their reputation as bad girls. Along with the drug addiction of some of the members, personality conflicts and creative differences also took their toll. By the end of 1984, Wiedlin left the band, and The Go-Go's broke up in May 1985.

Shortly before the break up, Schock had open heart surgery as the result of a congenital heart defect.

In 1990, Schock and fellow band members Caffey, Carlisle, Valentine, and Wiedlin reunited for a benefit concert for the California Environmental Protection Act. That led to a few more shows later in the year. Then in 1994, the band members got together to release the two-disc *Return to the Valley of the Go-Go's.*

Claiming she had not been properly paid for her contributions to the band since 1986 and citing a breach of contract regarding a songwriting agreement with Caffey, Schock sued the other members of the group in 1997. The suit was resolved by 1999 when the band reunited for a brief tour and finally began to resolve personal differences.

The Go-Go's have toured regularly since 1999, with their 2011 tour "Ladies Gone Wild" commemorating the thirtieth anniversary of the release of *Beauty and the Beat.*

In recent years, Schock has penned tween-pop hits for Disney artists Miley Cyrus and Selena Gomez. Gomez' *Kiss and Tell,* on which Schock had four songs, sold over half a million units and was one of the top ten selling records of the year. Said Schock: "I was so taken back . . . millions of records was no big deal a couple of years ago, now if you sell a million records, it's a big deal."

Interestingly, someone else in The Go-Go's started out as a drummer. Before co-founding the iconic pop group and becoming a successful solo artist, Belinda Carlisle played drums with the punk band The Germs under the name Dottie Danger.

Debbi Peterson

About the time The Go-Go's were doing their first tour outside the United States, another all-girl band was being formed in a Brentwood, California, garage. Guitarists Susanna Hoffs and Vicki Peterson, and Vicki's sister, Debbi, a drummer, formed the Bangles in December 1980. "The chemistry was there instantaneously. It just clicked," said Debbi. On the band's website, her sister Vicki recalls that within two hours of their first meeting to play and sing in the Hoffs' family garage, "we were a band, the three of us. And we still are."

Debbi, born on August 22, 1961, in Northridge, California, and raised in the San Fernando Valley, started drumming in her first band while still in high school. She says her musical influences were largely the result of her older sister Pam's record collection. "She would use her allowance and buy all the latest records of the great music from the '60s," Peterson said.

"I never really had any musical training, apart from one drum lesson," Peterson said. "I mainly watched other drummers and did a fair amount of air drumming! I started out wanting to be a bass player or guitar player, but a drumming opportunity opened up when I was fifteen and I took it."

"My sister Vicki had a band in high school that was in need of a drummer. I had never actually drummed before and sat down on a friend's kit and played like I had been doing it a while. Immediately I was asked to join."

She says her parents "endured hours of annoying rehearsals," but they were supportive, letting the girls practice in the garage/storage room and coming to as many of their shows as they could.

Peterson said the group changed over the years, and in one of the transition periods Vicki placed an ad in a newspaper for a guitar player. Guitarist Susanna Hoffs placed an ad for musicians in the same newspaper. Peterson said Hoffs called Vicki, and "they talked for hours—this was right after John Lennon's death in 1980. All of us got together soon after in Susanna's garage and jammed. We realized this was something special."

Initially the band called themselves The Colours, then the Supersonic Bangs. They shortened that name to the Bangs and became part of the Paisley Underground scene in Los Angeles, which featured music influenced by '60s folk-rock, but with a modern punk sound. In 1981 the band produced a single, "Getting Out of Hand," on their own label, Down Kiddie Records. Faulty Products, a label formed by Miles Copeland, then signed them.

Annette Zilinskas joined the band on vocals and bass, and they recorded an EP in 1982, releasing the single "The Real World." Because of a legal issue, they were forced to change their name to the Bangles, and that was the name that appeared on the released EP and the name they've kept since.

Zilinskas left the band to pursue her own projects and was replaced by Micki Steele, who had played with The Runaways. Their first full-length album released in 1984 by Columbia, *All Over the Place*, earned good reviews. They generated even more interest and visibility when Leonard Nimoy was featured in their video for the track "Going Down to Liverpool" and as the opening act for Cyndi Lauper on her "Fun" tour.

The band attracted the attention of Prince, so much so that he wrote "Manic Monday" for them. It became the number two hit in the United States, United Kingdom, and Germany, outsold only by another Prince piece, "Kiss." Their next album included the number one hit "Walk Like an Egyptian." Some of the group weren't completely sold on the song and were surprised to see it become such a hit.

"As the Bangles became more popular, we toured quite a bit and got to see a lot of the world," Peterson said. "We won a BPI award in '86 in the U.K. as the best international band and we were around some of our favorite people: Eric Clapton, Peter Gabriel, Kate Bush, Paul Simon, Mark Knopfler, to name a few. There was a time when us girls had a chance to jam with Prince at his recording studio. Also, I remember when we went to dinner with Duran Duran in San Remo, Italy. Ahh, fun times!"

As the band had more big sellers, including the multi-platinum *Different Light* and their biggest selling single, "Eternal Flame," Hoffs was being singled out more and more for recognition as the lead singer of the group. Actually all the band members, including drummer Debbi, shared singing duties on all the albums and each wrote or co-wrote their own songs.

Friction among the members caused the band to break up in 1989. "We went our separate ways, worked with other people, and grew up a bit," Peterson said.

Debbi Peterson joined the band Smashbox, which was short-lived and fell apart in 1991. In 1992, she formed the acoustic duo Kindred Spirit with Siobhan Maher. She met the former River City People vocalist at an Indian restaurant in Los Angeles, and the two teamed up to record a four-track single, "Here in My Eyes," in 1992. They also performed as the opening act for the British singer/songwriter Joan Armatrading. Kindred Spirit released a self-titled album in June 1995, and two years later Peterson and Maher went their separate ways.

In the early '90s, she had an opportunity to drum with Spinal Tap, which, in her words, "was inspiring to say the least." She also had a chance to perform with Bonnie Raitt, k.d. lang, and Emmylou Harris at a Roy Orbison tribute.

In 1999, the drummer rejoined the Bangles, who had been approached to do a song for the movie *Austin Powers: The Spy Who Shagged Me*. The group, comprised of Hoffs and the two Peterson sisters, stayed together after the film project and have continued performing and recording to the present day.

"When we joined back up with all four members, we had had ten years of gaining perspective when we were apart and were able to work together again quite well. Plus, having children definitely changes the way you see things," said Peterson, who was then the mother of two.

Steele left the group in 2004, and the rest of the group decided to continue on, but without a fourth female. "The original Bangles were a three-piece anyway," Peterson said. "So now we have a male bass player, Derrick Anderson. We've always had a male keyboard player—first Walker Ingleheart and then Greg "Harpo" Hilfman who has been with us since the late '80s."

In an interview after the release of their 2011 album *Sweetheart of the Sun*, Peterson said, "I think it's important for all of us to keep moving on and creating, because that's why we got into this in the first place."

Over the years she's performed with Cyndi Lauper, Tom Petty, and Elvis Costello—"all brilliant people and it was a joy working/performing with them."

Peterson says she gets her energy from the music. "I think it's the adrenaline rush that you get when you are in front of people performing. It's also the fear factor of not screwing up! There are so many elements that happen to you when you perform, that even if you're really tired before a show, energy manages to come from deep down inside and keep you going."

She says there were times she felt she was not taken seriously because she was a female. "At times I felt I had to prove myself as a drummer. The thing is, there weren't and still aren't that many female drummers out there, so I felt many challenges. On the other hand, the fact that I was female allowed more opportunities for me and more interest from a male-dominated industry."

She says perhaps the greatest lesson she's learned as a drummer is being patient with people and being flexible. "There were many times that plans have gone astray and I would have to reconfigure things in a moment's notice. Perhaps the unpredictability of drumming and performing has taught me that lesson."

Bobbye Jean Hall

Drummer Bobbye Jean Hall was still in her teens when she started playing clubs in her native Detroit, Michigan. In addition to drum kit, she became known for her skills on other percussion instruments such as bongos and congas and was a sought after session musician, a rare feat for any woman to this day. She was also the unaccredited percussionist for numerous Motown recordings. Her first studio gig, playing a full rock drum kit, is featured on Chris Etheridge's 1971 album *L.A. Getaway*.

In an interview with Melody Berger in the summer 2013 issue of *Tom Tom*, Hall says she didn't talk much as a child, but she did beat on pots and pans and garbage cans in the alley. They were her voice. Her mother took her to the Detroit Institute and was told, "Mrs. Hall, your daughter just needs to play. We don't want to disturb that."

Soon after she was "discovered" by Motown producer Paul Riser playing at a local sock hop, she found herself recording with The Temptations, Smokey Robinson and the Miracles, and Diana Ross and the Supremes. "It was really funny," she said, "because he'd have to pick me up because I was too young to drive."

After living in Europe for a few years, she moved to Los Angeles. Between 1971 and 1989, she worked with some of the top musicians in the industry, showing off her drumming skills on twenty-two songs that reached the top ten in the Billboard Hot 100, with six of those reaching number one.

Hall worked with Bill Withers on an album recorded at Carnegie Hall and also on his number one hit "Lean on Me." She recorded with Carole King on two of her studio albums and toured with her in 1973. The next year she was back at Carnegie Hall with James Taylor, after recording with him on two of his albums. In 1974 and 1976, Stevie Wonder called on her to provide percussion for some songs, including "Bird of Beauty," where her "artful quica work established a mood of Brazil at Carnival."

She released her own album *Body Language for Lovers* in March 1977, featuring instrumental work co-written by her and her husband Joe Porter.

Bob Dylan called on her in 1978 to join him for a world tour and offered her $2,500 a week, much more than she was making playing studio sessions at that time. Howard Sounes writes in his book *Down the Highway: The Life of Bob Dylan* that during the tour, the band stayed at all the best hotels and flew on a chartered jetliner. According to Sounes, Hall was invited by Dylan to join him from time to time to dinner. He also liked to entertain her with card tricks.

Hall, Sounes writes, was surprised to find that Dylan was a fan of soul food and observed him "to be infatuated by going out with black women . . . by that whole black thing, [even] eating the food." As the tour went on, Dylan became testy with the musicians, and Hall says that during that time, "when he spoke to us, he was not the poet."

Hall played percussion on Dylan's studio album *Street-Legal.* In between Dylan tour dates, she also played congas for Tom Waits' *Blue Valentine* album. In 1979, she joined Pink Floyd for their recording *The Wall.*

In the early 1980s, she recorded with Bob Seger's Silver Bullet Band and then joined Stevie Nicks for tours in 1982 and 1986 in addition to playing on her album *Bella Donna.*

Hall's diverse skills as a percussionist are also preserved in the soundtrack of the 1986 film *Little Shop of Horrors.*

Over her career she has recorded with a who's who list of top musicians in every genre: Lynyrd Skynyrd, Marvin Gaye, Janis Joplin, Rod Stewart, Dolly Parton, Joni Mitchell, Jerry Garcia, Dwight Yoakam, Mary Wells, Jefferson Starship, Kenny Rankin, The Manhattan Transfer, Boz Scaggs, Aretha Franklin, The Doobie Brothers, The Doors, Sarah Vaughan, Tracy Chapman—and that's just the beginning of the list.

In the *Tom Tom* interview, Hall states that at one time she represented five minorities: Black American woman, single mom, female drummer—and as a female drummer, representative of less than half a percent of women in the union, self-employed contractor and property owner.

She said her advocacy for single moms, in particular, was triggered when former Vice President Dan Quayle attacked *The Murphy Brown Show* for the lead character having a child without being married. "I'm a single mom by choice—not by chance," she said. "Some women just do certain things better on our own."

At the time of this interview, Hall had just returned from doing a drum class for her three-year-old granddaughter's preschool in Los Angeles. The granddaughter Olivia Lily is already an aspiring drummer, no doubt inspired by her "Grandmommy Bobbye." "I just gave her her first congas," Hall said.

As a professional musician, Hall describes herself as one of the most hired and most fired—"one day Carnegie Hall, the next day unemployed."

"When I go on a job, on a gig, on a session I am working my way out of that job when I leave there; it no longer exists," she says. But then when she turns on the radio and hears a song she had a part in, she just smiles and gets to relive the whole scene.

"Working in the music field has given me the task of always reinventing myself financially, we well as creatively," Hall says. "At this time in my life I cannot stress the importance in staying fit, emotionally balanced, and getting enough sleep." And to others she offers this sage advice: "Keep a clear vision to focus on, that will bring good success. Have no regrets. Have no debts."

And finally, "Live the life you love; love the life you live." It may not all be easy, she admits, but it's a beautiful life, all the same.

June Miles-Kingston

Drummer June Miles-Kingston started as an art student at the National Film School in the United Kingdom. In 1980, she helped film and music video director Julien Temple make the Sex Pistols' mockumentary *The Great Rock 'n' Roll Swindle*. In 1979, after moving in with Kate Korris of the Slits and Joe Strummer of the Clash, the music bug bit her big time, and she purchased a drum kit from Paul Cook of the Sex Pistols for forty pounds.

Over the next few months, she and Korris, with two friends, Jane Crockford and Ramona Carlier, formed an all-female punk band, the Mo-dettes. The Modettes toured for two years and broke up in 1982 after releasing one album *The Story So Far* on Derem Records. Their best known song, "White Mice," written by Crockford and self-released in 1979, was their first single and a number one indie hit.

When the band split, Miles-Kingston went on to become drummer for Everything but the Girl, the Fun Boy Three, Thompson Twins, and The Communards. In addition to drumming, she also provided backing vocals for several recordings. At the time this book went to press, she was working as a jazz singer and studying art at Central St. Martin's College of Art and Design in London.

Atsuko Yamano

Japanese drummer Atsuko Yamano along with her sister Naoko Yamano who played guitar and a friend Michie Nakatani who played bass formed the pop-punk band Shonen Knife in Osaka in December 1981. Shonen Knife, which translates into "Boy Knife," has been credited with putting the international into pop underground. The trio, known for its edgy instrumentation, earned a worldwide cult following and avid fans, including the late Kurt Cobain. The band is still active, touring and recording, after more than thirty years. They describe themselves as "oo-oo-ultra-eccentric-super-cult-punk-pop-band-shonen knife!"

When the group started, Atsuko played drums and provided backup vocals. A former fashion designer, she also designed the group's outfits. When Nakatani left the group in 2000, she switched to playing bass. Mana Nishiura, who took over drumming duties, was killed in a car accident in 2005 and was eventually replaced by Etsuko Nakanishi. Nakanishi played with Shonen Knife for four years from 2006 to 2010. She had formerly played with the Japanese band Pink Panda. Atsuko left the group when she married and moved to Los Angeles. However, she still plays with Shonen Knife when they are in the LA area on North American tours.

Hilary Jones

Hilary Jones, born March 25, 1964, in Baltimore, Maryland, started playing drums professionally at age sixteen. After graduating from the Baltimore School for the Arts, she enlisted in the U.S. Navy and spent her first six months of enlistment at the Armed Forces School of Music. As a drummer with the U.S. Navy Band, she took advantage of that opportunity to expand her knowledge of diverse musical styles, from big band to pop.

Upon discharge from the Navy, Jones moved to the San Francisco Bay area and joined Girlfriend, a group of musicians hand-picked by producer Narada Michael Walden. She also began working with artists such as Maria Muldaur, the Mamas & Papas, Angela Bofill, Clarence Clemons, Pete Escovedo, and Ray Obiedo.

Following a move to Los Angeles, Jones recorded and toured with Lee Ritenour, Dave Grusin, Scott Henderson's Tribal Tech, Eric Marienthal, Doc Severinson, Robben Ford, and Brazilian guitar virtuoso Badi Assad. She also played with bands such as Cecilia Noel and the Wild Clams, The Delphines, as well as her own band.

She released her debut CD *Soaring* in May 2001.

Julie Turner

Drummer Julie Turner was nine years old when she and her thirteen-year-old sister Jody, who played guitar and sang, decided in 1978 to form a heavy metal band. Inspired by the success of The Runaways, the girls formed Rock Goddess, a group that would eventually achieve cult status in their native Britain in the early '80s. Julie and Jody's father owned a music store in South London and used his connections to get the girls their first gigs. The backroom of their father's store also provided a convenient place for the band to rehearse.

With their father acting as manager, the sisters and two friends Tracey Lamb (bass) and Donnica Colman (keyboards) started playing London clubs and captured the attention of British record producer Vic Maile. Their performance at the Reading Festival in 1982 was so impressive that A&M signed the band to a recording contract. And after releasing their first single, they were invited to go on tour with UFO.

But the band ran into legal problems because Julie was still a minor in school. According to British law, the young drummer could not play more than six gigs in a row, and the UFO tour was for eight days. After the album was released, Julie was allowed to tour with the band in their stint as opening act for Def Leppard.

Jeff Treppel describes Julie's playing in an August 2012 *Decibel* magazine article: "The younger Turner sister hit the skins pretty damn hard for a fourteen-year-old (and had a kit that was way bigger than she was)."

Rock Goddess' second album *Hell Hath No Fury* was released in 1984, and the band toured in the United Kingdom and France. In 1986, the band made their first U.S. tour.

Until they disbanded in 1987, the band had numerous personnel changes, playing sometimes as a trio and sometimes as a quartet, but Julie and Jody remained the basis for the group's various formations. In 1988, Julie joined her sister in The Jody Turner Band, which featured two male musicians, but the group never made it beyond the local club circuit.

Rock Goddess reappeared in 1994 with a completely different lineup, including a different drummer, Nicola Shaw.

"Barbie"

A 1950s drum machine affectionately known as "Barbie" provided the beat for the Têtes Noires, when they formed in Minneapolis, Minnesota, in 1982. The first all-female rock band from that city started as a fun performance art project. Vixen, another all-female rock band, had started in St. Paul in 1980. The founding members decided to call themselves the Têtes Noires (French for "Black Heads"), not for zits but for their hair color. They were known for their unusual sound, witty and humorous lyrics, and original songs on a variety of topics, ranging from the Unification Church and world peace to the American family and gay murder.

"Barbie" was the drummer for the first two recordings by the sextet, critically acclaimed for their three- to six-part vocal harmonies. For their third album, a live drummer, Cristel Little, joined them. Jennifer Holt, the vocalist/violinist who was one of the main songwriters for the group, said they added the live drummer because there was a feeling "our music wasn't weird enough to get art grants, and yet without a drummer it wasn't accessible enough to a lot of people" (Huet, "Têtes Noires Will Turn Heads").

Although Little's "driving rhythms" were praised, the third album was not as universally lauded by critics as the first two. Some said it was too commercial. Others said it wasn't commercial enough.

Another Minneapolis all-female band, the Clams, emerged in 1985. Karen Gratz was drummer for the group, which, in live performances, was often compared to the Rolling Stones. The Clams were described as a "throwback" band. Many felt they never got the break they deserved. But in their hometown, Gratz and her fellow band members, vocalist/guitarist Cindy Lawson, and lead guitarist Roxie Terry, were heroes. In the words of critic John Dougan: "a great band that liked to powder their noses and kick some ass."

Lynn Perko Truell

Lynn Perko Truell earned her stripes as a drummer in the early American hardcore punk scene. In fact she's been one busy drummer since the early 1980s when she was an iconic fixture in San Francisco's underground, playing with the seminal hardcore punk band The Dicks and the blues leaning Sister Double Happiness. Today she continues winning praise for what *Spin* magazine calls her "killer combination of timing and texture" in her work with the indie punk band Imperial Teen. *Spin* praised the band as one of the top performing groups at SXSW 2012 and has listed Truell as one of the top one hundred drummers of alternative music.

Born November 2, 1963, in Palo Alto, California, Truell spent her teen years in Reno, Nevada, and started her music career in 1980 as drummer with The Wrecks, an all-girl punk band based in that city.

"The original drummer for the Wrecks was grounded for a month, and they needed help," Truell said. "I knew the girls in the band . . . next thing I knew I bought an old Ludwig Classic Kit, and it was a go from there. I was a classically trained pianist from age seven to fifteen. The piano is also a percussive instrument, so mechanically, drums made musical sense to me. My early influences were Robo from Black Flag, Janet Housden from Red Cross, Chuck Biscuits from DOA, Stewart Copeland, Tommy Lee, Martin Chambers, Clem Burke, and Charlie Watts."

After two years with The Wrecks, Truell relocated to San Francisco, where she joined The Dicks in 1983. Originally an Austin-based band, The Dicks reformed with new personnel when Gary Floyd left Texas for the California Bay Area. Along with Truell, other new members were Tim Carrol and Sebastian Fuchs. They released a few recordings and then dissolved in 1986.

Truell said her experience with the Dicks was often "tainted with the more delinquent side of hardcore: skinheads, rude and disrespectful people using punk to carry out their drunken rages, etc., but I had a lot of support from the punk/music community. For most of us, hardcore punk was a state of mind and lifestyle, thinking differently, standing out because we had something to say, not because we needed negative attention. It was a social movement based on music/lyrics/lifestyle. That's what I related to."

Truell and Floyd then co-founded Sister Double Happiness, an alternative blues-rock band. Over nine years they released four LPs, one EP, and one live record. They also toured with Nirvana during the release of *Nevermind*, Soundgarden, Dinosaur Jr, and Replacements.

"Sister Double Happiness was a totally different direction and was definitely based on punk ideas, but we were a blues/grunge band," Truell said. "I loved all the touring we did internationally. Also, being on SubPop (Records) still gives me street-cred."

When Sister Double Happiness disbanded in 1995, Truell went on to form Imperial Teen with Roddy Bottum, Will Schwartz, and Jone Stebbins. Imperial Teen did two major label releases and then were signed to Merge Records, their label since. The indie band's recordings have won universal critical acclaim for their distinctive symphonic pop sound. *Rolling Stone* named their 2007 album *The Hair the TV the Baby and the Band* one of the best of the year.

Truell and Imperial Teen, along with recording, have toured and opened for Hole, fronted by Courtney Love, and The Breeders. They also toured with the White Stripes, Pink, Cibo Matto, the Lemonheads, Lush, Dinosaur Jr, and The Go-Go's.

She said in the beginning of her career as a drummer, it was "often difficult to be taken seriously by some of the bouncers at rock clubs who would maybe not let me backstage or on stage because they didn't believe I was actually the drummer in the band. Or, I would often get some smirks and guffaws and little heh-hehs from some of the rock club bouncers or stage crews. Of course, that was absolute ammo for inspiration to do a kick-ass sound check and prove myself—something I shouldn't have had to do, but likely it improved my skills and intentions and intensity. As the years have passed, there are so many awesome female drummers, so obviously the club vibes and attitudes have changed."

In a March 3, 2008, interview with Nick Gio Barbiero from the *Austinist*, Truell said, "When the four of us get together more often than not we drift in the pop direction. And it's real fun to play these poppy songs live; we like audience participation and singing along. We are serious people—I think our lyrics express that—but we appreciate the chance to also express our musical bliss!"

"I gather inspiration from the other members of my band—always," Turell said. "Also, from the fans, the energy they give out, the physical satisfaction of drumming and feeling strong behind the kit. There really is nothing I can compare to a great show behind the kit. It's extremely satisfying."

She said she considered her "stumbling into drumming as some sort of career path" as a gift. "I am grateful for my experiences in and around songwriting, studio-recording, guest-drumming for projects, touring, meeting so many iconic musicians and artists, and having a second family in every band I've been in."

Roxy Petrucci

Looking back, Roxy Petrucci may not have known the Rock Gods were feeling frisky the day she was born in the City of Detroit well before the "Blue Ribbon" generation. As an Italian American brought up in humble beginnings, she said it was very clear at an early age she'd better be great at something.

Petrucci was well raised and schooled in a family of talented musicians. A first chair clarinetist in high school, then in college, she decided the "conservatory was too conservative," and drumsticks and black leather seemed a better fit. She gave up symphony rehearsals and formed the all-female band Pantagruel later to be known as Black Lace.

Inspiration then rocked Petrucci when, in her words, Bonham and Moon still rolled and her proverbial cup began to overflow. "Music was in my heart but metal was in my veins," she said, "and the road would soon call." Madam X proved to be her next outlet with a cast of characters that included "molten-lava" guitarist and sister Maxine Petrucci, bassist Chris "Godzilla" Doliber and vocalist Bret Kaiser. Visually stunning, their performances were described as "a brilliant blend of *Rocky Horror Picture Show* with *Spinal Tap* moments." The outrageous Madam X attained cult status as Petrucci paid her dues on an infamous four-year tour.

Fueled by Madam X, Petrucci continued to make noise of her own on the West Coast scene when she auditioned for David Lee Roth. The Roth opportunity, she said, was a "near miss" as master drummer Gregg Bissonette edged her out for the prized gig.

For Petrucci, the black leather got even hotter when 1986 proved to be the year of the Vixen. MTV and Vixen would be a match made in heaven, and the engine of one of the most successful all-female rock bands ever. Worldwide tours fronting notables as Ozzy, Scorpions, Deep Purple, and Kiss caused "the flames of success to burn too hot," according to Petrucci, so eventually she and Vixen parted ways in 1991 with occasional performances up to 2001.

Side projects such as Hell's Belles and Titania never caught fire, but in 2004 VH1 came courting the Vixen sirens when "Bands Reunited" found Petrucci hiding out in Germantown, Wisconsin. Leaving the fans wanting more, Vixen only performed a one-off performance, and Petrucci retreated back to her side project Roktopuss, featuring Lorraine Lewis of Femme Fetale and "face-melting" guitarist Jeff Young (Megadeth).

"It wasn't until 2010 that inspiration struck me once again like a bolt of lighting," she said. "While in Nova Scotia I was presented with the prestigious Cape Breton International Drum Festival Legends Award along with drum greats Carmine Appice, Alan White, Jerry Mercer, and Virgil Donati. It was at that specific time and place, in the presence of so much extraordinary talent when my circle closed on my destiny in music. Awards and accolades may look impressive on the wall but to inspire other potential rock legends is an unparalleled achievement and along with rock 'n' roll, will live forever."

She adds: "So they say lightning never strikes twice and you never know what the future may bring. It might be a Detroit thing but I will only speak for myself when I say; who the fuck are they and what do they know?" Ultimately they will find me slumped over my drum kit still grasping my sticks in my cold dead hands . . . but I'm not dead yet!"

CHAPTER 11

Wicked to the Max: The '80s Continued

> You know, that whole "show must go on" thing is real. The monitors are feeding back, the AC's gone off in the club in the heat of August, and your kick pedal is held together with duct tape, but by God you're playing, the crowd loves it, and that's what gets you up in the morning.
>
> —Kopana Terry

As all-female and female-fronted bands began to achieve long-sought chart success, female musicians in the '80s finally were winning some of that R-E-S-P-E-C-T that Aretha Frankin sang about in the late '60s. Bands like The Go-Go's and the Bangles proved to the music industry that females could play and be big money makers. The success of those bands also frustrated many women musicians who feared bands with reputations as "cute chicks playing music" would hinder them from being accepted as serious musicians. In response, they formed all-female metal bands or joined mixed bands that played heavy-hitting hard rock.

Bernadette Cooper

Klymaxx, started by drummer Bernadette Cooper, became the first self-produced all-female R&B and pop band in which every member played an instrument. Cooper dropped out of college to pursue her dream of forming an all-girl band. After numerous auditions in which she sought women who were not only competent musicians, but who exuded sex appeal and a sense of "I-am-woman-let-me-roar!," she chose vocalist Lorena Porter, bassist Joyce Irby, guitarist

Cheryl Cooley, and keyboardists Lynn Malsby and Robbin Grider. Solar Records signed them in 1981 and released their debut album *Never Underestimate the Power of a Woman.*

Cooper and the band went on to perform a number of chart hits, including the top five Billboard single, "I Miss You." Klymaxx also had the flattering distinction of being parodied on a 1985 *Saturday Night Live* sketch with Halle Berry playing the part of Bernadette. Their hit "I Look Good" was adopted by Bette Midler as the opening theme for her "Diva Las Vegas" show.

In 1991, Cooper released a solo recording, *Drama According to Bernadette Cooper*. In 2012, she started a solo tour "Diva and a Turntable," which encompassed hits she's written and produced for Klymaxx, other artists, and her solo album, all performed with a DJ. Regarding that undertaking, she said, "I have given years, time, and love to creating Klymaxx and its brand. Now it's time to be my epic self without compromise. In that sense Klymaxx is the theatre and Bernadette Cooper is the act" (Klymaxx, bbkingblues.com).

Two Metal Ladies

Carol "Control" Duckworth had already tested her chops in a number of bands before joining the all-female band Precious Metal. Born in Nebraska and raised in Riverside, California, her reputation as a drummer had won her the stage name Carol M. (Mass) Control before joining Precious Metal in 1985 to replace drummer and Precious Metal founder Susette Andres.

After leaving Precious Metal, Andres, of Long Island, New York, moved to California in hopes of finding other musical opportunities. She went on to form Wylde Hearts and another all-female group Bombshell, which played together for eight years before disbanding in 1999. Today the former drummer has a professional animal care business and she and her animals have appeared on the *Tonight Show*, *Animal Planet*, *Larry King Live*, and *Magic Mountain.*

Jody Linscott

Jody Linscott got into drumming purely by accident. She was in London studying to be a bookbinder and trying to earn a little extra cash by repairing household items. One of those items turned out to be a small conga drum. The owner never came back to claim it, and Linscott decided to give the conga a try. Her inspiration was a poster for a rhythm class to be taught by a master drummer from Ghana at the African Center in Covent Garden.

The master drummer was so impressed with her natural talent that he offered to give Linscott private lessons at his home. In a November 24, 1994, interview with Fred Shuster of the *Los Angeles Daily News*, she recalls going to his house three times for lessons. "The fourth time, he was dressed in these white robes, had a talking drum under his arm, proposed marriage, and started chasing me around the room. I couldn't really go back after that."

But even though the lessons stopped, her new interest in drumming was keener than ever. She built a full set of congas from fiberglass and located a blacksmith who could provide the hardware. She took a job as a waitress at a Camden Town club, and when the bands started playing, she'd take her drums out of the cloakroom and go onstage to jam with them. One night when Kokomo was the featured band, she stayed onstage for the entire set, which didn't sit well with club management. The club fired her, but Kokomo hired her a month later. Thus began an illustrious career, which saw Linscott performing and touring with more than forty-five well-known artists, including The Who, Paul McCartney, Jay-Z, Santana, Elton John, Eric Clapton, Phil Collins, David Gilmour, Tom Jones, Bryan Adams, Take That, and Avril Lavigne.

Linscott was a U.S. citizen who moved to England in 1977. The Boston native went there on holiday and never returned. After Kokomo gave the drummer her first professional break, she went to work with Robert Palmer on his album *Sneakin' Sally Through the Alley*. She toured with him for two years, and for that tour used her "handyman" skills to build her own percussion rack so that she could create a variety of sounds.

In a Q&A, which appeared in a 2009 Roland Drums blog, she spoke about spending time in New York and seeing musicians who were "doing a lot of jingles and stuff, just for the money." She said she never wanted a lifestyle or the kind of work where she would "get used to the money." Touring, she said, kept her from getting bored, and while recording sessions keep her busy, playing live was what she loved most. "The spontaneity and the way everything changes night to night is something I really like. I'm as passionate now about making music as I ever was."

Linscott stresses the importance of being open to all styles of music. In the Roland interview, she said: "If I don't like it I definitely try to make an effort to understand it so that I can appreciate it. I think everything's a form of art, so I just keep myself open. It's so easy as you get older to close yourself off from different styles of music, or new music. And I really try not to do that."

She recalls doing a gig with Jay-Z, and admits she went into it not being a huge rap fan. But after trying to get inside his music, to understand where it came from, so that she could play it, she said the experience was "fantastic and it opened a whole new door for me."

The talented drummer is also author of two children's books, published by Doubleday and edited by the late Jackie Onassis.

Suzy Zarow

Drummer Suzy Zarow became known playing with the all-female pop group Big Trouble in 1987 and 1988. The band was formed by television executive Fred Silverman in the tradition of the '60s group The Monkees. The rest of the group included bassist Julia Farey, keyboardist Rebecca Ryan, and vocalist Bobby Eakes, Miss Georgia of 1983 and future soap opera star.

Big Trouble was the "house band" for the television series *Comedy Break*, hosted by comedians Mack and Jamie. They were signed to Epic Records and recorded a self-titled album *Big Trouble*, which was released in 1988. Their debut single "Crazy World" peaked at number seventy-one on U.S. charts. Although produced by Grammy and Oscar winner Giorgio Moroder, the album was a commercial failure.

After the band spit, Zarow disappeared from the public eye, but is still deemed one of the best drummers of the era.

Teresa Taylor

Teresa Taylor, also known as Teresa Nervosa, started as a drummer in an Austin, Texas, high school marching band. She was drawn to the drums listening to and watching the University of Texas band at basketball games in the school's Gregory Gym. "The acoustics were great in the wooden bleachers," she said.

She joined the Butthole Surfers in 1982 after letting the band practice in an Austin downtown warehouse she was renting for forty dollars a month. Taylor joined King Coffey as a drummer for the group for six years. She and Coffey would drum in unison on separate, stand-up drum kits.

Music critic Austin Powell described the Butthole Surfers in a September 2008 article in the *Austin Chronicle* as "the physical embodiment of chaos theory, a flaming hemorrhoid of Texas psych, avant-garde expressionism, and iconoclastic noise ripping through the rectum of contemporary culture."

Front man and band co-founder Gibby Haynes said the band was "pure performance art with a musical soundtrack."

Taylor and Coffey were described by Powell as "two gods of thunder, hammering seismic beats that pressed the Surfers' live shows into the realm of spirit-possession ceremonies."

Taylor and Coffey often referred to themselves as siblings. Their physical resemblance to each other led many to assume they were related.

Taylor left the band in 1989 after the Hairway to Steven tour. In the *Chronicle* article, she's quoted as saying: "I didn't want to leave the band, but I really wasn't well. I was flipping out, drinking too much and all that. I had developed a really big fear of flying. I always thought the plane was going to crash. I couldn't figure out what was wrong with me. I started taking Prozac and trying to get better, trying to find someone who could help me."

She told Powell: "Our shows were pretty wicked at that time. We had the penis reconstruction video, the strobe lights, the fire, the naked dancer. Everything was getting really out of control. I didn't always think it was the most positive first LSD experience for someone to have. People were coming away scarred."

As the band began to make its name nationally with major label status, Taylor began suffering side effects, including strobe light–induced seizures. She was later diagnosed with an aneurysm and underwent brain surgery in 1993.

In 1991, Taylor took a role in Richard Linklater's film *Slacker* as "Papsmear Pusher," a woman trying to sell a Pap smear from Madonna. She appears on the movie's poster and home video media covers.

Taylor also played in the '80s punk band Meat Joy with Gretchen Phillips of Two Nice Girls and John Hawkes. In 2008 and 2009, Taylor was drumming for the Butthole Surfers once again when the band reunited for their Classic Lineup Tour.

Kate Schellenbach

Kate Schellenbach of Beastie Boys and Luscious Jackson fame is working these days as a television producer (*The Ellen DeGeneres Show* and *Lopez Tonight*), but back in the 1980s she was, in the words of Beastie Boys' rocker Dave Parsons, the "gal in the downtown music scene whom everyone admired and followed around" (Beastiemania website).

A hardcore punk fan from the get-go, Schellenbach would try to make every show that came to her hometown, New York City. Once she started performing and demonstrating her skills on drums, she began winning fans for herself as one of the Big Apple's premiere drummers, first with Beastie Boys and then with Luscious Jackson.

In a March 2012 interview with Mia Jones posted on AfterEllen.com, Schellenbach talks about being a teenager in New York: "We grew up in a really amazing time, the girls from Luscious and the guys from Beastie Boys, because we all met as teenagers, going out to clubs, and there was a big mish-mosh of music that was really influential on us like rap and punk and the mixture of the two. And it has really informed our music in different ways. So we feel really blessed to have grown up in a time when we could sneak into clubs as fifteen-year-olds and dance around to The Slits."

Along with her talent as a drummer, Schellenbach, says Parsons on the Beastiemania website, also had "an artistic gift of reproducing venue entrance stamps on the hands of her underage friends." According to Parsons, she always had a pouch of colored pencils and markers. When someone went into a club and came back out, she would duplicate whatever the stamp design was for that night, so that all her friends could get into the club. "She could do any stamp design," Parsons said. "Back then they had some interestingly complex ones, but she was quite an artist."

Parsons said she was a "ring leader" for all the "little girls" who followed her. Eventually guys like the Beastie Boys' Adam Yauch and Michael Diamond were following her around, too, and soon she found herself playing drums as an original member of that group. Although Schellenbach was only with the Beastie Boys from 1981 to 1984, her contributions to the hardcore punk band were significant.

In a September 1998 *Spin* article, "The Story of Yo: The Oral History of the Beastie Boys," former Beastie Boys member Thomas Beller tried to explain Schellenbach's departure from the band. "No one ever actually said, 'Kat you're out.' She went away for a weekend, and Rick [Rubin] bought the other three members matching Adidas sweat suits, red and black warm-ups, and sneakers. They were at the Manhattan club area dressed up like a trio and Kate bumped into them—by accident. She just started crying because it was obvious that there was not going to be a woman in a band that's, like, going to have an inflatable penis on stage."

During her time with Beastie Boys, Schellenbach was featured on the 1982 recording *Polly Wog Stew*, *Cooky Puss* in 1983, and *Some Old Bullshit* in 1984.

Before joining Beastie Boys, Schellenbach played with other bands, including the Carcinogens from 1978 to 1979, Toxic Shock in 1980, and the X-Patriots and Nagasaki Newsboys.

After leaving Beastie Boys, Schellenbach helped form Luscious Jackson. During that time she became one of the first out lesbian musicians, according to Mia Jones, who interviewed Schellenbach for AfterEllen.com.

Luscious Jackson, made up of Schellenbach, singer/bassist Jill Cunnif, singer/guitarist Gabby Glaser, and keyboardist Vivian Trimble, released four albums. Before disbanding in 2000, they also left their mark on '90s pop culture, being featured in the soundtrack for the movie *Clueless* and the TV series, *Buffy the Vampire Slayer*, along with starring in a Gap commercial. In 2011, the group reunited for a new album, but instead of going with a traditional label, decided to self-produce the recording with the help of fans through Pledge Music.

Georgia Hubley

Georgia Hubley of the New Jersey underground band Yo La Tengo started playing drums in her late teens. When she and her friends went to clubs to see bands, it was always the drummer who drew her attention. "It looked like it would be fun to play," she told Clare Longrigg in a 2004 article in *The Guardian*, entitled "Not Bad—For a Girl." "I was very causal about it. . . . I started to play drums, and it didn't seem far-fetched."

She said she got her first kit when she was thirteen. In a May 2012 *Tom Tom* magazine "Drummer 2 Drummer" conversation with Decemberists drummer Rachel Blumberg ("Yo La Tengo's Georgia and Rachel"), Hubley is quoted: "I remember my dad took me to this decrepit apartment complex, and I remember we walked into this apartment and it was just filled with pot smoke and the heads all had pot leaves and flowers drawn on them and we brought this thing home, and it had two kicks and four rack toms. It was two kits together. It was a crappy old giant kit. I didn't know the value of it. I love playing vintage drums now."

Her mother never discouraged her interest and allowed her to set up the drum kit in her Manhattan studio where she ran a business by day. At night, Hubley would practice, not always to the delight of nearby tenants. Mostly she played along with records—especially anything by the Rolling Stones. She also took a few informal lessons from friends of friends who were drummers and picked up "little things" here and there.

When she went to art school, she was invited to join an all-girl band by a woman she met in a life drawing class. The band never had a name and never played a show during the time she was with them. When they finally got their first show, they named themselves The Dangerous Curves. Hubley said that was pretty much what happened with Yo La Tengo, too. As quoted in the *Tom Tom* article, "We didn't have a name until we had a show!"

Hubley and her husband, guitarist/vocalist Ira Kaplan, formed Yo La Tengo in 1984. They had started as friends, often running into each other in record stores and at shows. Sharing a love of music and the New York Mets, they were soon hanging out together and jamming.

Yo La Tengo started as a party band playing covers and eventually evolved into its own thing. Mostly ignored by mainstream radio, the group still managed to win cult status and a reputation as the quintessential critics' band. Hubley, as the drummer and vocalist, has been recognized as the heart of the trio's sound.

Writer Sabrine Crawford, in a 2001 article in *DRUM!*, described the notoriously shy Hubley as "the ultimate anti-rock star." Her shyness and unassuming demeanor, however, haven't kept this "bashful basher" off the lists of most creative indie drummers.

Kopana Terry

Kopana Terry was born and grew up primarily in West Liberty, Kentucky, an Appalachian, she claims, by ten or more generations. She says her dad's side of the family was "not particularly musical." In fact, she said, "Dad can't carry a tune in a bucket. Poor guy can hardly tap his foot. He doesn't even like music, really."

Terry got her musical genes from her mom's side of the family. Along with playing guitar and piano, her mother also was a snare drummer in the high school band, and "that was cutting edge for a girl back in the 1950s, especially in Appalachia." She said her mother had a "ton of records—Elvis, Tom Jones, Aretha Franklin, and Mahalia Jackson, with a smattering of Stevie Wonder, Beatles, Dionne Warwick, and the Platters thrown in."

But in Eastern Kentucky, there was nothing on the local radio but country. "I got plenty of Loretta Lynn, Conway Twitty, Johnny Cash, and Tammy Wynette and George Jones. And always, there was Bluegrass. That's what Papaw played and what a lot of locals played, and with being raised in the Pentecostal church, I was inundated by southern old-time gospel, which in that church was not too dissimilar from Black Gospel."

To fill in the musical gaps, her friends and other family members turned her on to Deep Purple, Blue Oyster Cult, the Carpenters, Jimmy Buffett, and Simon and Garfunkel.

"My interest as a child was drumming," Terry said. "That's all I wanted to do, when I wasn't playing outside—in the creek or running the hills. I was a tomboy for sure. When I was tall enough to reach the kitchen drawer, I used butter knives as drum sticks. I destroyed quite a bit of furniture until my grandmother, still cooking with lard in those days (it was the 1970s) would save her empty lard buckets for me. Eventually, I destroyed those, too."

She said when she was four, her parents gave her a skin-covered tambourine, which "didn't quell my desires at all," and at age six, her mom bought her a tiny set of bongos from a friend's little head shop. Next, she graduated to JC Penney kits with paper drumheads. "The longest any one set lasted was fifteen minutes."

"When I was eight, a blue sparkle snare drum arrived on our doorstep. That was only one drum and didn't quench my thirst long. My parents finally accepted the fact that I was going to be a drummer no matter what, and in 1975, when I was ten, my mother found an off-brand real set of red sparkle drums at an antique store, which she bought for $110. I've had a drum set ever since!"

In middle school, Terry started playing trumpet at her mother's urging, but switched to drums after a year. Lacking an inspiring teacher and classmates, she soon lost interest. "I just wanted to rock. I wanted to play kit. I wanted to be in a throw-down, kick-ass, screaming guitar rock and roll band. Mind you, this was the disco era, and I listened to it like all the other kids, but to play? I wanted to be in Deep Purple and Blue Oyster Cult! Of all the music I heard growing up, those were the bands I wanted to be in. They were raw, primal, heart pounding, butt grabbing, in-your-face music; not like marching band at all. I had absolutely no interest in rudiments or structure or Sousa."

Terry says by the time she was twenty, she was kicking herself for not sticking with marching band. "I could only teach myself so much. Rudiments are fundamental to other forms of rhythmic development, from switching time signatures to reading simple drum charts. I got myself a book and learned the rudiments, but I never fully developed the speed the way I could have if I had stayed with it."

Her first drumming gig was with a band called The Countrymen. She was fifteen at the time and her mother had to drive her to the gig. "It was an OK gig, but the guys, as I recall, weren't especially friendly. They didn't want to have to change the name of the band just to have me in it. So, they didn't, but it was a first gig, and ya gotta start somewhere."

In 1985, after receiving a certificate in audio engineering, she moved to Barrow, Alaska, to take a job with a local radio station. Terry was only there five months and when she returned to Kentucky, she responded to an ad her mother found in a Lexington paper placed by a local punk band looking for a drummer. She got the job with Kiya Heartwood's band Radio Café, which a few months later changed its name to Stealin' Horses.

Her experiences with that band ran the gamut: "from a major label deal replete with MTV music video, tour support, major players, and a producer, rubbing shoulders with huge names, playing Farm Aid to fifty thousand people and millions more via TV, to playing every stinking beer dive from Santa Barbara to the Jersey Shore, living out of a suitcase in roach-infested hotels, driving sixteen hours to the next gig, and having absolutely no money for food for days at a time. It was the best of times, it was the worst of times, as the story goes."

After quitting Stealin' Horses, Terry went back to Kentucky and enrolled in the College of Fine Arts at the University of Kentucky. She played in a couple of original pop bands, but says she had the most fun in a couple of blues bands, U.S. 27 and La Vida Loca—the best bands, she says, no one ever heard. "Learning to play good blues taught me more than all the other bands combined. I learned how to finesse feel, swing, and really, really listen."

When Terry joined Heartwood's band Wishing Chair, she said her blues experience helped her considerably on the two CDs she made with that group. At the time of this interview, Terry said she and Heartwood were revisiting the idea of a band, and with two others were writing and piecing together a recording project.

She says the main thing she's learned from her musical experiences was how to deal with dysfunction. "Seriously, being in a band, any band, is like being in a dysfunctional family of your choosing. It teaches you how to deal with various personalities, situations, think on your feet, play in any situation. You know, that whole 'show must go on' thing is real. The monitors are feeding back, the AC's gone off in the club in the heat of August, and your kick pedal is held together with duct tape, but by God you're playing, the crowd loves it, and that's what gets you up in the morning."

Terry, in addition to being a professional musician, is a librarian at the University of Kentucky and has a master's degree in library and information science. She's also a photographer and has a daily blog called "the outhouse."

Her advice for young women who'd like to be professional drummers: "Take lessons. Learn as much as you can. Learn the rules, then learn how to break them. Explore, be adventurous, never take no for an answer, and never ever let a group of middle-aged white men tell you they won't change the name of their band because you're a girl. Go make your own fucking band and wipe the stage with them!"

Terri Lord

Terri Lord didn't waste any time honing a skill that would eventually earn her a reputation as one of the top punk rock drummers in Austin, Texas, in the 1980s. In fact, the Austin Rock Hall of Famer formed her first band at age seven: Terri and the Termites. She and girlfriends from the neighborhood, playing whatever instruments they could—flute, piano, you name it, with Terri on toy drums—found a second home in her basement "studio" grooving to Herb Alpert records. Terri even put Christmas lights on an old dining room table as a stage for her go-go dancers. Her "play" recording studio had a little red light and mic dangling from the ceiling. If the red light was on, the girls were playing.

"My parents told me we went to an ice show when I was three and I threw a fit until I could see the drummer," she said. Growing up in a musical family was a big help, and her parents never discouraged her from pursuing her drumming passion. "My father played guitar and always carried it around with him. In the 1960s he went to a New York club in the Village, and a new folk group asked him to join them. He turned down the opportunity. The folk group later became famous as the Kingston Trio."

Terri, who was born in Massachusetts and grew up in Colts Neck, New Jersey, said she had fond memories of family gatherings where her father and relatives would pull their chairs together and jam. "My aunt played spoons, and I had an uncle who played ukulele. My grandmother's husband sang and played guitar."

Terri got her first real drum set—a red sparkle—at age nine. She says she took drum lessons for about two months—mostly over the phone—and then a friend of her father sat with her for about three hours and taught her how to master a 4/4 beat, using what she called a "hooked-on-phonics" approach. "Since the majority of music is in 4/4, if you can master that major beat, you can play just about anything," she said.

In high school, she and some fellow members from the school basketball team formed a band called Paradise. In keeping with the band's name, she put a cover on the red sparkle and painted it with a tropical scene. She also played with some guys she met in study hall, and they practiced in her basement/recording studio where she taped everything they did.

As a high school senior, she quit the basketball team and decided to try out for the Kit Kat Club drummer role in the musical *Cabaret*. "I had to convince the teacher that I actually could play." She got the part and as a result has loved playing for musicals and plays ever since. "It's like putting on a show in the garage, and the band is over before everyone can hate each other," she laughed.

After graduating from high school, Terri moved to Austin in 1978 to study film at the University of Texas. "I came to Austin for the heat. I hate cold," she said.

Before moving, she sold her drums to a paperboy in New Jersey, something she regretted once she realized how the punk rock scene was exploding in Austin. Her roommate, Lisa Rhodes, was constantly encouraging her to answer ads for drummers. "I was really shy," Terri said. "Besides that, I didn't have any drums and hadn't practiced."

Lisa finally convinced her to buy a drum set she found for sale on a local bulletin board—a red sparkle for three hundred dollars—"the same drums I started with and the same drums I play now," she said.

"I was so excited. I lived in an apartment, and the manager came in and said you have to stop. So I rented space in a warehouse that had electricity."

She joined an all-girl band, the Sirens, which she said broke up pretty quickly because all the girls started having affairs with each other. She recalls the first show they played, "Big Boys was on the bill, and it was a benefit for an island trying to save its monkeys."

She then started drumming for Aces 88, a New Orleans "cool wave" band—two guys and two girls—in which all members had hair dyed jet black. "We practiced every night—unlike most bands now that may only practice once a week. Our favorite words then were, 'Practice is cancelled.'"

Along with Aces 88, Terri played in the Jitters, Airhead, Mind Splinters, Bad Mutha Goose & the Brothers Grimm, Girls in the Nose, Power Snatch, Lord Douglas Phillips, and the Applicators. She won her biggest national audience as the drummer for Sincola. She's gigged with Dirty Hearts and her emo-pop band Dreadful Sorry and has done theatrical work as well as songwriting, recording, teaching, volunteering for Girls Rock Camp, and running her own Terri Lord School of Badass Rock.

She compares the energy at a rock show to that at a football game. "The audience is as much a part of it as the band," she said.

She says like so many other women drummers, she's been assaulted with comments through the years such as "You're really good for a girl" and "Are you setting up the drums for your boyfriend?" At a 1988 gig in Brownsville, Texas, the poster read, "Featuring Terri, the Female Drummer!" "It's still a girl music ghetto," she said.

In addition to being musicians, Terri says, "All drummers are plumbers and magpies, collecting shiny metal things," referring to the many times drummers have to jerry rig equipment to make it through a rehearsal or performance.

She said her drumming experience had taught her to be tenacious. "If you stop, the train will stop. You have to make it to the end of the song."

CHAPTER 12

Awesome Times Two

> I picked up a pair of sticks, and it was the most natural-feeling thing I've ever done.
>
> —Karen Carpenter

> To me the stage is like my living room, or my home, and when you come over to my house, I have to be a hostess and invite you in so that we can have a great time.
>
> —Sheila E.

Karen Carpenter

Karen Carpenter entered high school in the Los Angeles suburb of Downey, California, in the fall of 1964 at the age of fourteen. Not relishing the thought of sweaty morning runs on a track field, she was delighted to learn she could substitute a band credit for P.E. And when it came to choosing between school choir and geometry, singing easily won over mathematical theorems.

The young girl who would become a musical legend was born in New Haven, Connecticut, on March 2, 1950. Her family moved to California in 1963, and not long after that Karen discovered her passion for drums.

As a new member of the marching band, Karen was assigned to glockenspiel by band director Bruce Gifford. The young Miss Carpenter was underwhelmed, to say the least. She found the glockenspiel awkward and didn't care for the tone. To her ears, it was a quarter step sharp with the rest of the band's instruments. Other pieces in the percussion section were far more fascinating to her, particularly the drums played by her classmate and close friend Frankie

Chavez. Chavez had played the drums since he was three and shared Karen's passion for music.

After two months with the glockenspiel, Karen met with Gifford and expressed her desire to change instruments and join the drum line. As quoted in the book *Little Girl Blue: The Life of Karen Carpenter* by Randy L. Schmidt, "I used to march down the street playing these stupid bells, watching Frankie play his tail off on the drums. It hit me that I could play drums as good as nine-tenths of those boys in the drum line, outside of Frankie."

The band director tried to discourage Karen, telling her, "Girls don't play drums. That's not really normal."

The stubborn Miss Carpenter refused to let such comments deter her, and Gifford finally acquiesced, assigning her to cymbals. She ultimately ended up playing snare, and it wasn't long before she was one of the top players on the drum line. According to biographer Schmidt, she would spend countless hours rehearsing before and after school and then go home to assemble the kitchen barstools and pots and pans in a makeshift drum kit, using her father's chopsticks as drumsticks.

In another quote, which appears in Schmidt's book, she says, "I picked up a pair of sticks, and it was the most natural-feeling thing I've ever done."

Rod Fogerty, in the May 1983 issue of *Modern Drummer*, quotes her brother Richard saying she took to the drums "in nothing flat." Her big influence was Joe Morello, drummer for the Dave Brubeck Quartet. In just a year she was playing the "intricate, odd-time rhythms" of Brubeck's "Take Five" and "It's A Raggy Waltz."

She and her pal Chavez spent hours together talking drums and listening to jazz. But her parents were skeptical and thought her obsession with drums would soon pass. At her brother Richard's urging, they finally agreed to purchase a three hundred dollar entry-level Ludwig drum kit.

Her first lessons were with her friend Frankie. She then began studying with Bill Douglass at Drum City in Hollywood. Douglass was a well-known jazz drummer who had played with Benny Goodman and Art Tatum.

After two months, Karen was ready to trade in her drum kit for a 1965 Ludwig Super Classic in silver sparkle with double floor toms and Super Sensitive Snare—the same drum kit used by one of her drumming idols, Joe Morello. Her parents balked at first but had a change of heart. Karen was one happy kid on Christmas morning.

Her first gig was playing with her brother as a piano and drum duo for a local production of *Guys and Dolls*. She then became drummer for an all-girl band Two Plus Two, comprised of her Downey High School classmates. One member of the band, Linda Stewart, recalled one of Karen's favorite songs was the Beatles "Ticket to Ride." She hadn't heard Karen sing, but said, "I had never heard such a good drummer in my young life at that time." The band broke up after a band member's mother refused to let her go to a gig at a local pool party.

When Richard graduated from high school in 1964, he went to California State University at Long Beach and met bassist and tuba major Wes Jacobs. The two clicked musically and decided to form an instrumental jazz trio with Karen on drums. "Within three weeks she could play drums better than anyone that I heard at the college," Jacobs said (Schmidt 28).

In 1966, the trio won first prize in the Hollywood Bowl Battle of the Bands. Karen's drum solos were already being described as "an explosion of energy and chops" and "a real tour-de-force for a drummer just past her sixteenth birthday."

Trumpet player Dan Friberg, who played with the Richard Carpenter Trio on a recurring basis, said Karen's idols at the time were Louie Bellson and Buddy Rich. Their pictures and pictures of other great drummers graced the walls of her room. "Her goal was to be as good as they were. She was great then, by all I could tell, but not good enough for her," Friberg said (Schmidt 29).

When she graduated from high school in 1967, Karen was presented with the John Philip Sousa Band Award, considered the highest achievement for high school band students. In a yearbook message to Frankie Chavez, she thanked him for getting her interested in drums, for teaching her, and for inspiring and guiding her.

The Carpenters released their first album for A&M in 1969. On the album, which was originally released as *Offering* and later reissued as *Ticket to Ride*, Karen is drummer on all tracks. Music writer Rod Fogarty in the *Modern Drummer* article "Karen Carpenter: A Drummer Who Sang," describes the performance of the nineteen-year-old drummer: "Here we witness a drummer in full command of her technique, assured and full of fire, playing imaginative fills and great hand/foot combinations. Her drumming is alive with the joy of self-discovery."

Later when Karen's talents as a singer were uncovered, she still liked being surrounded by her "battery of drums." Not particularly tall at five feet, four inches, the drums made her barely visible during performances. Her kit by now had grown to include four melodic toms. She liked to brag that hers was only one of three such drum kits in the world. The other two belonged to Hal Blaine and Ringo Starr.

In 1971, reviews began to note the lack of a focal point for the group. One critic in Omaha, Nebraska, wrote: "Hire a drummer. Why stick a lovely girl with a tremendous voice behind a set of traps and have her pump high hat cymbals and shoot an occasional rim shot when by rights she should be in front moving to the music while she sings?"

Their manager, Ed Leffler, agreed with the chorus of critics who believed the drums were in the way and "disconnecting" her from audiences. He told Karen, "You can't sing like that and hide behind a drum set" (Schmidt 84).

Karen was reluctant to make the change. Those close to her felt the drums had become for her a security blanket of sorts. Sherwin Bash, who played bass with the group, is quoted in Schmidt's book: "This was a chubby young lady who could hide some of that chubbiness behind all of these drums. She was kind of a tomboy, and the drums were traditionally a male instrument. She was kind of asserting herself in a certain way. The girl vocalist out front was a role that she wanted to achieve, but she was insecure about getting out there. She wasn't sure she was slim enough, svelte enough, pretty enough, or any of those things."

Karen disagreed with suggestions that she abandon the drums for a spotlight in front. She argued that there were already enough "chick singers" forming groups and that she could best demonstrate her skills behind a drum set.

The truth was Karen had more passion for and was more comfortable playing drums than being a star in the spotlight. She loved her drums and didn't want to leave them. According to the late composer Allyn Ferguson, who worked with The Carpenters on their television series, Karen's poise and self-confidence took a dive when she was absent her drums. "Her confidence was sitting behind those drums. It was a part of her, and she was a damn good drummer. When she was not behind the drums her confidence and her security just disappeared. . . . She was not a stand-up singer in any way because she didn't believe in herself that way" (Schmidt 85).

Indeed, Karen thought of herself as a drummer who sang—not a singer who played drums.

Hal Blaine, who eventually took over some of the drumming duties for The Carpenters, was quoted in Fogarty's article in *Modern Drummer* magazine: "I always said that Karen was a good drummer. I knew she could play right away when she'd sit down at my drums on sessions. She played on a lot of the album cuts, and she played when they performed live, as well. But after their third or fourth hit, I remember saying to her, 'When are you going to get off the drums? You sing too good and you should be fronting the band.'"

Karen eventually began to take front stage on ballads, but for up-tempo numbers, she remained seated behind her beloved drums.

Another drummer who played with The Carpenters, Cubby O'Brien, is quoted in the Fogarty article: "Karen was a very good player and very knowledgeable about the drums." He said it wasn't always easy because Richard always wanted everything played exactly as it was on the recordings, and it was hard for someone other than Karen "to take over the drum chair."

Percussion features were sometimes worked into live performances so that Karen could show off her chops along with her impressive vocal capabilities.

In 1973, The Carpenters recorded *Now and Then* with Karen playing drums on every track except one. Of her performance on "This Masquerade," Fogarty writes: "Karen lays down a Latin rhythm that can only be described as elegantly hip. With a stick and a brush, she weaves an almost ethereal groove. Hi-hat accents and an uncluttered clave offer a textbook example of musical and creative drumming."

Others took notice of Karen's drumming skills. In 1975 *Playboy* magazine's annual opinion poll, readers voted Karen the Best Rock Drummer of the Year. John Bonham of Led Zeppelin came in second and was *not* pleased. He states in the book *John Bonham: The Powerhouse Behind Led Zeppelin*: "I'd like to have it publicized that I came in after Karen Carpenter in the *Playboy* drummer poll. She couldn't last ten minutes with a Zeppelin number."

Despite Bonham's putdown, even Buddy Rich considered her an extraordinary drummer. In Fogarty's *Modern Drummer* article, Cubby O'Brien is quoted: "I remember one time when Karen and I went to see Buddy's band. I knew Buddy fairly well so before the show I took her backstage to meet him. I said, 'Buddy, this is Karen Carpenter.' He said, 'Karen Carpenter, do you know that you're one of my favorite drummers?' As tough as Buddy could be on drummers sometimes, he always respected someone who played the instrument well."

Karen Carpenter died February 4, 1983, at the age of thirty-two. She suffered a heart attack brought on by her seven-year battle with anorexia. But her legacy as a drummer who sang lives on. She would be pleased to know her name appears on nearly every list of top women drummers, and that she is respected as much for her drumming chops as her vocal abilities.

Sheila E.

When Prince met drummer Sheila Escovedo for the first time he teased her, telling her he and his bassist were fighting over who would be the first to be her husband. He also predicted that one day she would be part of his band. The year was 1978. Six years later, his prediction became reality. In 1984, when Prince recorded Purple Rain, Sheila E. was there recording with him, drumming and providing vocals to "Let's Go Crazy" and "Erotic City." That would begin a musical collaboration that would span more than two decades. But even before Prince "discovered" the talented Sheila E. and made her his protégé, this remarkable musician had already made quite a name for herself.

From the moment she was born December 12, 1957, in Oakland, California, Sheila Escovedo was destined for a life of making music. Of Mexican-Creole heritage, she was the eldest child of Juanita Gardere Escovedo, a worker in a diary factory, and famed Latin percussionist Pete Escovedo. Her godfather was Latin jazz artist Tito Puente, and her uncle was Alejandro Escovedo, founder of the punk band The Zeros. Another uncle, Mario Escovedo, fronted the indie band The Dragons. Another uncle, Coke Escovedo, played with Santana. By the time she was three, Sheila had picked up drumsticks and was making music. Later she added to her musical skills by learning to play the tuba, guitar, and violin.

Her father, with whom she still performs frequently, was a great influence, and as a young child she spent hours watching him rehearse with his band Azteca. At age five, she made her "concert debut" when her father invited her on stage to play a solo. Performing before a group of three thousand at the former Sands Ballroom in Oakland, California, the young drummer had an inkling of her future, even though at that time she had other plans.

In an interview in the *Washington Post* (May 17, 2013), Sheila told writer Lauren McEwen that as a child her aspirations were to be "the first little girl on the moon." She later decided she'd settle for being a Gold Medal Olympic runner, and actually trained for the Olympics, as a teenage track star. But a performance with her father at age fifteen changed all that. She knew then her true destiny was and had always been performing and making music.

At age seventeen, she was performing professionally, and in 1976 made her recording debut on "Yesterday's Dreams" with jazz bassist Alphonso Johnson. By the time she was in her early twenties she had already built an impressive resume as a session and touring musician, playing with George Duke, Lionel Richie, Marvin Gaye, Herbie Hancock, and Diana Ross. Through the years, that list would grow to include other renowned artists such as Prince, Babyface, Billy Cobham, Natalie Cole, Gloria Estefan, Herbie Hancock, Stevie Nicks, Patti LaBelle, Cyndi Lauper, Ringo Starr, Don Wise, Stevie Wonder, Tito Puente, her father, and many others.

According to her official website, she caught Prince's attention in 1983, changed her name to Sheila E., and with his help recorded her first solo album, *The Glamorous Life.* The album-titled first single won critical and popular acclaim and was nominated for multiple Grammy and American Music Awards. It also won MTV's Best Video Award. A follow-up single from the album, "The Belle of St. Mark," was another hit. For three months, on the heels of the album's success, she performed for sold-out performances in Europe and United States. Her association with Prince catapulted her into international superstardom. She also had a brief romantic fling with Prince, which captured tabloid headlines, further increasing her name recognition and visibility.

In 1984-1985, she began touring as the opening act for Prince's 1984–85 "Purple Rain" tour. At the same time she was busy working on her second album *Romance 1600,* which was released in August 1985 and featured the mega hit "A Love Bizarre." After a headlining tour in spring 1986, she signed on for a three-month engagement, opening for Lionel Richie.

The drummer was also attracting the attention of movie producers and in 1986 made her acting debut in the film *Krush Groove.* The following year she appeared in *The Adventures of Ford Fairlane.*

Her third album *Sheila E.* included the hit single "Hold Me," which topped the *Billboard* charts at number one. Rather than touring to promote her own album, she chose instead to go on tour with Prince, playing drums and percussion in his "Sign o' the Times" European tour. In a *Rolling Stone* readers' poll, that tour was ranked as the fifteenth best tour in music history. She joined Prince again in 1988 and 1989 for his "Lovesexy" tour.

Between tours, she joined her father Pete Escovedo and godfather Tito Puente for a concert of Latin jazz where she had an opportunity to show off her skills as a virtuoso percussionist. The concert *Latina Familia* was later released on video and CD.

A collapsed lung caused numerous health problems, and Sheila was forced to take a hiatus for the next few years. Then in 1994 she started E-Train, a band that combined her eclectic musical tastes: soul, Latin, jazz, funk, fusion, and gospel. E-Train toured Europe in 1994 and four years later released a CD, *Writes of Passage.*

When Magic Johnson asked her to become music director for his short-lived *Magic Hour* in 1998, she became the first female bandleader for a late night TV show.

Ringo Starr, a great admirer of Sheila E.'s drumming skills, signed her on as a member of his "All-Starr" Band in 2001. She did two more stints with Starr in 2003 and 2006. Her comic drum duets with the former Beatles drummer were a highlight of the show.

In 2004, she was back with Prince on his "Musicology" tour, with sell-out crowds totaling over 1.5 million people.

In the *Washington Post* interview with McEwen, Sheila E. talks about performing live and how important it is for her to build rapport with the audience. Known for bringing audience members on stage, she said, "Engaging with the audience lets them now I'm approachable. To me the stage is like my living room, or my home, and when you come over to my house, I have to be a hostess and invite you in so that we can have a great time."

Over forty years, the woman who is considered among the best female drummers alive has built a long and impressive list of credits that include performing at the thirty-fifth Academy Awards with Placido Domingo and at the 1996 Summer Olympics, touring and recording with Japanese artist Namie Amuro, and being featured on countless albums, including Gloria Estefan's *Mi Tierra* and the soundtrack to *Prince of Egypt* with Whitney Houston and Mariah Carey. She is particularly proud of her participation in the "We Are The World" session that provided support for African famine relief.

She has performed for past and present U.S. presidents and their families, has worked as a musical director with superstars such as Jennifer Lopez and Beyoncé Knowles, and has been a featured artist and producer/arranger at numerous awards shows, including the Grammy Awards, MTV Video Music Awards, Image Awards, ALMA Awards, and the Latin Grammy Awards.

In 2010, she received an Emmy nomination for Outstanding Music Direction for "Fiesta Latina, A Performance at the White House." She also is the recipient of an honorary Doctorate of Music degree from the Musician's Institute.

The multi-talented musician is also known as an astute businesswoman and philanthropist. She is the founder and president of her entertainment company Stiletto Flats Inc. and co-founder of the Elevate Hope Foundation, a charitable organization that uses music and art to help abused and abandoned children. The foundation's work for her is especially personal. She is quoted on the Elevate Hope website: "At the tender age of five I was sexually abused by a babysitter. Growing up, I struggled with the shame of my childhood experience, but fortunately I had an outlet. Not until I was an adult did I realize how my exposure to music at an early age assisted in the healing process."

Her philosophy of life is simple: "I believe we are here to help people in this lifetime. We must give something of ourselves to truly live."

She says being a woman drummer in the '80s was a rarity. The *Washington Post* article quotes her: "When I started performing with other artists and would walk into the room to play with other percussionists, they didn't know of me—they kind of talked bad to me and tried to disrespect me."

She said her parents' advice was to learn her craft, play well, be prepared, and have confidence. "If this is my best, this is all that I can give you. I don't have to prove anything to you. This is my gift. It's not a competition," she said.

"Even now, some women come up to me and say, 'I always wanted to play, but it wasn't the female thing to do.' This was a man's instrument. But gender isn't attached to music. And music, itself—percussion or whatever it may be, is an open door to communication."

Viola Smith, original "hep" girl, 101 years young, courtesy Viola Smith.

Honey Lantree (top) and Honey Lantree with the Honeycombs (bottom), courtesy Paul R. Moy.

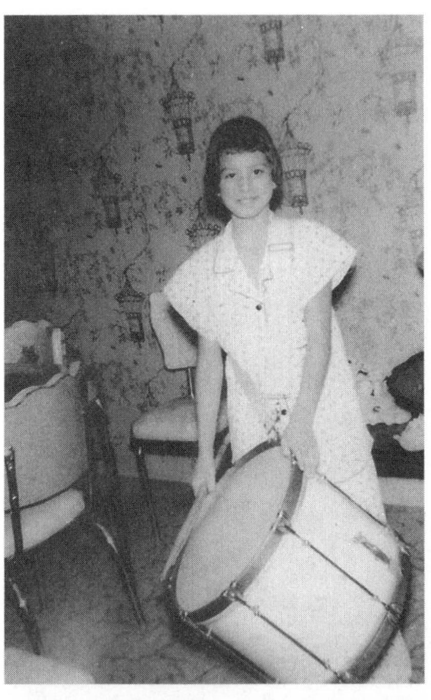

Ginger Bianco of Goldie and the Gingerbreads, with her first drum, courtesy Ginger Bianco (top), and Ginger Bianco today, courtesy Robbie Michaels (bottom).

Jenny Jones, courtesy Jenny Jones.

Crissy Lee, courtesy Jude Medhurst.

Alice de Buhr of Fanny, courtesy Alice de Buhr.

Palmolive, courtesy Palmolive.

Gina Schock of The Go-Go's, courtesy Arnold Neimanis.

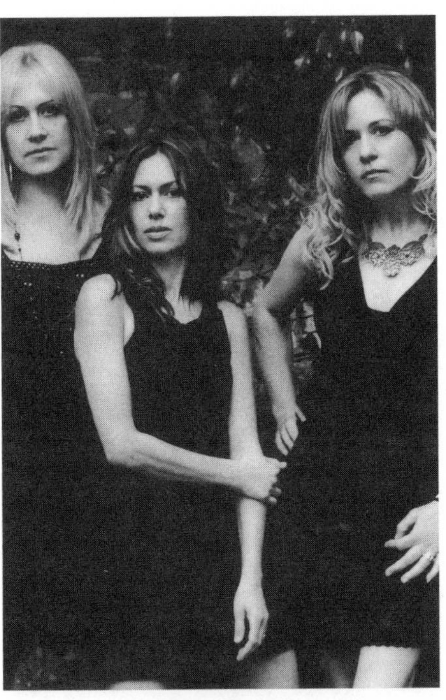

Debbi Peterson with the Bangles, courtesy Rebecca Wilson (top), and Debbi Peterson, courtesy Casey Rodgers (bottom).

Lynn Perko Truell, courtesy Peter Ellenby.

Roxy Petrucci, courtesy James Schmelzer.

Kopana Terry with Stealin' Horses, courtesy Kopana Terry (top), and Kopana Terry, courtesy Kiya Heartwood (bottom).

Terri Lord, courtesy Shelley Hiam.

Karen Carpenter, courtesy of the author (top) and courtesy PhotoFest (bottom).

Sheila E., courtesy Sheila E.

Cindy Blackman Santana, courtesy Jimmy Bruch.

Dawn Richardson, courtesy Jeff Graianette.

Patty Schemel, courtesy of the author.

Dena Tauriello, courtesy David Sokol.

Linda McDonald, courtesy Robert John Photography.

Debra Dobkin, courtesy James Cruce.

Meytal Cohen, courtesy Meytal Cohen.

Carla Azar, courtesy Autolux.

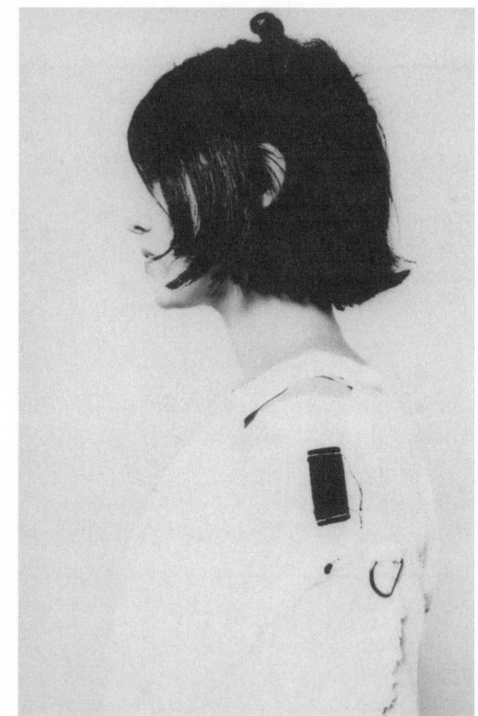

Rachel Blumberg, courtesy Sara Toor.

Rachel Fuhrer, courtesy Rachel Fuhrer.

Lisa Pankratz, courtesy Jon Noe.

Jyn Yates, courtesy Jyn Yates.

Karen Biller, courtesy George Brainard.

Michelle Josef, courtesy Malu Baumgarten.

Carol Dierking, courtesy Rick Moore.

Dottie Dodgion playing with Benny Goodman (top) and today (bottom), courtesy Dottie Dodgion.

Allison Miller, courtesy Desdemona Burgin.

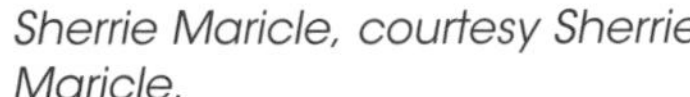

Sherrie Maricle, courtesy Sherrie Maricle.

Dame Evelyn Glennie, courtesy Mike Blake/Reuters.

Julie Hill, courtesy Julie Hill.

Alessandra Belloni, courtesy Alessandra Belloni.

Mindy Abovitz, founder/editor of Tom Tom *magazine, courtesy Brad Heck.*

Carla Black, founder of MEOW, courtesy Carla Black.

Sara McCabe, Ladies' Rock Camp graduate, courtesy Sara McCabe.

Moe Tucker of the Velvet Underground, courtesy Ruth Leitman.

Lauren Malloy, Austin McCallum High School student and future drummer in the making, courtesy of the author.

CHAPTER 13

Bangin' and Slammin': The '90s

> Thank god for punk and rock music. You could be whoever you wanted to be.
>
> —Patty Schemel

Women came roaring into the '90s, musically and otherwise. They worked at jobs and careers that affirmed their self-sufficiency and independence. They reveled in diversity, change, and their sexuality. They were comfortable in their skins and confident in what they could accomplish. The Spice Girls' lyrics said it all: "She's a power girl in a '90s world, but she's a downtown swingin' dude."

For women musicians, the decade was a whirlwind of activity. To quote a Rock Czar blogger: "The '90s were without a doubt the decade of the female. From Madonna and Mariah Carey's pop dominance to Garbage, No Doubt and Alanis just killing it on the rock side, there has simply been no better musical decade for women."

Cindy Blackman Santana

Drummers such as Cindy Blackman Santana, who had spent most of the previous decade playing jazz, became rocker chicks in the '90s. Blackman teamed up with Lenny Kravitz in 1993 after giving him a sample of her drumming over the phone. Up to that time, she had recorded, composed, and led her own band, developing a reputation for her driving groove. Her stint with Kravitz lasted eleven years.

As a jazz artist, Blackman was used to playing in small, intimate venues. She recalls in a *Drumhead* interview with Andrew Vargas her first experience playing in a big arena: "The first time I played in a really large concert with Lenny was at an outdoor festival called Pinkpop. We played for about seventy thousand people. It was in the summer so most people had just t-shirts or tanks, a lot of guys had their shirts off, so you just see skin and hands, and they're doing this wave thing. I almost lost it; my equilibrium was teetering. I wasn't used to seeing that many people. I was disoriented. I just had to stop looking and start focusing." She said Kravitz teased her for years afterwards about that.

"The big arena is like being on a big ship," she told Vargas, "and you're getting ready to take off into the stratosphere. With that amount of people there's a lot of energy coming at you. You have to push back."

In another interview with *Toronto Star* writer Ashante Infantry, Blackman said: "I like dance music and I like making the music feel good. To drive an audience of one hundred thousand into complete oblivion by playing a groove so strong . . . I love doing that. I love the chance to show versatility."

Blackman says playing with Kravitz gave her the opportunity to play with rock's finest and to perform with people such as James Brown, Prince, Mick Jagger, and Iggy Pop. "I've been exposed to a lot of stuff and I'm glad for it."

Some of the other "stuff" included performing with artists Pharoah Sanders, Cassandra Wilson, Bill Laswell, Joss Stone, Joe Henderson, Buckethead, Don Pullen, Hugh Masekela, and Angela Bofill.

Blackman, whose artistry in jazz-rock fusion is universally recognized, got her first toy drum kit when she was about five or six. She says her mom claimed she was born "hitting things and making rhythms." At age thirteen, she got her first professional drum set and started playing in the school band.

After high school, she moved from Connecticut to New York where she began what would become an illustrious career as a street musician. There she was exposed to abundant opportunities to see great drummers such as Max Roach, Al Foster, Jack DeJohnette, Roy Haynes, and Art Blakey play live. She also counted Clyde Stubblefield, John Bonham, and Mitch Mitchell among her drumming influences.

Her 2010 album *Another Lifetime* is a tribute to the legendary drummer Tony Williams, who she considers her mentor. A teen-aged Blackman met Williams at a clinic he did in a drum shop in her hometown. On her website, Blackman says, "I loved everything about Tony's playing," she said. "He changed the sound of music several times with different tunings and configurations, and innovated with every limb. His attitude and bravado behind the kit was incredible, and his technique was impeccable."

Blackman is best known today for her work with her husband Carlos Santana. She met Santana while on tour with Kravitz. To quote her website bio, "Electricity onstage generated chemistry offstage—Carlos proposed to Cindy during a July 2010 concert, and they married in December." She and Santana both believe in the transcendent nature of music. "To me, music is completely spiritual. It's the way you connect with your higher self, with the universe," she said. "It's also a way to share light with millions of people. They don't need to speak your language, have your beliefs, or be in the same place you are. The music speaks; it channels good energy, and makes a difference in people's lives. Carlos and I are both conscious of doing that."

Blackman says on her website, "I think of playing as controlled freedom, and in jazz, especially, that's exactly what you have. I love it. You know the forms of the songs, but you have the freedom to stretch over them. You want the music to grow and breathe, and you want to invite creativity from all the musicians. As you're going along you can change the color, the feel, the mood in different ways, or go off the chart and open it up to something new. Controlled freedom is an incredible discipline in itself, requiring a lot of focus. Improvisation like that is art in its highest form."

Blackman has established a reputation as an innovator who's always experimenting and pushing creative boundaries. *International Herald Tribune* music critic Mike Zwerin is quoted on Blackman's website: "Some drummers act, some react. Some keep time, others create it. Cindy Blackman Santana is among the few who can."

Dawn Richardson

As a rocker chick, Blackman was in good company. Take Dawn Richardson who helmed the drums for 4 Non Blondes. The mostly female rock group, formed in 1989 in San Francisco, released its first album in 1992, and their song "What's Up" became a massive radio hit and MTV smash. The album sold over six million copies worldwide. Richardson replaced drummer Wanda Day, who left the group before they made the hit recording. She and the band won international fame, touring with Neil Young, Pearl Jam, Bob Dylan, Aerosmith, and Prince.

Richardson said "I got the urge to learn drums at age twelve but before that I had tried piano and trombone. I actually played brass instruments—the trombone and then the baritone horn—for six years as a kid. Piano didn't last quite as long—maybe a year. I think some other kids at school were talking about learning the drums and it sounded cool."

About the time she started drumming, she was listening to bands like Aerosmith, Cream, and Led Zeppelin, and decided "drums figured into those bands better than the baritone horn." She started taking lessons with a local drum teacher, Jim Volpe, who inspired her when she had a chance to see him play live in the LA club scene.

Richardson, thanks to her parents' support and their investment in "many private lessons along the way," became a proficient percussionist, playing in rock groups, marching band, concert band, orchestra, and percussion ensembles. She received a Bachelor of Arts degree from Cal State Los Angeles and studied with Raynor Carroll, the principal percussionist of the Los Angeles Philharmonic as well as noted studio musicians Steven Houghton and Greg Goodall.

She joined the San Francisco rock band 4 Non Blondes in 1991 with bassist Christa Hillhouse, guitarist Shaunna Hall, and vocalist/guitarist Linda Perry. At the time the group had just been offered a major record deal with Interscope. After struggling and playing with so many LA groups that had tried to make it, Richardson said she was thrilled to have the opportunity to work with a group that "clearly had the songs to make it all happen."

During the two years Richardson played with 4 Non Blondes, the group received gold and platinum records for sales in the United States and abroad. She said highlights of that experience, along with recording the album and having a hit song, was the opportunity to tour North America and Europe with some of her favorite bands and musicians. "We were on a lot of TV shows including the *Late Show with David Letterman*, *The Conan O'Brien Show*, *The Billboard Music Awards*, and *Top of the Pops*. Playing the drums and being a member of that group taught me a lot about both the music business and playing music."

Richardson said breaking into the music field as a professional is a challenge for anyone. "There are so many uncontrollable factors involved in the entertainment business; it just doesn't work like most other businesses. I think the best you can do is be as persistent and as prepared as possible. You have to have a certain amount of good luck and be ready for plenty of challenges and disappointments along the way."

After leaving 4 Non Blondes, Richardson had a chance to work with artists such as The Martinis, Go Go Market, Penelope Houston, Vicki Randle, Erika Luckett, Kindness, Dolorata, The Loud Family, Holly Vincent, and Angel Corpus Christi, to name a few.

"I have to say touring with Tracy Chapman in 2009–2010 was a standout experience," she said. "She was great to play with—a generous musician and person. Plus I was up there with my pal Joe Gore on guitar/bass. He's an amazing talent. We had so much fun that we started a duo project, Mental 99, when we got home!"

Her current gigs have included working with Mental 99 and with singer/songwriter Shana Morrison, the daughter of Van Morrison.

Richardson also teaches. "I really enjoy passing along what I can and helping anyone and everyone who wants to give it a try no matter the age or skill level. I love the drums, so why wouldn't I want to share that as much as possible in as many ways as I can."

She's written five books to help people learn to play—all of them published and distributed by Mel Bay. She's also done a series of video lessons for www.onlinedrummer.com and was in discussions regarding plans for an Online Drummer School. "With new technology comes new ideas and concepts, but you can take all of the old school background. I am just going to keep doing my thing and see where all of this takes me."

Her advice to young women who aspire to be professional drummers is to "Follow your heart and your dreams. Of course, it is not an easy path, but you can't know what will happen if you never even give yourself the chance to try. Don't be afraid—be prepared. Practice, learn, and be open to different ideas and perspectives at every turn. Flexibility is key in life—especially the life of a professional musician."

She says playing music in so many varied situations has taught her to be mindful of others. She said this mindfulness, working hard, and thinking about how your actions and interactions may resonate with others can make one a better partner, teacher, friend, daughter, sister, or anything else you might be. "Work, dedication, and perseverance really do count, no matter how cynical our culture can sometimes be about those things."

For Richardson, music continues to be a "journey and constant learning experience." She says, "It is the place I can best focus and create. Depending on the project, it might be the type of musical situation that requires me to connect with other musicians and help express someone else's musical vision. Other times it can be more of my own musical vision and I might have the latitude to improvise more and be creative on-stage. I appreciate that every situation is different, but I do my best to give it my all every time out."

Patty Schemel

The alternative rock band Hole won critical acclaim during the '90s along with their prolific drummer Patty Schemel. Schemel was born April 24, 1967, and grew up in rural Marysville, Washington, where the hub of the social scene was the local Dairy Queen. She started playing drums after her father bought her a drum kit at age eleven. She said she chose drums because it was a "guy thing to do." She also says that like so many other kids, she wanted to be a rock star but didn't think that would ever happen.

At age fifteen, she and her brother Larry formed the band The Milkbones, which played in the school cafeteria. After forming another band, The Primitives, she and her brother joined Sybil, later renamed Kill Sybil, because the original name belonged to another artist.

In the 2011 documentary *Hit So Hard*, Schemel said she was one of three or four kids in high school who were into punk rock. The others were "farming kids and cowboys" who were "always going to the Dairy Queen and trying to beat us up."

She joined the Seattle all-female punk rock band Doll Squad in 1987. The band, which was active until 1989, gained a big indie following and released a demo. They also played alongside Nirvana. According to an interview with Hole founder and front woman Courtney Love, her husband Kurt Cobain considered Schemel as a replacement for Nirvana's drummer Chad Channing when he left the band. Dave Grohl ended up getting the job, but Cobain and Schemel became good friends.

Love recruited Schemel for Hole after original drummer Caroline Rue left in 1992. Schemel, in addition to playing drums, also played guitar on her first recording with the band. But it was her drumming on the second and Hole's most successful album *Live Through This* that caused people to take notice. While on tour in 1995, she became the first woman ever to appear on the cover of *Drum World* magazine.

It was also in 1995 that she revealed she was gay in the August 21 issue of *Rolling Stone*. "When I realized I was a lesbian, it was weird," Schemel said. "Thank god for punk and rock music. You could be whoever you wanted to be."

Over the next two years, Schemel recorded with Phrank, playing drums on their EP *Goofyfoot*. She also played drums on Hole's cover of Fleetwood Mac's "Gold Dust Woman," which became the first song on the soundtrack to *The Crow: City of Angels*.

In 1997, Schemel was in the studio again with Hole to begin recording *Celebrity Skin*. She wrote much of the album's material, but a session drummer played her parts for the actual recording. She left the band and was replaced by drummer Samantha Maloney.

In 2001, she joined Bastard, a short-lived band started by Courtney Love. She also recorded with the punk rock band Juliette and the Licks. Schemel and her brother Larry were composers and performers on Courtney Love's solo album, *America's Sweetheart*. She also toured with Imperial Teen.

When Schemel left, Courtney Love put the blame on Schemel's drug habit at the time. In the early 1990s, Schemel became addicted to heroin. She had refused to be part of Kurt Cobain's drug intervention in 1994, claiming that would have been hypocritical since she was doing the same thing.

Schemel said she left the band because of "musical differences." She and *Celebrity Skin* producer Michael Beinhorn didn't get along, and she felt that the band had betrayed her when they brought in a session drummer for the recording. Feeling her artistic integrity had been questioned, Schemel began a personal downward spiral.

In the *Hit So Hard* documentary, Schemel says she "made a trip to crack heroin heaven" and "stayed there for a long time." After being arrested, going to jail, and running out of money, she went "straight to the streets." She described her life as a homeless person. "Part of it was anger. Screw you guys—I'm on the streets pushing a shopping cart."

She recalls from her life on the street going into a church and seeing an "old crappy drum set." She realized then she had once played the drums but had been so totally into being a homeless person, only living for the next fix, that she had forgotten about that part of her life.

"One day I decided I couldn't do it anymore. I called my dad and told him I needed help. I went into rehab." As of 2011 when the documentary was made, she had been sober more than six years.

In 2010, she formed the band Green Eyes, and in 2012 released an album *The Cold and Lovely* by her all-lesbian trio of the same name.

Along with her music, Schemel owns a dog walking/boarding/day care business. "I love dogs as much as I love music," she said. She has also been involved in supporting causes related to women's recovery from drug addiction to sobriety. A woman who's been successful in exorcising her demons, Schemel gives back by playing for benefits and as a mentor at rock 'n' roll camps for girls.

Dee Plakas

Demetra "Dee" Plakas became a drummer the day she joined the Chicago punk band Problem Dogs. An earlier event, however, may have foretold her destiny. In a 1995 interview with Andy Doerschuk in *DRUM!* magazine, she tells of hanging out with some punk pals at a Cheap Trick concert when drummer Bun E. Carlos flung a broken a stick out into the crowd, which landed "right into Plaka's unsuspecting hands."

Plakas was born November 9, 1960, in Lansing, Illinois, and spent her childhood in the suburbs near Chicago. As a teen, she took the requisite piano lessons, but didn't feel called to a musician's life. At that time her ambitions were leaning toward a career as a radio DJ.

Then six months after she accidentally caught Carlos' drumstick, she was partying with some pals from Problem Dogs and learned they were looking for a drummer. In the *DRUM!* interview, she says, "I knew a guy who was a drummer and asked him to show me how to alternate the kick, snare, and ride cymbal. He taught me the most basic beat, and I sat there for half an hour playing it over and over again. I eventually threw in a roll in and decided, 'Yeah, I could do this.' Piece of cake, right?" She says she practiced for two weeks and then played her first gig.

After a few years doing the Chicago music scene, Plakas talked the group into relocating to Los Angeles. She had grown bored with the Chicago music scene and wanted to escape the brutal Midwestern winters. She didn't have to twist many arms before the group was packing its gear in a rental truck and heading west. The band didn't exactly find instant success after the move and had to settle for whatever gigs came their way. "Most of them were pretty bad," she said in the *Drum!* interview, "like the first band on a Monday night playing for your friends and five other people."

It was at one of those gigs in 1987 that she met an *LA Weekly* stringer who told her an all-female band called L7 was looking for a drummer. She was flattered when Donita Sparks, one of the guitarists and vocalists for the group, called her and asked her about her availability. Not ready to desert her friends in Problem Dogs just yet, she turned Sparks down and L7 lined up another drummer. However, two months later Problem Dogs decided to call it quits. She called Sparks, and as fate would have it, L7 had fired its drummer and was scouting for a new one.

The foursome, which took its name L7 from a 1950s slang phrase meaning square, was soon winning acclaim and packing clubs. They released a number of albums and a hit single "Pretend We're Dead." They played the Lollapalooza and Warped tours and became an international smash after releasing their fourth album *Hungry for Stink.*

The band also built a reputation for shocking its audiences. During a live show in London in 2000, L7 offered a one-night stand with Plakas as a raffle prize. The lucky winner got to spend a night on the band's tour bus.

In 1991, L7 formed a pro-choice women's rights group called Rock for Choice. The first Rock for Choice concert organized by L7 and Sue Cummings, *LA Weekly* music editor, was held October 25, 1991, and featured Nirvana, Hole, L7, and Sister Double Happiness. For a decade, Rock for Choice held concerts in the United States and Canada, featuring other big names such as Pearl Jam, Red Hot Chili Peppers, The Foo Fighters, Joan Jett, Melissa Etheridge, the Bangles, Stone Temple Pilots, Joan Osbourne, Iggy Pop, and Rage Against the Machine. It was considered a cultural bridge between the baby boomer feminists of the 1970s and the generation X feminists of the 1990s.

Riot Grrrl

About the same time as the Rock for Choice concert series was getting started, the Riot Grrrl movement was gathering momentum in Washington state. The underground feminist punk rock movement played a key role in changing the musical landscape of the '90s. Both Rock for Choice and Riot Grrrl were formed in response to the early 1990s bombings of abortion clinics by fringe elements of pro-life groups. Although the two were often associated together, very few Riot Grrl bands were ever featured in Rock for Choice concerts, held from 1991 to 2001.

The subculture Riot Grrrl movement saw the rise of numerous bands such as Bikini Kill, Bratmobile, L7, Huggy Bear, and Team Dresch addressing in their music issues such as rape, domestic abuse, sexuality, racism, patriarchy, and female empowerment.

Until the '90s, hardcore punk rock was dominated by males. Piero Scaruffi writes in his book *A History of Rock and Dance Music*: "Girls were excluded from hardcore the same way they were excluded in society from many other male-only rituals, whether street gangs or USA football. The 'riot grrrls' movement of the 1990s changed the sociopolitical landscape of punk-rock by introducing the 'girl factor' into the equation of frustration/depression/desperation/anger."

The movement started in the Pacific Northwest in the Seattle/Olympia, Washington, area, which at that time boasted numerous all-female bands. According to Scaruffi, an article entitled "Women, Sex and Rock and Roll," published in *Puncture* in 1989, became the movement's first manifesto. Young women who felt marginalized in the predominantly male punk scene began to articulate their anger and frustrations by creating garage bands and cut-and-paste fanzines that covered a range of political and feminist topics.

The Riot Grrrl movement coalesced in 1991, some speculate in response to attacks by the Christian Coalition's Right to Life attack on legal abortion and senate judiciary hearings in which Anita Hill accused Supreme Court Justice Clarence Thomas of sexual harassment, resulting in her being mocked by the media.

The underground music phenomena focused on lyrics rather than music. As Scaruffi writes: "mostly, the vocals were quite unattractive (they tended to imitate a scream, rather than enhance a melody) and the playing was quite amateurish. The female voice had been treated as an instrument (a sound) in the male-dominated musical culture; it now became a vehicle for a message. The rest of the music was largely redundant and/or optional."

Tobi Vail

The formation of the band Bikini Kill at Olympia's Evergreen State College in 1991 marked the beginning of the Riot Grrrl musical revolution. Bikini Kill drummer Tobi Vail, whose zine *Jigsaw* was one of the first punk zines to explicitly address gender issues, is considered a leader of the movement. Vail, who had been playing since age fifteen, wrote in *Jigsaw*: "I feel completely left out of the realm of everything that is so important to me. And I know that this is partly because punk rock is for and by boys mostly and partly because punk rock of this generation is coming of age in a time of mindless career-goal bands."

Vail, born July 20, 1969, and raised in Naselle and Olympia, Washington, began playing with The Go Team, an experimental punk project started in 1985 by Calvin Johnson. The group released several recordings on K Records, an independent label, mostly on a seven-inch vinyl format. Billy "Boredom" Karren, a guitarist who played with that band on a rotating basis, like Vail, would also go on to play with Bikini Kill.

Vail also played in all-girl teen band Doris from 1986 to 1988, which played shows throughout the Northwest. They made a demo that was never released. After The Go Team disbanded, Vail played in other project bands and was the featured drummer in a recording made by Some Velvet Sidewalk.

The drummer became best known during her years with Bikini Kill, the band she formed with singer/songwriter Kathleen Hannah. Hannah, who, along with music interests, studied photography and supported herself as a stripper, first collaborated with Vail on a fanzine called Bikini Kill, which eventually became the name of their band. Bikini Kill, which was active from 1990 to 1997, developed a reputation for its wild live performances, controversial lyrics, and political zines, which dealt with topics such as racism, vegetarianism, anti-capitalism, and a range of feminist issues ranging from rape and domestic violence to body image and eating disorders.

The band released several LPs and singles on the Kill Rock Stars label and toured extensively in the United States, Europe, Japan, and Australia.

Vail also started the band The Frumpies in 1992 in Washington, DC. They did a U.S. tour with Huggy Bear in 1993 and toured Italy in 2000 with Dada Swing.

Molly Neuman

When Vail started The Frumpies, she was working with another drummer who also played a key role in the Riot Grrrl movement. Molly Neuman played drums with the iconic band Bratmobile. Bratmobile and Bikini Kill are considered by many the two most influential first generation bands in the Riot Grrrl movement.

Bratmobile was the brainchild of University of Oregon students Molly Neuman and Allison Wolfe who had collaborated on the feminist fanzine *Girl Germs*. The two women had written some songs but didn't play any instruments. Since they performed a cappella, they considered themselves a "fake" band. When they were invited to play a Valentine's Day show with Bikini Kill and Some Velvet Sidewalk, they agreed and asked friend Robert Christie who played with Velvet Sidewalk to help them. He provided rehearsal space and equipment and advised them to listen to the Ramones.

Wolfe, who shared drumming duties with Neuman, is quoted in the book *Girls to the Front* by Sara Marcus: "Something in me clicked. Like, okay, if most boy punk rock bands just listen to the Ramones and that's how they write their songs, then we'll do the opposite and I won't listen to any Ramones and that way we'll sound different."

Wolfe and Neumann ended up writing five original songs, and Bratmobile played its first show on February 14, 1991, with the two women taking turns on drums, guitar, and vocals.

During spring break that year, Wolfe and Neuman went to Washington, DC, to follow Beat Happening and Nation of Ulysses on tour. With the addition of two musicians, Jen Smith and Christina Billotte, they recorded and released the cassette *Bratmobile DC*. In July 1991, the group began playing as a trio with guitarist Erin Smith joining Neuman on drums and Wolfe on vocals.

Bratmobile released the classic album *Pottymouth* and EP *The Real Janelle* on the Kill Rock Stars label.

Until their onstage breakup in 1994, the band's live performances were known for their "raw, high energy punk style, sexiness, playful and political onstage banter, and Allison's signature dance moves" (Mitchel, Reid-Walsh 200). Their music incorporated elements of pop, surf, and garage rock.

After the breakup, Neuman moved to the San Francisco Bay Area where she began working at the punk label Lookout! Records, which she now co-owns. She also played for The PeeChees and The Frumpies. In 1999, Bratmobile reunited for a show in Oakland and then relaunched to tour with Sleater-Kinney. A year later, they released on Neuman's label their second full-length album, the critically acclaimed *Ladies, Women and Girls*. Their third album *Girls Get Busy* was released in 2002.

In recent years, Neuman has started her own indie label Simple Social Graces Discos. She has managed acts such as The Donnas, Ted Leo, and The Locust, and is Director of Label Relations for eMusic, a subscription online service.

The entrepreneurial drummer has also started a Brooklyn-based food venture that provides personal chef, catering, and health consulting services with an emphasis on natural and whole foods. She shared her expertise related to that topic sitting on a 2013 SXSW panel on healthy diets and lifestyles for musicians on tour.

Sara Lund

Sara Lund of the Corin Tucker Band wrote in the September 2010 issue of *Modern Drummer* magazine that as a female drummer, she still felt "like a novelty act." When she started with a band called Unwound in 1991 in Olympia, Washington, she says she was "a surprisingly rare specimen known as a female drummer in an otherwise male band."

"There were not many of us that I knew of at that time," she said. "Arika Casebolt of Circus Lupus, Amy Farina of the Warmers, Katherina Bornefield of the Ex, Janet Weiss of Quasi—all stupendous powerhouse, kick-ass drummers, regardless of gender." She said in the early '90s, "people could not believe their eyes or ears when they discovered that a woman could be marginally competent on the drums."

Lund started playing drums in school band at age eleven. By fourteen, she had her first drum set and started her first band. She wrote in *Modern Drummer*: "We didn't have a name; we were just three dorks jamming in my bedroom after school. My first real band with a name and gigs was the Fixations from Bloomington, Indiana—the one and only all-girl band I ever played in."

After the Fixations, Lund joined the garage/experimental band Belgian Waffles and in 1991 moved to Olympia to enroll in Evergreen State College and to check out the exploding music scene there. In short time, she found herself playing with Witchy Poo, "kind of Olympia's version of Belgian Waffles," she said, "experimental, no permanent members, pretty much indefinable."

In the summer of 1992, she joined Unwound after their original drummer Brandt Sandeno quit and stayed with that group until 2002. She wrote in *Modern Drummer* that the decade she spent with that band was invaluable. "We operated as a classic power trio . . . our music sounded the way it did because of the styles each individual player brought to the table."

She and fellow band members Justin Trosper on guitar and vocals and Vern Ramsey on bass were eighteen and nineteen years old at the time they started playing together. Over the years, they formed what Lund described in the *Modern Drummer* article as a "psychic connection, allowing us to communicate musically in some realm outside of ourselves, outside of our words or our head. Our notes and rhythms found one another without much prompting. And believe it or not, we didn't really take that many drugs!"

After Unwound dissolved, Lund formed her own band, Hungry Ghost. In 2010, she joined the Corin Tucker Band.

Self-taught except for three years in school band where she says she learned how to hold her sticks and count rests, Lund says she has spent "years of my life, listening to the drummer."

In her words: "I believe drums are a musical instrument and should be played as such. Listen, drummers, listen. And if you're lucky, the other players will listen, too."

CHAPTER 14

Mega to the Max: The '90s Continued

> My favorite and happiest inner feelings percolate and are at their peak when I am performing live. . . . It's reaching out and connecting and sharing the joy that inspires me. Got gigs? I'll take it!"
>
> —Linda McDonald

More women drummers emerged in the last decade of the twentieth century, leaving their imprint on a music scene increasingly dominated by grunge and hip-hop. During the decade rock music felt the growing impact of technology and electronica. Artists such as Bjork and Moby, instead of hiring live drummers, began using sequenced drumming software in their recordings. Dance clubs replaced live bands with DJs and their turntables. While many drummers fell victim to technological change, others saw it as a challenge to push the envelope and find new ways to show their virtuosity.

Linda McDonald

When it came to change, Linda McDonald certainly wasn't a casualty. One listen to her brother's copy of Iron Maiden's *Maiden Japan* EP and a few hits on one of his friend's drum kits were all the inspiration she needed to eventually become one of the best drummers of the '90s. As a youngster, she tried her hand at piano for eight years and dabbled at violin and classical guitar. "All very beautiful, melodic instruments," she said, "but as a teen, I desired more than beauty. I wanted girth! I was angry and needed to feel something deeper and heavier and more physically satisfying and powerfully expressive."

McDonald had her first opportunity to give the drums a try when her brother's drummer friend left his kit at her house one weekend. "It was everything I hoped for and I was hooked." She said her brother John encouraged her to get a drum set of her own so that she could jam with him when he played his guitar. "He's my favorite brother," she said, "well, he's my only brother, but still, he's my favorite one!"

Born in Great Falls, Montana, half Irish, half Japanese, McDonald already was moving in that direction at age four when she started banging on her mother's Tupperware with chopsticks. She said she was lucky to have a supportive family who always allowed her to play whenever she wanted "until 8 p.m.," put up with her bands practicing in her bedroom and garage, went to all her shows, and helped her move her drums in and out of the house at all hours of the day and night.

Self-taught, McDonald started her musical career in 1987 with a short stint in the original three-piece female band, Andromeda. "When I was getting started people thought it was cute that a 5'1" young, shy girl wanted to play drums and it was hard to be taken seriously without having to prove yourself all the time."

As a founding member of Phantom Blue, her first band signed to a label known for its artists' musicianship, McDonald said the group "was met with many crossed arms at our shows until we started to play." The band won critical acclaim, and McDonald was given much credit for the band's energy, style, and sound.

McDonald said Phantom Blue gave her an "amazing opportunity to live the childhood dream of being a rock star—well . . . to a small degree, anyway," she laughed, "with other girls who shared that vision and work ethic. All of the extraordinary experiences we had as very young girls and growing together through the scary traps of the industry, traveling the world and just learning and growing so much so fast during that time period was something I will never forget. I really wish the band could have held it together better and longer with the original lineup; I think it would have been a great success today."

"It was the whole experience of that journey that was so amazing to me," she said. "It all happened so fast it didn't really seem real. I met a group of girls who just melted my face off when I heard their material, and that was that! I had never heard this style of playing from a group of girls, or let alone from men, either. It was so fresh. We broke ground for a lot of girls in the future is what I am still constantly being told by fans of the band and fellow musicians today. We were recording a demo one day, and suddenly, we were signed to a popular and well-respected independent label, were on MTV, in all the magazines, toured all over Europe, came back, got signed to Geffen Records, toured again. It was a dream come true, and then things got out of control. Typical story, but I still wouldn't trade it for anything."

McDonald said when Phantom Blue "was put on the shelf" in 1991, she was the only original member remaining. "I love what the band stood for, but the problem was that I honestly didn't feel the same spark or integrity within the band," she said. "I was very frustrated with the band and with the whole music scene in general at that time so we decided to hang it up for a while. I really thought I was done with the business, and then Iron Maidens came to be."

Iron Maidens

McDonald said the inspiration for Iron Maidens came about when Phantom Blue was scouting out a bass player to do some East Coast dates with them. The bass player they were checking out was featured in a co-ed tribute group to the heavy metal band Iron Maiden. She wasn't right for Phantom Blue, but the idea of an all-female Maiden tribute was born, and McDonald and her guitarist Josephine were recruited for that effort instead.

"I never really understood the big deal about tribute bands, but did get a flashback of memories when hearing them play," McDonald said. "The local music scene was suffering pretty badly during this time period, and people just wanted to go to clubs and be entertained and hear music that they knew and loved instead of miscellaneous original bands who were less than mediocre and unfamiliar."

She said the concept of a tribute band to Iron Maiden seemed a natural fit since Iron Maiden and Clive Burr were the main reasons she started to play drums to begin with. "If you are going to be in a tribute band and really do it right, you have to spend a lot of time with the music to get every nuance down and I can't think of another band I would rather listen to that closely and under such a microscope than Maiden."

As a member of that group, McDonald took the stage name "Nikki McBurrain," a play on the names of Iron Maiden's former drummer Clive Burr and their current drummer Nico McBrain. The British glove puppet Sooty adorns McDonald's drum kit just as it does McBrain's.

McDonald has also shown off her drumming skills recording for various projects including two releases from Carina Alfie and sharing drumming duties with Gene Hoglan on former Phantom Blue bandmate Michelle Meldrum's release "Blowing Up The Machine" with her original project called Meldrum. She also performed with the now defunct Ozzy Osbourne tribute band, The Little Dolls—"All Female, All Ozzy, All the Time"—and on *Surfing With The Alien*, a tribute to Joe Satriani, and cover bands The Valley Dolls, Crabby Patty (I'm So Unclear!), and Unholy Pink.

She said whatever the group and whatever the venue, she loves live playing. "My favorite and happiest inner feelings percolate and are at their peak when I am performing live. There is nothing else that brings that out of me like that. I love playing to people and sharing the energy of the music and bringing out smiles, metal horns, dancing, or whatever reactions the style of music being played brings out of them. It's reaching out and connecting and sharing the joy that inspires me. Got gigs? I'll take it!"

McDonald and Maidens' bandmate Courtney Cox joined other former Phantom Blue members for a reunion concert on May 26, 2009, to benefit brain research in memory of Phantom Blue co-founder Michelle Meldrum, who died of a cystic growth in her brain in 2008.

In 1997, McDonald won "Best Drummer/Performance of Drums and Percussion" at the Seventh Annual LA Music Awards in the very first co-ed category for drummers. However, she says she considers her greatest accomplishment is having someone she doesn't know tell her that she inspired them to play the drums. "Being told that I am somebody's influence and favorite drummer means I made a difference in somebody's life through drumming and music in a positive way. That is a major achievement, in my opinion."

To young women who aspire to be professional drummers, she says: "I can't stress how important it is to believe in yourself. Be fearless and brave and just play. Practice a lot! You will not regret it later. Practice, listen to a lot of different styles and genres of music, mingle, skip the excess partying, and love what you do. I would even learn to play another instrument as well to help with writing. And another thing—if you don't get the audition, it doesn't mean you suck. It just means it wasn't the right gig for you!"

Her advice to everyone: "Take things one beat at a time. Your own world will keep in time with you so you don't need to rush through life; enjoy and take in the moment. It always feels so much better that way."

Samantha Maloney

The future might have been quite different for drummer Samantha Maloney had she decided in 1993 to give up her drum seat with the band Shift and accept one of several scholarship offers from colleges to play basketball. Along with being a percussion major at the High School of Performing Arts in New York City, Maloney was also a star basketball player who could have easily taken the athletic route. Instead, according to her official website, she decided to "soldier on" in music.

Maloney was born December 11, 1975, in Manhattan and raised in Queens. She received her first guitar for Christmas at age four, and a year later at age five, her first drum kit. In elementary school she played baseball and listened to Madonna, Michael Jackson, Lisa Lisa & Cult Jam, and Phil Collins. At the age of twelve, she was introduced to the metal/hard rock of Guns N' Roses, and for her that was a life-changing experience.

She joined the post–hard core band Shift as their drummer when she was sixteen and continued playing with them when she went to Hunter College to study music and urban studies. In an interview on the website, she said the male band members were extremely supportive, but sometimes audiences were reluctant to take them seriously because they had a female drummer. While she was with them, the band was signed first to Equal Vision Records, then eventually Columbia Records.

In 1998, Maloney got a call informing her that Patty Schemel was out of Hole and she should go to Los Angeles and audition. Of the more than twenty girls who made the audition, Maloney got the job and ended up touring with them for two years. In 2000, while Hole was on hiatus, she was offered a job with Mötley Crüe—for her "a dream come true." She was initially told she would be doing a couple of gigs to substitute for the drummer who had a problem ulcer, but ended up doing their entire North American summer tour and going with them to Japan. She admitted she was a "little intimidated" by taking over the seat once occupied by one of her all-time favorites, Tommy Lee.

In 2001, Maloney joined The Chelsea, an all-female group, which played one show and disbanded. The group's moniker would be reincarnated in 2004 by Hole front woman Courtney Love who asked Maloney to help write, record, and assemble a live band for her solo album.

From 2005 to 2007, Maloney toured with both Eagles of Death Metal and Peaches. In 2009, Maloney and fellow musician Corey Parks started an all-star-all-cover band called Chelsea Girls who had a monthly residency for over a year at the Roxy Theatre.

In addition to working with other groups such as The Herms, Scarling, The Desert Sessions, Billy Ray Cyrus' rock band Brother Clyde, and the Crystal Method, Maloney also scored an award-winning documentary called *Bounce: Behind the Velvet Rope*, contributed to the music for Daryl Hannah's documentary *Stripnotes*, and worked with Hans Zimmer on the soundtrack for *Black Hawk Down*. She has also made appearances in television and film, including the air drumming comedy *Adventures of Power*.

She says the job of a drummer is to listen to a song and create grooves to go with it. "It's not how fast you can play or how many triplets you can place in one bar."

She says not enough girls are playing drums, because they haven't seen that many girls playing. Her tip for learning how to play is to "listen and play along to your favorite CDs. That's how I got my grooves and chops. It's not what you play—it's how you play it."

Yael

Yael knew she wanted to be a drummer after going to a Broadway show in New York at the age of five or six. In a video on the Vic Firth Drums website, she says she doesn't remember anything about that show except the drummer and being in awe of what he was doing and wanting to be him. Six months later, she had her own set of drums.

In the sixth grade, a music teacher told her, "Little girls like you should play the flute." He gave her a drum rudiment book, which she used as her focus for practice over the summer. By the time school started the next fall, she found herself a place in the band.

In high school, she worked as a pizza delivery girl, but also had an opportunity to study with teachers who kept her serious and focused on developing her drumming skills.

"I have had a love for drums and rhythms and patterns for as long as I can remember," Yael wrote in a 2009 article in *Modern Drummer*. "I made a little name for myself in New York City straight out of high school playing some double kick heavy rock with an all-girl band called Meanstreak."

Four days after she joined that band, they played to a sold-out two thousand capacity crowd with Anthrax at L'Amour Brooklyn. Soon they were opening for bands such as Motorhead, Iron Maiden, Overkill, and King Diamond.

Growing up in a house that listened to world music and Stevie Wonder, Yael wrote that she loved the "release of big, loud drums resonating through my feet to my head." She found herself performing at Lollapalooza '93 with Arrested Development, Alice in Chains, and Fishbone, which took her into an even funkier direction.

Always experimenting with microphones and recording tools, she decided to get a college degree in audio engineering, an interest she had since being an audio intern in high school.

Her Lollapalooza experience led her to begin experimenting with a fusion of rock, hip-hop, and world music. At the time Yael was playing with the band 1stborn7. They toured Morocco where, Yael said, she "got my paws on so many little drums, I was in heaven" (*Modern Drummer* 2009).

When she got back to New York, she started playing with the band Tung. Then one day she loaded her drums in the back of her Jeep and headed for the west coast.

Between New York City and LA, the "mélange of genres" had begun. According to Yael's DrumAddict website, she and her collaborator and "partner in the crime of music loving," producer Nik Chinboukas, started recording a "ton of experimental stuff"—everything and anything from Buddha Bar vibes to '70s rock sprinkled with Latin and Middle Eastern touches.

After her move to Los Angeles, Yael toured Europe, the United Kingdom, and the United States with Creins, My Ruin, and Fireball Ministry. She also was drummer on numerous records produced by Chinboukas, moving from "super heavy and fast to smooth backbeats and jungle setups."

"My setups change according to the style I need with the artists I'm working with," she said. "Your best bet as a drummer is to be a good listener in those situations, and, of course, to practice" (*Modern Drummer* 2009).

She was able to combine her passion for music and film and audio skills as producer, editor, and director of the 2010 CD/DVD *The Love Project Journey*, featuring musicians from around the globe.

In the Vic Firth video, she gives advice to those seeking to break into the music field: "Just do your homework. It doesn't just happen." And this important reminder for all drummers: "You're not just a drummer, you're a musician." On her website, she defines a musician as someone "you put in a room with a cardboard box, a wooden spoon, and some marbles and they'll make music."

"I've never tried to be number one," she said in the video. "Life is too short for that, but I will be number one for the moment I'm doing something."

Juanita Parra Correa

Juanita Parra Correa started her musical journey at age three. She was the daughter of Gabriel Parra, once considered by the British press one of the top three drummers in the world. Parra, who died in a car crash in Lima, Peru, in 1988, was the original drummer for the acclaimed Chilean group Los Jaivas. Juanita is the only woman to play in the band over its fifty-year history.

Juanita took her father's place in the band three years after his death. She was nineteen years old at the time. In an interview, she said she took to her new role "very naturally" and was able to combine the playful, creative side of her father with the quiet disposition of her mother. "On stage I move, dance, and surrender my soul to the music. In the dressing room I am totally opposite of an artist hyperventilating—calm and thoughtful. People are amazed at the contrast," she said.

Over the years, Juanita has become known for her distinctive style, a successful mix of Latin and progressive rock.

Debra Dobkin

Drummer Debra Dobkin was born with a good ear. "From the time I was very little, I would sing harmony with my sisters, play folk songs on guitar, and pretend that I could read the music my piano teacher was giving me, but it was really all 'by ear,'" she said.

Dobkin who has drummed with some of the greatest, including Bonnie Raitt, Richard Thompson, Don Henley, Jackson Browne, Shawn Colvin, Al Jarreau, Marcia Ball, Stephen Bruton, Ann and Nancy Wilson of Heart, and many others, says Chicago radio stations and records were her "salvation" all through grade and high school.

"I listened to the blues, the Beatles, folk, R&B, and jazz. Music was all so new and amazing. I find it really interesting that although I wasn't conscious of it, whatever song was on the radio, stored itself in my brain. I'm amazed at the amount of material that I can call up when performing or recording a track."

When she first started playing in bands, Dobkin was a vocalist and utility player. "If rhythm guitar, a keyboard part, or hand percussion was needed in a song, I would jump in. It became clear to me that if I was going to ever be really good at music, I needed to go to school for it."

Dobkin said she had planned to major in composition. "I was playing in bands until three in the morning and then getting up to go to music school by 8:30 a.m. I lasted a few semesters until that school of 'earn while you learn playing bars' won out."

While she was in music school she met some fellow musicians who turned her on to Brazilian and African music. "I completely fell in love with the earthiness of the instruments and the rhythms. I found my voice as a player from it. Moving to percussion and drums was a very natural transition for me. I was able to use those different flavors to make whatever kind of music I was playing move and feel good. I have never been a purist when it comes to any particular style of music. I use whatever works for the song. All of my early influences inform the way I play now," she said.

Dobkin said she was seventeen when she got her first paying gig. She said none of the members of the band were twenty-one, and all lied about their ages so that they could get bookings in bars.

Dobkin left Chicago and moved to Los Angeles in 1976. "The band I was in at the time got a record deal, but as that faded, I found I was on my own. As a working musician you always have to reinvent yourself to fit the situation, so I worked hard at learning how to be a good side person. I found it to be so much more rewarding musically, more fun, and it suited my personality better than being the main focus."

Dobkin said she learned from a good friend that Don Henley was putting together a band. The friend suggested she audition. "Luck was with me and I wound up on Henley's 1985 'Building the Perfect Beast' tour. That was my first major tour and I was able to keep working steadily from there developing the emphasis on drums and percussion."

She says her career has been filled with "musical high moments," such as "playing on stage in a collaboration featuring Sonny Rollins, the David Sanborn Band, Leonard Cohen, and a few of us from Was (Not Was) on a show called *Night Music*. I look back at that video clip, and the memory comes flooding back. I recall looking around the stage thinking, 'This is incredible. I'm here and I'm not dreaming.' Another highlight would be sitting in on drums with Spinal Tap and living to tell the tale."

Since 2003, Dobkin has been playing with Richard Thompson in a trio for "1000 Years of Popular Music" and then in a fully staged production of "Richard Thompson's Cabaret of Souls." "These particular projects are special for me because I was able to incorporate all the different facets of my musical knowledge."

"So much of becoming a good musician is the intense study and physical mechanics of playing. Over time, my setup has evolved into an unorthodox mixture of drum set with various hand drums, and small percussion. As I've gotten more confident on my instruments and found my own unique voice, I'm able to turn off my mind and let the music flow through me. It has taken a long time to get there, but well worth it," Dobkin said.

"There is no other feeling like having the music sweep you up into the moment and to ride that wave of feeling. Traveling to amazing places and playing with many great talented people are all perks of a career in music, but the bottom line is, we really play music for that chance of all at once, feeling grounded to the earth and flying, and we get to experience this with other players! I count myself as extremely lucky. People say you make your own luck, so I'm going to keep working on my craft so I can serve the music best."

Dobkin is also a songwriter, producer, and a visual artist. Of the latter, she says, "Painting and playing music are one in the same for me. Just as I would use my palette and brushes, drums and percussion become the medium. The blank canvas has infinite possibilities, and I will fill in the lights, shadows, and colors."

CHAPTER 15

Sweet! A New Century

> The only thing that pisses me off is when you hear guys say, "You're the best girl drummer I've ever seen." What the hell is that supposed to mean? But you'll never not have that. No matter what, they're always going to say that. And it's not as bad as it used to be. I only hear it like once a week now.
>
> —Stephanie Eulinberg

As the new millennium dawned, music—like everything else—entered the digital age. By 2012, digital stores such as iTunes became the primary outlet for buying music, eclipsing mass merchants such as Target and Wal-Mart, once rulers of the market. CD sales continued to plummet as people chose instead to download music to their iPhones and iPads. Surprisingly, vinyl also made a comeback, with special appeal to those looking for better sound quality than digital could offer.

Music sales in 2012 totaled $16.5 billion, compared to $30 billion ten years earlier. Rather than investing in whole albums, one could purchase single tracks, or take advantage of streaming offered by Spotify or Pandora. YouTube became the popular source for music videos. While no doubt giving artists more exposure, these services didn't do much to pad an artist's pocketbook. Exacerbating the problem was the billions of dollars lost as a result of music piracy. Ironically, one study found free music downloaders also were also the biggest spenders when it came to record purchases, buying about 30 percent more music than non-moochers.

With advanced software, it was now possible to create high-quality music and backing tracks with a single laptop computer. New genres developed that mixed rock with digital techniques and sounds. Drum machines were refined to the point that a professional electronic kit was nearly indistinguishable from a quality acoustic set.

In this digital age women began to dominate mainstream pop and become the top-grossing recording artists. But the female drummer—especially the female drummer recognized as an equal among her male peers—remained an oddity. When *Rolling Stone* in 2011 polled its readers to name the one hundred best drummers of all time, not one woman made the list. When Hillary Clinton declared at the Women in the World Summit in April 2013 that equal rights and opportunities for women are "the unfinished business of the twenty-first century," probably more than one female drummer would have joined in the thunderous ovation given the former secretary of state.

Meg White

Despite the failure to make some of music's male-centric top one hundred lists, numerous women have proven they have the chops to equal anyone when it comes to groove-making. Consider Meg White. White, born December 10, 1974, in a Detroit suburb, is best known as the drummer of The White Stripes. She and her husband at the time, John Anthony "Jack" Gillis, formed the alternative rock duo in 1997.

White was working as a bartender in the early 1990s when she met Gillis, and the two married in 1996. Gillis took his wife's name and began using the stage name Jack White.

White had never played drums until 1997 but took to the instrument, feeling liberated as she learned to play. According to Jack, Meg had a unique style on the drum that gave the band its distinctive sound. While some drummers would "feel weird" about being overly simplistic, Meg valued the primal feeling of the drums and approached her playing with that attitude.

The White Stripes had a signature sound that blended punk, country, folk, and blues. Their music was noted for Meg's intense drumming, the music's fast pace, and memorable lyrics. In 1999, they released their debut album on an independent California label, followed by a tour with the independent rock bands Pavement and Sleater-Kinney.

In 2000, Jack and Meg divorced but continued to work together and released the album *De Stijl*, which was praised by critics for its primitive sound. In 2001, they released *White Blood Cells*, which gave them international fame, and in 2002 they won three MTV Video Music Awards.

Their albums continued to win critical acclaim in both the United States and United Kingdom, and they won Grammy Awards for Best Alternative Music Album in 2003 (*Elephant*), 2005 (*Get Behind Me Satan*), and 2007 (*Icky Thump*).

Although Jack was the main vocalist on most recordings, Meg began making a greater contribution as a vocalist in the later albums.

In 2007, Meg began suffering acute anxiety attacks, also known as panic disorder. At the time The White Stripes had been touring in Canada and were scheduled to play Hawaii. That show along with eighteen others in Glasgow, Manchester, Birmingham, and London were cancelled, and disappointed fans were given refunds for the tickets they had purchased.

Meg and Jack apologized to fans on their website and asked for their continued loyalty during their time of hardship, but no announcement was made regarding future tour dates.

After releasing a reissue of The White Stripes' first three albums in 2010, the duo disbanded in February 2011, ending a career that had spanned more than a decade. According to their official statement, the breakup was not for health reasons or artistic differences—only "to preserve what was most beautiful about the art and music the group presented during their time performing and recording together" (megwhite.com).

Meg married guitarist Jackson Smith in 2009. Since retiring from The White Stripes, she has modeled and made appearances on *The Simpsons* and *Josie and the Pussycats*. She was also the subject of a song by Ray LaMontagne in which he compliments her: "Playin' those drums is hard to do. . . . And nobody plays them quite like you do."

Drummer and Foo Fighters founder Dave Grohl also gives high praise to Meg's drumming skills. In a January 28, 2013, interview with the British music publication *NME*, he said he considered White, who was sometimes criticized for her primitive style, one of the best drummers of all time and that he held her in the same esteem as iconic drummers such as Keith Moon and John Bonham. "Nowadays," Grohl said, "I think it could be hard for a kid to find a favorite drummer, because a lot of that personality is being robbed from these musicians for the sake of perfection and it's kind of a drag. It's nice to hear drummers like Meg White—one of my favorite fucking drummers of all time. Like, nobody fucking plays the drums like that."

Stefanie Eulinberg

Stefanie Eulinberg, born December 11, 1967, knew at the age of two she wanted to make music. Growing up in her native Cleveland, drums were her passion and by fifteen she was playing pop and rock everywhere: in hotel bars, cruise ships, prisons, wherever a cover band was needed.

In 1998, according to her bio on the Kid Rock website, she had booked a studio in Milwaukee to record a solo album when her pal DJ Swamp called her and told her, "This Kid Rock guy in Detroit has a record on Atlantic, and he needs a drummer. Like now."

After playing an extended game of phone tag, Eulinberg and Kid Rock connected, and she learned she was one of the top three drummers being considered. He had never heard her play, so Eulinberg decided to use her reserved studio time to make an audition tape. She sent the tape overnight, and within days she was part of Kid Rock's back-up band, Twisted Brown Trucker.

She said making the transition from playing nothing but pop covers was a "cinch." The hardest part those first years was "living in an RV with twelve of us on top of each other. I'm glad those days are over."

Eulinberg, who is known for hamming it up on stage, takes her drumming seriously. She plays "hard and smart (and barefoot)."

On whether being a female drummer helped or hurt, she had this to say: "The only thing that pisses me off is when you hear guys say, 'You're the best girl drummer I've ever seen.' What the hell is that supposed to mean? But you'll never not have that. No matter what, they're always going to say that. And it's not as bad as it used to be. I only hear it like once a week now."

Janet Lee Weiss

Janet Lee Weiss was born September 24, 1965, in Hollywood, California. At age sixteen, she started playing guitar. After graduating with a degree in photography from San Francisco State University at age twenty-two, she took up the drums and after two weeks started playing and touring with an all-girl trio, The Furies.

Weiss moved from San Francisco to Portland, Oregon, in 1989 and formed the indie rock band Quasi with her ex-husband Sam Coomes. She later became drummer for the now defunct Sleater-Kinney in 1996. When Sleater-Kinney disbanded, she joined The Jicks, Stephen Malkmus' band.

After making that transition, she was asked in an interview with *Gothomist* writer/editor John Del Signore if she missed the type of percussion she did with Sleater-Kinney: "Sometimes I do miss being in a complete sweat when I'm done playing. But I loved playing in that band so much it would be unusual not to miss it. I miss those fans; I miss that sort of amped-up energy level. But I play a lot of stuff that I love in the Jicks that I didn't get to play in Sleater-Kinney, and there's no one band that encompasses all your abilities. That's why I always like to be in a few bands. I'm not very monogamous in the band world."

In recent years, she has played for Bright Eyes, performing with them on the *Late Show with David Letterman* before joining their European tour in 2007. She has also played for Junior High, The Shadow Mortons, The Go-Betweens, Sarah Dougher, Elliott Smith, Goldcard, and most recently Wild Flag.

In a 2012 interview with Jen Long in the *Line of Best Fit*, Weiss said she wasn't "quite ready to pack it in just yet." She said the idea of being in a new band was "sort of exciting, sort of scary, and a little bit intimidating." She also liked the possibility of "starting fresh—something where you could actually surprise people with what you were doing and they wouldn't know what to expect."

She said with the computer age, new things were given more attention. She said this became painfully obvious when her band Quasi, after eighteen years of performing, would go on tour and no one would be there. "You feel like you're doing this really good work, but then people have seen you already, and people don't have money to go to every gig, so they pick this new band they've never heard."

Another new project for Weiss is Drumgasm, an all-drummer super group made up of Weiss, Matt Cameron (Pearl Jam/Soundgarden), and Zach Hill (Hella/Death Grips). They were to release their first album in 2013 on Jackpot Records, a Portland label.

Weiss is also keen on her responsibility to be a role model for young women and has been a volunteer for the Rock 'n' Roll Camp for Girls, a nonprofit organization started in Portland. She feels the most valuable aspect of the program is that it gives girls self-confidence. "I think that it's really half the battle, getting the confidence to make a lot of noise, and not feel embarrassed about it," she said in a March 28, 2008, article in the online magazine *BYT*. She said it was important for girls to find their voice and not be afraid of it.

Weiss, who didn't start playing drums until the age of twenty-two, said she never had that problem herself. She said the moment she thought she could do it was the moment she did it. She told *BYT* she had no experience when she joined her first band, and that in itself took a "certain amount of gumption and self-confidence to go on stage when I was really not that good at what I was doing."

She went on to say, "I'm not exactly the most girly girl in the world; it's not like I'm up there in heels trying to play. I pretty much fit in with being dirty and carrying things. . . . I just wanted to get better at playing my instrument. I wanted to be as good or better as any of the guys were, and I didn't think there was any reason why I couldn't be, and I think that's true for all women in most fields."

She said this was something she knew in her heart; it wasn't something she was taught. She also feels young girls who have strong female role models have a real advantage. "I didn't really have that; I just had to learn myself, feel it in myself."

Weiss also feels the real role models for young girls are not to be found in pop culture. She says pop culture is for the mainstream; there's nothing there that's edgy, scary, or alternative. In BYT, she's quoted as saying: "There are lots of role models for girls outside of the mainstream . . . a gamut of strong women writing music, dressing differently, and behaving in a non-traditional way. I think if people want to look at the mainstream, then that's what they're going to get . . . it's meant to be middle of the road. If you want to be a serious musician you best look somewhere else for your inspiration."

Carla Azar

Carla Azar grew up in Huntsville, Alabama. Her mother was a pianist, so music was a constant around her house. At the age of four, she saw a marching band for the first time at a local football game and found herself gravitating toward rhythm-based things. In tenth grade, she started playing percussion and mallet instruments in the orchestra, but didn't take up the drum set until after high school.

Although she's now best known for playing drums, Azar is a multi-instrumentalist. She says that she doesn't consider herself technically proficient on other instruments, but playing other instruments has made her a more musical drummer. In an April 2011 interview in *Tom Tom* Magazine, she said, "I have always felt that if you record something with a band and mute all of the instruments except for the drums after everyone has finished, the drums/percussion should sound beautiful and musical without all of the other instruments in."

Azar feels that whomever she's playing with determines how she plays and that studio recording and live performance are two completely different forms of expression. "How much to play depends on the song or the feeling in the room at any given moment. I love drummers that do everything—simple and hypnotic at times and completely unpredictable, insane, and out of control at other times. And everything in between."

Azar gained critical attention as the drummer for the Los Angeles–based experimental rock band Autolux, in which she shares some vocal duties as well. She recalls how the band started in 2001: "Eugene Goreshter and I were friends but started playing music together for the first time when we were asked to write a score for a play. We performed the music live to the play, pretty much every night, for six weeks. Immediately after, we formed Autolux. Greg Williams fell out of the sky and landed on us. Band complete."

Autolux is known for its eclectic post-punk sound. A year after forming, they released a self-produced eight-track EP *Demonstration*, which they sold at shows. They were then signed by DMZ, a small label created by T-Bone Burnett and the Coen Brothers after Burnett saw them performing live in Los Angeles.

In May 2002, Autolux opened for Elvis Costello. After the performance, Azar went to jump down from the stage, tripped on a cable, and shattered her elbow. She underwent experimental surgery the next day and made a full recovery in four months.

In the fall of 2002, Azar and Autolux went into the studio to begin recording their first full-length album, *Future Perfect.* T-Bone Burnett produced the record, which was released in 2004 and met with critical praise. The band toured heavily throughout 2005, including opening for The White Stripes, where Azar met Jack White.

In early 2006, Autolux was asked to write the music for the "Sonic Scenery" exhibition at the Natural History Museum of Los Angeles. Throughout the next couple of years, Azar said she and the band "wrote quite a bit along with playing live to work out new ideas."

During that time, they were also collaborating with visual artist Mark Whalen by creating music for several art installations for his solo exhibitions in Los Angeles. Also during that period, Azar was asked by PJ Harvey to play drums on the PJ Harvey/John Parish album, *A Woman a Man Walked By.*

In 2010, Autolux released their second full-length album entitled *Transit Transit.* The next year Jack White asked Azar to play drums on his first solo album, *Blunderbuss.* In early 2012, White invited her to tour with him on one of his two touring bands: one all female, one all male. The twist was that the decision of which band would play each night would be decided by White the day of the show; the audience never knew which band would be performing. Both bands toured throughout 2012—their last performance being the 2013 Grammy Awards. *Blunderbuss* was nominated for three Grammys, marking the first time Azar had played on a Grammy-nominated album.

Azar said she felt "extremely lucky to have had the opportunity to play with Jack. And I'm also proud of the playing I did on his record."

Asked if she had ever felt any discrimination as a female drummer, she said, "Yes, but not until recently. The first time *Tom Tom Magazine* (a magazine dedicated to female drummers) asked if they could do a piece on me, I remember e-mailing them and saying that they were the first drummer magazine to ever ask me to do an interview. It was strange, but a reality."

Her advice to aspiring female drummers: "There's no right and wrong way to play an instrument. Freedom without boundaries is a good place to reside. That's a good start."

Shauney "Baby" Recke

Considered one of the top female drummers working today, Shauney "Baby" Recke has performed with Sting on the *Ellen DeGeneres Show*, toured with the Pussycat Dolls, will.i.am, been house drummer for the *Keenan Ivory Wayans Show*, and played with Natalia Kills, Robin Thicke, Nicole Scherzinger, Paulina Rubio, Wounded Couger, and Hilary Duff.

As a child, Recke was fascinated by the drummer at church who played at choir practice and services. At the time she was about seven or eight and singing in the kids' choir. If no one was playing, she would get on the drums herself and "mess around" until one of the older church women walked up and said, "Honey, you can't get on the drums."

"I was inspired by music in general, but when I listened to the music, the drums were what stood out most. It was definitely about rhythms and patterns. I loved movement, dancing, etc.," she said.

Recke is a native of Washington, DC. Her father was a founding member of the 1970s R&B group the Delfonics, so music was part of her family heritage. In high school, she was a voice major in the School of the Arts until eleventh grade when she switched to percussion. She got a scholarship to study percussion at the University of the District of Columbia and then later graduated from the prestigious Duke Ellington School of the Arts.

In an interview on the TAMA Drums website, she says percussion was as much a wonder to her as a music major as it was when she was a seven-year-old child. "I was really fascinated and amazed at the different sounds that drums could make, depending on the type of music and how they were played. You could play melodically or you could do a solo; there were so many different ways that you could make drums sound."

She said as a college student she was really into jazz. Her mentor was the great trumpet player Wallace Roney. At the University of DC, she also got to try her chops at marching band, which she admits wasn't her strong suit. In the TAMA interview, she's quoted as saying: "It was really strenuous. I was playing snare and I had to wear this heavy drum and run around the field. And, especially in the summertime, it was really hot . . . there was a lot of rehearsing, so my hands would hurt and I had all these blisters. And then, we would march and practice our routines, and I would always laugh because everything was funny to me . . . that's why I got put out of the marching band . . . because you had to have a serious face, and I didn't realize that. That was one thing I learned."

Shauney said she also played in the concert band. "It was really cool. I learned a lot, but at that age, I was like, 'Man, I just want to play music,' but there are all these rules."

While in school, she and some of her musician friends put together an all-girl go-go band called Pleasure. The group toured "from DC all the way down to the Carolinas and everything in-between." They also got to tour with some big-name rappers, including Salt-n-Pepa, LL Cool J, and Queen Latifah.

After leaving school and moving to Los Angeles, Shauney became a sought after drummer by some of the day's top talent. In 2010, she was approached about doing a music video with Disney star and singer Hilary Duff. She's been playing drums for Hilary ever since. She says it's a pop gig, but it's still fun because of the audiences. "The kids, and the comments I get from them, and how me just being a female drummer inspires them to do anything, not just drumming. So many little girls are inspired to fulfill their dreams, whatever they may be."

She says young boys are inspired, too. "They're totally blown away, because they're like, 'wow, chicks can play drums'" (TAMA interview).

Recke has written a book called *The Female Musicians' Guide to Surviving the Road*, based on the lessons she's learned.

"I'd like to travel all over the world talking about passion, perseverance, gratitude, and all that comes with being a female—definitely confidence and self-love," she said. Meanwhile, she's sharing thoughts on those subjects via Twitter and her fan page on Facebook.

Torry Castellano

If it hadn't been for tendonitis and a bad shoulder, Torry Castellano might still be playing today. Instead, the former drummer of the all-female rock band The Donnas has put away her drumsticks to study political science at Stanford University, with hopes of later pursuing a law degree. At age thirty-two, she became one of rock's most youthful retirees.

Torrance "Torry" Heather Castellano was born January 8, 1979, in San Francisco. She met her Donnas bandmates in Palo Alto, where they all grew up and became friends in the eighth grade. That year (1993), they formed a band to play for a school event. Castellano, like her friends, was a self-taught musician, and they spent every day after school practicing in Castellano's garage. They started out calling themselves Raggedy Anne and then changed the name to The Electrocutes.

As their high school days were ending, they decided to form another band that would be a "softer" version of the metal queen Electrocutes. For the new band, each of them took on the first name Donna and connected it to the first letter of their last name. Torry Castellano became "Donna C."

Their first two albums were released on Darin Raffaelli's Superteem! Label. During their senior year, they took off a week to tour Japan as The Donnas and were then signed by Lookout! Records. In 2001, they were signed to the major label, Atlantic.

The punk-pop Donnas were reminiscent of the popular 1970s all-girl band, The Runaways. In the early 2000s, they achieved commercial and mainstream success, touring the world and appearing on shows such as *Saturday Night Live, The Tonight Show with Jay Leno*, and the *Late Show with David Letterman*. In

2003, they played the main stage at Lollapalooza. Their music was featured in numerous film and video game soundtracks.

Band members, according to *Los Angeles Times* writer Susan Carpenter in a November 11, 2004, article, conveyed an image of "Pabst-swilling, sex-crazed party animals," but, in reality, they were "just regular girls who liked iced tea, candy, and watching TV."

Castellano herself admitted in an article entitled "Drummer Hits the Books," which appeared in the *Stanford Magazine*: "There [were] many crazy nights, many crazy tours. I don't want to kill the fantasy image of rock 'n' roll life. But there's a lot of work that goes into being successful, and I was always involved in the business decisions."

Before The Donnas released their album *Gold Metal* in 2003, Castellano developed tendonitis. After surgery in October that year, she had to take drum lessons to relearn how to hold the drumsticks in the correct way. She was able to make the recording while recovering, but could only play for short periods of time.

A shoulder problem forced Castellano to withdraw from The Donnas' tour after a show at the House of Blues in Anaheim, California, on December 27, 2008. Drummer Amy Cesari of The Demonics filled in for the rest of the tour, and when Castellano officially left the band in 2010, Cesari replaced her.

Adrienne Davies

Before Adrienne Davies joined Earth and eventually married Earth's founder Dylan Carlson, she was a teenage fan of the Seattle-based band. "I was a big fan of Earth before I had the pleasure of playing with them." In a 2011 interview that appeared in the metal blog *Invisible Oranges*, she talked about being a seventeen-year-old girl using a fake ID that belonged to a twenty-eight-year-old man, who happened to be "effeminate with a unisex name," to get into shows. At the time she was living in Olympia, Washington, and the grunge scene was going strong.

She met Carlson as a teenager but lost touch with him when he left for California. She ran into him again in 2000, and after they started jamming together she was invited to join the band.

Davies started drumming for school bands as a fifth grader. Her first drum set—a used Ludwig from the 1970s—was her "pride and joy." Coming from a musical family, she said she had to fight off her four brothers to keep them from destroying it. In the *Invisible Oranges* interview, she also said her family never discouraged her interest or told her, "You're a chick, and you need to play the flute." She admitted they did get a little annoyed when she played for three hours.

She said she lost "the vibe" while she was in high school or college and then began playing with some friends in garage bands. But it wasn't until she actually joined Earth that she began to take her drumming seriously—"to do it right."

Until Davies joined the group, Earth had never had a live drummer. As she said in the *Invisible Oranges* interview, "Everything was done on a machine Dylan programmed. That wasn't their desire; they just couldn't find someone who fit with their musical taste." She said her goal was to fit into the band musically. "I'm all about keeping songs as simple as possible and serving the song. I'm not a showy drummer. I like to find the heartbeat, the feel of a song . . . give it movement and dynamics. There are tons of showboating drummers in rock, but in this band and format, we could never have a twenty-minute drum solo."

Davies says she's most comfortable playing "relaxed and laidback." She says while everyone has fun getting a drum set and banging the skins and playing as loud and fast as possible, it's not always fun for the listener. "I like drums that build the song and stay out of the way."

She says in the beginning she had some issues with stage fright and nerves. "I'm a perfectionist, and I had this fear that it would be a complete disaster, or that I would screw the whole set up. These negative things were paramount in my mind. I just realized if I completely blew it, the world wouldn't stop turning. I was making a bigger deal of it than I needed to and taking the fun out of it. Your brain eventually just needs to wrap itself around reality. It's not perfect now, but it's so much better" (*Invisible Oranges*).

Davies also said in a January 2013 interview with *Tom Tom* TV that when she started playing professionally, she was under the impression she had to live up to a "caveman style of drumming." She realized later the "less is more" approach worked better for her and allowed her to bring in a jazzier influence with subtle, delicate washes that brought in the dynamic.

In the *Tom Tom* interview, she commented that she keeps an "eye out" for her fellow female drummers. Ten years ago if you were a female who went into the drum section of a music store, chances were you would be asked, "Are you buying drumsticks for your boyfriend?" It would never occur to them, she said, that you were buying the drumsticks for yourself.

Meytal Cohen

"Meytal Cohen" is a pretty common Israeli name, according to the drummer who happens to have that name. It also just happens to sound like her favorite genre of music.

Cohen was born August 9, 1983, and raised in Ramat-Gan, Israel, the youngest of seven children. Her four sisters and two brothers all went on to become lawyers and doctors. Her father was killed by a drunk driver when she was in the second grade, and she and her siblings were raised by their mother.

She initially studied theatre but took up the drums at age eighteen despite the typical view, "you're making noise, you're wasting time, you're spending money, and this will never amount to anything." At the same age she was drafted into the Israeli army and served her two years of mandatory service. In her official website bio, she says, yes, she can shoot a gun, and yes, she can kick your ass.

At age twenty-one, after serving her army stint, she moved to Los Angeles to pursue a drumming career. While attending the LA Music Academy, she broke her back in a car accident and went back to Israel to heal. Within a year, she was back for more study and graduation. She said finding work and making it as a musician was hard at first, but she did some small tours and "ridiculous gigs" and kept up her practice, mostly playing by herself to her favorite tunes.

After posting an audition tape for *America's Got Talent* on YouTube, she suddenly found herself a YouTube sensation. She began to upload more videos and today she has over sixty million YouTube views and over 350,000 Facebook followers.

Andy Doerschuk in the July 2011 issue of *DRUM!* Magazine called her YouTube drum covers a "total disconnect—here's this smiling adorable girl in a sun dress and bare feet nailing every note to classic tunes from Pantera, Rush, and Tool with total accuracy and great feeling."

At the time of this interview, Cohen was working on her first original album. "I feel very fortunate to be working with such an amazing group of people," she said. "My first single will be launched soon, and I have a feeling this will mark the beginning of a new age in my musical career. Other than that, I've just finished shooting *Maximum Meytal*, an instructional DVD set, which was shot in Canada. It will be an amazing learning tool that I'm very excited about."

In looking at her experience as a female drummer, she said, "I personally had put a lot of pressure on myself to prove to the world that girls can play. In most auditions, it felt like people were more curious to see if I could play than the other guys that were auditioning. I felt like I was representing the whole female gender, and that if I suck I'm ruining it for girls everywhere by supporting the stereotype that said girls can't play, 'you play like a girl'—kinda silly, thinking about it now. I think that starting out relatively late, not really getting much encouragement, and being super critical of myself made me relate to drumming in such a way. I don't think this is necessarily how things are, but that was my personal experience."

Mercedes Lander

Mercedes Lander was twelve when she founded the all-girl heavy metal band Kittie in 1996. Three years later, at age fifteen, Kittie recorded and released their first album *Spit*. Their second album *Oracle* was released in 2002. Both have sold over 1.5 million copies worldwide.

Lander has won wide respect in the competitive world of metal drumming. American record producer Steve Thompson, who worked with Guns N' Roses, said, "I've worked with a lot of rock bands in the guy department that couldn't hold a candle to Mercedes' style and timing. I mean it is very rare when you can work with a drummer who doesn't require a click track. I hate click tracks" (artist bio on Zildjian website).

Frankie Rose

Brooklyn drummer Frankie Rose was a founder and the original drummer for Vivian Girls and later drummer and occasional vocalist in Crystal Stilts and the Dum Dums. A San Francisco native, she also played with the Bay Area all-female band Shitstorm until she moved to New York; the group changed its name to Grass Widow with Lillian Maring taking Rose's seat as drummer.

Most recently, Rose has been doing solo work, and in 2012 released the acclaimed album *Interstellar*, a follow-up to her equally well received *Frankie Rose and The Outs*.

In a 2009 interview with *Tom Tom* Magazine ("Legend in the Making"), Rose said she started playing drums in her first band. "No one except the guitar player really knew how to play anything so I just sat down behind the kit, and it was decided that I would be the drummer."

Aixa Vilar

Aixa Vilar saw Santana in concert at age one. Although she obviously doesn't remember that experience, she does know that music was ever present when she was growing up: "either on the record player or someone was playing it."

In an interview in the zine *The Cover Zone* ("Go Betty Go"), Vilar said the best day of her life was the day she walked out of a store with her first drum set. She knew she wanted to be a drummer after going to her first punk show at a local gym, featuring Officer Negative. "The music was loud, fast and I knew that I wanted to be up there playing just as hard."

Vilar and her sister Nicolette along with Michelle Rangel and Betty Cisneros were founding members of the punk band Go Betty Go, formed in Glendale, California, in 2001. The band was prominent in the California punk scene of the mid-2000s.

Dena Tauriello

Dena Tauriello decided to become a drummer after seeing Karen Carpenter in concert and then having the opportunity to meet her idol backstage. At age eight, the New Jersey native had graduated from banging on pots and pans and was taking private lessons. By the time she was thirteen, she was playing in garage bands along with the school band, orchestra, and other ensembles. At thirteen, she also had her first paying gig, and the young drummer was hooked for life. She cultivated her musical tastes, listening and playing to the rock 'n' roll classics.

Music took a backseat when Dena went to college. At Penn State, she majored and earned a B.S. in Human Development and Family Studies. Back at home, she started taking gigs with local theatre productions, cover bands, and her own projects. She continued doing live shows and studio work while completing a postgraduate degree at Seton Hall University.

In 1998, she received a call from the New York City–based female rock band Antigone Rising. After a successful audition, she toured with the group for several years, doing as many as 160 shows a year. The band also released a successful recording *From the Ground Up* for the Starbucks Hear Music Debut series.

Dena and the band have opened for The Rolling Stones, Aerosmith, Allman Brothers, Rob Thomas, and Joan Jett. Their television appearances have included the *Today Show*, *Tonight Show*, and a VH1 special.

Dena has also worked with Lisa Loeb, Bernie Worrell, and Robert Randolph. She is a certified drum therapist, clinician, private teacher, and professor of music at Passaic County Community College.

She said it would be hard to pick a particular highlight in her career. "I feel very blessed to have had some truly incredible opportunities and surreal moments. I think perhaps one of the best was when the Allman Brothers asked if they could come up and jam with us. That alone was a huge compliment—but then to be onstage playing, looking around at Derek Trucks, Warren Haynes, and Gregg Allman was just unbelievable."

Asked if she ever felt discrimination as a female drummer, Dena replied, "Absolutely. People automatically assume you can't play because you are female. Then you get comments like, 'Wow, you hit pretty hard for a girl.' It is far less prominent today than in my earlier years."

As a musician, Dena says she's learned "Life isn't fair. Working hard and doing the right thing doesn't necessarily translate into financial success. However, if you are passionate about something and have the courage of your convictions to stay the course and follow your heart, you are far richer in so many other ways. And isn't that really why we are all here?"

CHAPTER 16

And the Beat Goes On (To Be Continued)

It's not a boy's club anymore.

—Rachel Fuhrer

In an article, which first appeared in *DRUM!* magazine, Paula Bocciardi wrote about a drum clinic in San Francisco where a grand-prize cymbal giveaway went to a woman drummer in the audience. Some guy in the audience yelled out, "Hey, that's not fair! She can't be a drummer!" While many female drummers are still fighting the battle to be recognized as legitimate contenders in the popular music world, each year that number grows. Here are a few more women who, by proof of their talent, are evidence the game's far from over.

Alicia Warrington

Alicia Warrington grew up torn between two ambitions: to be a drummer or professional wrestler. Warrington, born August 30, 1980, in Saginaw, Michigan, says while other kids wanted to go to the circus, she preferred the excitement of a good wrestling match. Her mother started taking her to wrestling matches when she was just four years old. The young fan of all things wrestling even collected wrestling action figures.

But music was also a passion, and she grew up hearing and appreciating an eclectic mix—everything from her grandparents' polka music to her mother's R&B and classic rock to her sister's and uncle's heavy metal. "I love music. Period," she said.

Her uncle had a drum set, and around age eleven, Alicia picked up sticks and taught herself to play, drumming along to cassettes of her favorite bands.

Warrington was raised by a single mom who, according to a May 2012 interview in *Tom Tom* magazine, didn't bat an eye when her daughter started playing in local punk and metal bands and hit the road to tour at age fifteen. By the time she was eighteen, she had performed in thirty states. In the *Tom Tom* interview, she talks of relocating to Los Angeles "with a crappy fake ID and seven hundred dollars to my name." She was homeless for a while, "sleeping on friend's couches, in her car or a dirty band rehearsal space with broken windows. She kept knives and a crowbar nearby and bought a gym membership so she could shower."

Her first big break came when she replaced Kelly Osbourne's drummer on the MTV reality show *The Osbournes*. She toured with Kelly in eleven countries and performed on her 2003 album *Changes* as well as the DVD, *Kelly Osbourne: Live at the Electric Ballroom*.

Since then, she has performed with Selena Gomez, on the Disney hit series *Hannah Montana*, Dawn Robinson of En Vogue, Gore Gore Girls, and Canadian pop group Lillix.

Another project is the All-Girl Boys Choir with guitarist Marlene "The Hammer" Hammerle. She co-wrote, produced, engineered, and mixed the duo's 2009 LP, *Walking Miracles*. Explaining how the name of the group came about, she said, "Music is a very male-oriented business—hence, The All-Girl Boys Choir. Haha! I love being a female musician in a position to hopefully inspire and motivate other females to follow their dreams and achieve their goals of being a professional musician."

When asked what drove her, Warrington said, "There is nothing in life that I would rather be doing—career-wise—other than music. I come to life when I perform. The live crowds, traveling, the fans, lights, stage, tour buses, airports, different hotel rooms every night—all of those things motivate, inspire, and give me the energy to perform."

She said she loved the opportunity to play with different artists as opposed to being in one particular band. "Constantly performing in different genres, with different musicians is motivation for me to be a better player and to constantly challenge myself."

Warrington said she's learned that drumming "is very similar to communicating with people and behavior in relationships. In drumming, as well as in any relationship, you have to learn to compliment and accent. There are moments to follow instead of leading and vice-versa. You don't always have to be loud to be heard. You don't have to give everything you've got in one conversation; save something for the next conversation—or song."

Hannah Billie

In junior high, Hannah Billie used to hang out in the band room after school messing around with the drum kit. She played saxophone in the band, but was attracted to the drums. While waiting for her father, who happened to teach in the school, she took advantage of the time to explore that attraction.

A few years later, Billie became the drummer for Gossip, a three-piece indie rock band formed in 1999 in Olympia, Washington, featuring singer Beth Ditto and guitarist Brace Paine. She joined the band in 2003 after the original drummer Kathy Mendonca left to pursue a career as a midwife. Billie had established herself on the punk music scene as drummer for Shoplifting.

After Billie joined the band, Gossip recorded the acclaimed LP *Standing in the Way of Control*, which earned gold record status in the United Kingdom. In 2007, they signed with Sony's subsidiary Music with a Twist, which focused on lesbian, gay, bisexual, and transgender acts. The band has made four other recordings featuring Billie on drums, including the 2012 release *Joyful Noise*.

Beyoncé's Drummers

A trio of enormously talented and skilled female drummers have been locking down the groove for superstar Beyoncé's all-female touring band, The Sugar Mamas. Beyoncé said she put the band together to provide more female role models for young girls, and there's no doubt Kim Thompson, Nikki Glaspie, and Marcie Chapa have helped promote the cause. Prince drummer Cora Coleman-Dunham has also played with Beyoncé.

"When I was younger, I wish I had more females who played instruments to look up to. I played piano for like a second, but then I stopped," Beyoncé said in a statement before the band performed at the 2013 Super Bowl. "I just wanted to do something which would inspire other females to get involved in music so I put together an all-woman band" (Rivas).

Nikki Glaspie

Sugar Mama band member Nikki Glaspie honed her skills working as a full-time drummer for her church. Born to a family of Black southern ministers, Glaspie was playing drums in church by the time she was eight. She moved to Boston in 2001 to pursue her musical dream of becoming a performance artist.

At Berklee College, she learned technical and theoretical skills to further her aspirations. At Wally's, one of Boston's most famous jazz clubs, she was able to put her drumming skills to the test, proving she could "hang with the baddest cats in the area."

After four years in Boston, the young drummer had no problems lining up gigs with some of the most talented artists around. In 2006, after returning from a European tour with "soul rebel" Martin Luther McCoy, she was chosen to be a member of Beyoncé's new all-female band. She appeared in the debut performance of The Sugar Mamas on the 2006 BET Awards and toured with Beyoncé in 2007.

Glaspie has also performed with Chaka Khan, Jay-Z, Kanye West, Destiny's Child, and George Michael.

Kim Thompson

Kim Thompson was born in Los Angeles and raised in St. Louis, Missouri, and has performed internationally in over thirty-three countries. She became a fixture on the New York City club scene, playing venues such as the Stellar Blue Note, Avalon, and The 55 Bar.

In 2003, she received a degree in Jazz Performance and Composition from Manhattan School of Music.

Beyoncé tapped her for the debut 2006 BET Awards performance and for her upcoming 2007 tour to promote her CD *B-Day*.

Along with Beyoncé, Thompson has worked with an impressive lineup of artists, including Jay-Z, Terri Lyne Carrington, Wallace Roney, Gary Dourdan, Mike Stern, and Jason Moran.

Marcie Chapa

Marcie Chapa joined Beyoncé for her 2009 world tour with an impressive resume spanning musical genres, from salsa to gospel music.

In a February 2009 interview with Kristin Bartus in *DRUM!* magazine, Chapa said she was introduced to the drums in a Houston-area elementary school band. Her mother, not wanting her "running the streets," encouraged her to get involved in some sort of school program. Her older brother played trumpet in the band, and Chapa liked the idea that traveling and playing with the band sometimes gave him the excuse to miss school. Not particularly fond of school, she found that aspect of band participation especially appealing. The band director, unlike some who might steer a young girl from playing drums to a more ladylike instrument, thought the drums would be a great fit for her personality. "He said I was a hyper child," she said.

Chapa was soon proving she and the drums were a good match, and before too long was ready for her own drum set. She bugged her parents until they finally relented, and she was off on a new adventure, playing to the radio and mimicking everything she'd hear. After playing along with all the top forty stuff, her jazz-loving brother encouraged her to play some "real music." Out came the Miles Davis, Maynard Ferguson, and Buddie Rich, and a new-found appreciation for jazz by the young drummer.

In the *DRUM!* interview, Chapa recalls how during her sophomore year in high school, the band director encouraged her to go see Sheila E. She was blown away. "I was like, WOW, it's a girl playing. I saw her playing the timbales and just going crazy and then playing drum set and then switching over to congas. That's when I realized, this is exactly what I want to do."

Cora Coleman-Dunham

Cora Coleman-Dunham, also known as Queen Cora Dunham, began playing drums in the ninth grade when she became active in the marching band and concert band at Kashmere High School in Houston, Texas. After graduating as valedictorian of her senior class, Cora went to Howard University in Washington, DC. In a fortunate twist of fate, she changed her major in the middle of her freshman year from computer science to music.

As a student, she performed not only in university ensembles but also with the Washington Symphony, The American University Orchestra, and the Washington Ballet and with artists such as Marvin Stamm, Yusef Lateef, Greg Osby, Donald Byrd, Grady Tate, and Larry Ridley. She was the first female section leader of Howard's Thunder Machine drum section and the university's first recipient of the Avedis Zildjian Scholarship for Outstanding Percussionist.

After receiving her bachelor's degree in 2002, Cora moved to Los Angeles. In 2003, she entered the Guitar Center's Annual National Drum-Off competition and beat out over five thousand drummers to become not only the first female to make it to the national level but the first female to earn the annual title of the Nation's Best Amateur Drummer. One of her first gigs in Los Angeles was drumming with the all-female group Angaza. Then after touring with Zac Harmon and the Midsouth Blues Revue, she joined Frank McComb's band. After seeing Cora perform at a McComb concert, Prince was so impressed that he sent the drummer a custom-made eight-piece drum kit for Christmas.

In 2005, after a tour in Japan with McComb, Prince put together a new band with Cora as drummer and her husband Joshua Dunham on bass. Named the After Party House Band, they performed at the Grammy Awards, Academy Awards, and NAACP Image Awards shows. She has been the drummer for most of Prince's live appearances and has worked with him on and off in the studio to the present day. She says one of her most memorable experiences was performing in the rain with Prince at Super Bowl XVI.

She has also jammed, performed, and toured with Najee, Billy Miles, Pink, Rick Fante, Lalah Hathaway, Tom Schuman, Phil Upchurch, Foley, El Divo, Michael Bearden, India Arie, Everett Harp, Norman Brown, Peter Michael Escovedo, Mandrill, Herbie Hancock, Sheila E., and many others.

In May 2011, Cora joined Beyoncé's band.

Hannah Ford

Hannah Ford confesses that, like most kids, when she was younger she wanted to be famous. But she later realized "in the long run becoming a good musician is a much more appropriate and fulfilling goal."

Ford ended up achieving both—as a sought after artist, bandleader, and studio drummer. In 2012, she became part of Prince's New Generation touring band.

Ford was introduced to the drums in her third grade music class. According to her official website, it was "love at first sight."

Born and raised in Louisville, Kentucky, Ford moved to Chicago when she was twelve. She had the opportunity to study with some of the world's greatest drummers and teachers, including Diane Downs, Louie Bellson, Ruben Alvarez, Jerry Steinholtz, and Ndugu Chancler. She also studied and performed with mentors such as Peter Erskine, Stanton Moore, Danny Seraphine, and Johnny Rabb.

After high school graduation, Ford received a scholarship to study at the College of Performing Arts at Roosevelt University where she continued studies with Paul Wertico. While expanding her musical knowledge playing in the university's different ensembles, she was also able to work with major touring musicians such as Ignacio Berroa, Wynton Marsalis, Butch Miles, Jeff Berlin, and others.

With college behind her, she became a much in demand session drummer for some of the top pros in the business. She also started her own bands: The Hannah Ford Band and Bellevue Suite. Ford also writes and teaches. Before joining Prince's New Generation Band, she was the stage drummer for Whoopi Goldberg's musical *White Noise.*

Ford is also an enthusiastic supporter of young drummers, especially young female drummers. During off-times, she appears at school assemblies with her multimedia show "Peace, Love, and Drums," and as a clinician and teacher at drum workshops and summer music camps.

She's quoted on her website: "It used to be that telling someone they hit like a girl was a put down, but after watching the way women like Karen Carpenter, Gina Schock, Sheila E, and Cindy Blackman play the drums, I'll take it as a compliment. After all, what's better than playing kick-ass drums in a rock 'n' roll band, doing what you love . . . and getting paid for it?"

Athena Lee

Athena Lee may never have started playing drums if it hadn't been for a fit of anger. The younger sister of Mötley Crüe's Tommy Lee recalled in a 2006 interview in *Modern Drummer* how she wanted to go a dance but for some reason couldn't go and was "super mad." Her brother took her to his soundproof studio downstairs, handed her some sticks, and told her to take it out on the drums.

That was the first time Athena had sat behind a kit, and the instant she started hitting the drums, she realized she was having fun. She was about fifteen or sixteen at the time.

Her brother was already a huge star at the time, and she said she couldn't wait until he left to go on tour so that she could try her hand at the drums again.

At the first show she played, she said Jon Bon Jovi, Ann and Nancy Wilson from Heart, and Aerosmith were there. "I was shaking. I thought I was going to die because I had never played live before. But I went out there and kicked ass."

Athena played with the all-girl band Hardly Dangerous and the punk group Butt Trumpet. She played with ex-husband James Kottak in the heavy metal band KrunK, which became Kottak. Athena was named *Access Magazine*'s Best Female Drummer and was the first female ever nominated for Best Drummer in the LA Music Awards.

A breast cancer survivor, Athena is still actively playing today. She is also a celebrity commentator on VH1's *Behind the Music* and *E! True Hollywood Story*.

In an August 2011 interview with Jessica Messina, when asked what her most memorable moment was, she replied: "One really awesome night in San Diego. Opening for Mötley Crüe."

Leah Shapiro

Leah Shapiro has been described as the "drummer with a gaze of steel." The drummer is known for the intense death stare she gives the audience as she pounds away, providing the beat for her band, Black Rebel Motorcycle Club (BRMC).

The Danish-born drummer joined the Los Angeles–based BRMC in 2008 after playing with the Danish garage band the Raveonettes and the Portuguese band Dead Combo. She replaced Nick Jago, who had been with the group since its start in 1998.

In an interview with Lily Moayeri, which appeared in *Boxx News* in March 2013, Shapiro said the first female drummer to inspire her was Cindy Blackman who she saw in a Lenny Kravitz video. "She just looked so fucking cool and powerful. I later found out she was actually a really incredible jazz drummer. Aside from that, the first drummer that was sort of forced on me was Ginger Baker. When my dad found out I wanted to play drums he made me sit and listen to Ginger Baker drum solos quite a bit."

In that same interview, she said she hadn't had too many negative experiences as a female drummer, but that she did sometimes come across the attitude that men were "inherently better" drummers than women. "That's laughable, not true, and should really just be ignored."

Stephanie Bailey

Black Angels drummer Stephanie Bailey drove her parents crazy as a kid with her loud and incessant pounding—so much so that they forced her to put maxi pads on her sticks.

Born and bred in Houston, Texas, Bailey's passion was playing drums even though she never had formal lessons. She put away her sticks while attending the University of Texas, but once she graduated, she decided to turn her passion into a career and auditioned for the Austin-based Black Angels. The Black Angels have performed at Lollapalooza and South by Southwest and on tours with groups such as The Black Keys and The Raveonettes. The band is also featured on the soundtrack to the Twilight movie, *Eclipse.*

As the drummer for Black Angels, Bailey has won rave reviews such as this one after a 2011 performance in New York City from *Pop Break* editor Bill Bodkin: "While the band as a unit was super-tight and all killer all night, it was drummer Stephanie Bailey who stole the show. A true 'goddess of thunder,' she really dominated the performance, setting the tempo, pace and energy for every song. Truly a drummer that percussion fans need to check out."

Stella Mozgawa

When twelve-year-old Stella Mozgawa told her mum she wanted to play drums, the response was "No fuckin' way!" Fortunately, mother and daughter finally sorted things out, and Mozgawa went on to become recognized as one of the top hard-hitting rock drummers today.

A native Australian, Mozgawa currently resides in Los Angeles and is the featured drummer for the indie rock band Warpaint. She said she decided she wanted to play drums after a boy in her primary school told her she couldn't.

Music was actually part of the Mozgawa family tradition. Her mom was a vocalist and her father a bass player who played as a duo in their native Poland and then in bars and clubs across Australia. Mozgawa in a Q&A entitled "Interview with a Drummer," which appeared in *Flab Magazine*, said, "It would have been totally unnatural for me to not play an instrument."Ignoring her mother's counsel to stay away from drums, young Mozgawa fed her passion pounding rhythms on pillows until her father gave her a drum kit for her thirteenth birthday. At age fourteen, she started playing in high school rock bands, pretending to be a twenty-year-old Polish immigrant with no ID.

Six years later, she joined the Sydney band Mink. To quote her artist's biography on the Zildjian website: "Australian born Stella is to the band as what, say, Charlie Watts is to the Rolling Stones: cool as #%^& and the driving force behind their sound."

Mozgawa joined the female psychedelic band Warpaint in 2009, replacing drummer Shannyn Sossamon who left to focus on an acting career.

In the *Flab* Q&A, when asked about her "calling" to be a musician she said: "Sure, I can romanticize my vocation . . . but I don't think there's anything esoteric involved in me becoming a musician. My parents were both musicians. I was intrigued by it from an early age and knew that playing drums made me feel more fulfilled and creative than I'd ever felt in my life. I'm committed to learning everything I can about drums and am always open to following my whim when it comes to what inspires me. I don't tend to glorify what I do . . . I feel like that puts you on some sort of pedestal where you're more entitled to play drums than others who haven't experienced that intangible sensation. I've just followed my muse since the moment I started playing, and I don't feel like the well is running dry. I predict I'll be obsessed with music til the day I die."

Jen Ledger

When Jennifer "Jen" Ledger joined the Christian hard rock band Skillet, she says she had to "learn how to play and sing on the fly."

Born in Coventry, England, on December 8, 1989, Ledger moved to the United States at age sixteen to attend a Christian school and study drumming in Kenosha, Wisconsin. Before leaving England, she had played in a local band and had been a finalist in the U.K. young drummer of the year competition in 2006.

In Kenosha, she played in a worship band called The Spark, but since that band already had a drummer, she found herself playing bass instead.

In December 2007, drummer Lori Peters left Skillet and the band started auditions for her replacement. Eighteen-year-old Ledger beat out numerous other drummers for a coveted spot with the Grammy Award–nominated alternative band.

In a December 2011 interview with Stephen Losey in *Modern Drummer*, Ledger says when she joined Skillet, she had never sung from behind a kit. "I had to sit with drum pads, figuring out which hand and which foot goes with which vowel and which word. I even worked out where I could play one-handed at certain spots while grabbing the mic stand."

Ledger says one of her inspirations is Dave Grohl of the Foo Fighters who taught her feel was more important than chops. "I get in that groove and throw my whole body into the performance," she said.

She says after hearing Grohl for the first time, she has never played the same. "Grohl doesn't win you with finesse or skills," she said in the *Modern Drummer* interview. "He wins you with passion." She said she had learned from personal experience that "a kick on the one and a snare on the two can really move an audience. When you give everything you've got, most crowds will realize it."

Poni Silver

Poni Silver of the garage rock revival band The Ettes says playing drums was for her "a happy accident."

Silver grew up in Queens in a Dominican home where salsa was the radio mainstay. She played piano and clarinet and was a dancer for about fifteen years, which she says definitely helped her transition to drummer. In the early '90s, she discovered hip-hop, but when that genre "became more about rapping about money and bitches and whatever, I was a little lost. So I did what any little sister would do and went snooping into my brother's room and came up with some mixtapes that had all these punk bands on them like the Ramones, Dead Kennedys, and the Misfits. Never looked back. I was a changed woman," she said in a 2012 *Ghettoblaster* Magazine article.

In a Q&A in *Tom Tom*, she talks about her first drum lesson with "a nice man" who lived in the Los Feliz Hills: "When I showed up for practice, we went into his garage and he closed the door behind us in the dark and I thought, 'Well, I guess this is how it ends.' I really thought he was going to kill me and wear my skin! Luckily, that wasn't the case." She added that he gave her some solid lessons and advice that she still uses. The rest of her training she gained on the job.

Along with her drumming skills, Silver is also known for her great fashion sense. She was a student at the Fashion Institute of Technology in New York City and was working in a clothing store in Melrose in Hollywood with fellow band member Coco when the idea for The Ettes was conceived in 2004.

In addition to four recordings, The Ettes have opened for sold-out tours by The Black Keys, Kings of Leon, and Dead Weather.

Rachel Fuhrer

Reviewer Lance Higdon described Texas drummer Rachel Fuhrer as a "funky, punk-rock metronome in human skin" (Artist Profile on Gretsch website). The Austin drummer is well known for her "deceptively subtle cave-woman bashing" when she gets behind her stripped down kit with her band Ume. The Austin drummer also plays with the post-hardcore We'll Go Machete.

Fuhrer started playing drums as part of a church gospel band with her father in Long Island, New York. She grew up in a musical family so instruments were always around the house. "My dad was a musician, my mom was an artist and musician, and my brother was a drummer, too. We were a very noisy family," she laughs.

She remembers at age nine going to a party with her dad and finding a drum set in one of the rooms. She decided to try it out. "Someone came up and asked me how long I had been playing. I said 'five minutes.'"

Her early musical influences were mostly determined by her dad who was into classic rock: Jethro Tull, Creedence Clearwater Revival, Cream, The Beatles. In junior high, she was into heavy metal and hard rock.

Fuhrer never went the marching band route and instead learned drum notation and honed her skills with private lessons. "I was quiet and shy, and nobody in school even knew I played drums," she said. "It was a big surprise and shock when people discovered I could play."

She majored in music at the University of North Carolina and continued studies with Rod Morgenstein at Berklee in Boston. She moved to Austin in 2006, drawn by the music scene there.

In addition to playing, Fuhrer also teaches. She's a co-owner of Austin's Mercury Music, which offers private and group lessons in a variety of styles. When it comes to gender, she says her studio is half and half. "Drums are for everybody. There shouldn't be any gender discrimination going on." She said one of her students she's especially proud of is a fifty-year-old gal named Robin.

Fuher takes pride not only in the versatility she encourages in her students but in her own playing as well. She's played with a wide range of artists, in rock, funk and electronic, experimental, and metal bands. She also plays for theatre productions, operas, soundtracks, and small ensembles.

She described herself as "the eternal student" who was always learning something every time she performed. "I do kinda good under pressure," she joked. "I can come up with things on the fly. It keeps me healthy and sharp."

She said being a drummer has taught her how to be organized and methodical in all that she does. "Being a teacher has broadened my horizons—learning how other people work and approach things. It's taught me to compromise and how to be part of a team. My way might not be the best way."

As a female drummer, Fuhrer said she had been "oblivious" to any gender discrimination. "I'm sure there was whispering going on that I wasn't aware of," she said. "I didn't want to get pigeon-holed by playing in all-girl bands, although I was part of one, Chelsea on Fire. I actually replaced a male drummer in that band, so we became an all-girl band inadvertently."

"More and more women are seeing that there is no divide," she said. "If you're driven, gender has no bearing. It's not a boy's club anymore."

Elaine Bradley

Elaine Bradley of Neon Trees was about five when she started banging on pots and pans with wooden spoons. In a July 2010 blog entry in *Modern Drummer*, she says she asked her parents for drums frequently, "but they thought it was a phase that would pass. After several years, and tireless begging, they bought me a Sears drumset . . . I thought it was the coolest thing, ever!"

Bradley says she wasn't very good, but that didn't keep her from playing, and within a year, "that little set was destroyed." Her parents decided she was serious and gifted her with her first real set, a black Tama Rockstar with Paiste cymbals.

She joined her first band her freshman year in high school and says she played the drums until they could find a "really good drummer." Once they found one, she moved to guitar, and she says, weird as it may sound, that's when she became a better drummer. As she says in the *Modern Drummer* blog, "I would listen to and watch our drummer, and then I would air drum to everything in the car or at home. I learned to think of drumming in a way I hadn't before—as an equal instrument, capable of evoking feeling just like bass and guitar."

After that band broke up, Bradley went to Germany on a mission for her church and then moved to Utah where she started drumming again and eventually joined Neon Trees.

She said she had never thought of herself as a girl drummer. "I just think of myself as a drummer. I don't want to be 'really good for a girl'—I just want to be 'really good.'"

Emmanuelle Caplette

Canadian Emmanuelle Caplette has been earning kudos for her drumming skills since age nine when she joined a local drum and bugle corps in her native Quebec. During the eight years she played snare with different groups, she won numerous awards, including first place at the Quebec Provincial Individuals' Championship four years in a row.

In 2001, she entered Drummondville College to study pop/jazz drumming with Camil Belisle, and while there collected a few more accolades for her resume. In 2003, she represented the college in a Rising Star Contest at the Montreal Drumfest. After getting her degree, she continued studies with Paul Brochu at the University of Montreal, and at the end of her first year, was hired by Michel Cusson's troupe Cavalia for their American tour.

In 2007, Caplette was touring with pop artists such as Ima and Marilou. The next year she was recording and playing on a popular Canadian children's television show.

She has been a featured artist at numerous international drum festivals and has led workshops in Canada and Europe.

Waldo the Squid wrote in the September 2009 issue of *DRUM!* magazine: "Her sense of time, tasteful ghost notes and effortless independence will no doubt impress, but it's the passion for the craft that stays with you."

Rachel Blumberg

Rachel Blumberg became known for her work as the drummer for the indie rock band The Decemberists. When Chris Funk and Colin Meloy from that group first asked her to play with them, she thought it was just for fun. It turned out they were looking for a drummer to join them on tour as the drummer who had recorded with them on their first record had moved on to other things. "I ended up playing drums and singing with them on that tour, and it went so well they asked me to stay." She was a member of The Decemberists for about four years before leaving them to play with M. Ward.

Blumberg also played with the indie rock band Bright Eyes and, during a tour that took them to the Oxygen Festival in Dublin, double drummed with Janet Weiss while REM looked on from side stage. For her "that was a real pinch me moment."

Blumberg's dad started her on the drums when she was in fifth grade. "He was the band teacher at our school and brought home a lot of instruments for me to try, but I didn't show any promise on the woodwinds and brass." She said she was "already really into tap dancing so another rhythmic outlet seemed natural."

Early on she played mostly orchestral and jazz music, but in high school, she was influenced by the drumming in bands such as The Minutemen, Husker Du, Echo and the Bunnymen, and REM. She joined her first rock band at age eighteen.

When she was starting out, she said she was lucky not to face any particular challenges as a female drummer. "Maybe it was because I was always first chair of the drum section from fifth grade through high school. Even though I was one of only two females, I was always better than the boys! I didn't encounter any kinds of challenges or attitudes about being female until I started touring." Until then, she said she'd never thought anything of it before.

Despite any challenges, her life as a musician has been filled with numerous "pinch me" moments: playing with Bright Eyes on a seven-night stand at New York City's Town Hall with Lou Reed as a special guest; being with Yo La Tengo's for their Eight Nights of Chanukah at Maxwell's in 2011 and playing drums for them on a few songs on two different nights; and playing a tiny house show in San Francisco with her old pop band Boycrazy. For the latter, she says, "We were in a very tiny apartment in a very tiny kitchen, and the room was packed full of wonderful people and everyone was dancing, just bouncing up and down. It was completely joyful."

She adds to that list the first show she ever played in Europe, in Switzerland, with Norfolk & Western, on a tour opening for Sparklehorse. "The audience was so attentive and interested. It was eye-opening. I realized how music can be appreciated as art and not just entertainment."

She counts among other career highlights "every show I've ever played with Michael Hurley"; playing drums and vibraphone in Paris with Mirah, Tara Jane O'Neil, Hurley, the Cascadia Ensemble and Lovers at the Pompidou for the "Keep Portland Weird" Festival; "the time when The Decemberists opened for the Pixies and David Lovering did magic tricks for me"; and a wild recording session with The Decemberists that ended with "a drunken tap dancing session."

Recently, Blumberg has been working with her pop band Arch Cape and an experimental project Manzanita. "I name all my musical projects after magical places on the Oregon coast," she says. Blumberg started work on Manzanita while on tour with M. Ward. "I discovered I could make music with my computer and got really into looping. I recorded vocals in bathrooms, in hotel rooms and venues. I wrote most of the music in moving vans and buses." She put together two versions of the band in Portland and after moving to Providence a third one.

Blumberg is also a visual artist. "I used to curate an art exhibit during MusicFest NW in Portland called 'Two-Timer: Cheatin' on our Art, Cheatin on our Music.' The shows were always great and I had lots of amazing artist/musicians like Georgia Hubley (Yo La Tengo), Tim Rutili (Califone), Ryan Dobrowski

(Blind Pilot), Tara Jane O'Neil and many others. I asked them if there were any lessons they learned from art that carried over to life. All their answers, plus my own personal reflecting made me realize that really, art is art. Music can be more collaborative and art solitary, but sometimes it is also the opposite. And in the end it all stems from the same seed. In the end the most important lessons I've learned from both are that of just working really hard, doing good work, being a humble person in the process, and trying to always have beginners' mind no matter what you are working on."

Laney Santana

In high school, Laney Santana played in the rock band Fellow Freak. The Fort Worth–based band was selected as one of top five bands in America to perform at a battle of the bands at Berklee College of Music. "Our band won second place," Santana said, "but I was named 'Musician of the Night'!"

Santana started playing guitar in the second grade, and shortly after that her brother got a drum set and started taking lessons. "I decided to get behind the drum kit and see what kind of noise I could make. I taught myself how to play by listening with my headphones and playing along with the tracks I liked," she said. She said she had no formal training, "unless you count watching a few instructional drumming DVDs."

Her family never discouraged her. "Once they learned how serious I was about music, they bought me a PDP Platinum Series, which is the kit I still use now."

At the time this book went to press, she was a student at St. Edward's University, majoring in criminology.

She says as a female drummer, she's faced the usual gender discrimination. "Most times when I'm loading my drums into a venue, I get these judgmental looks as if people are doubting my ability to play. But every time after I play, people come up to me and tell me how badass I am and that they are impressed by my talent."

As a drummer she's also learned this important truth: "Sometimes it pays to carry a heavy load."

CHAPTER 17

Honky Tonk Angels

> The country drummer's job is to keep time, know how to play a killer country shuffle, have a great groove, and make people dance.
>
> —Karen Biller

If women drummers are still the exception to the rule in the popular music world, they are even more so in the realm of country music. For that matter, even the use of drums is relatively new to this idiom.

Even though the late Jimmie Rodgers used a drummer as early as 1929 in his recordings of "Desert Blues" and "Any Old Time," and Bob Wills hired Smokey Dacus as drummer for his Texas Playboys in 1935, drums were scorned by early country musicians as being "too uptown," "too loud," and "not pure." At the Grand Ole Opry, drums were expressly forbidden until Bob Wills defied the ban and performed there December 30, 1944, with Monte Mountjoy bringing his entire drum set onstage. Grand Old Opry management was not amused.

After the performance, Opry bosses reaffirmed their ban, pronouncing no drum sets would be allowed on stage. In 1954, country singer Carl Smith hired Nashville big band drummer Buddy Harmon to play for a performance. Opry management relaxed the rules to allow Harmon to play a snare drum with brushes. The only condition was that he play behind a curtain and not be visible to audience members. Unfortunately, that wasn't enough for Opry manager Dee Kilpatrick who imposed the drum ban once again.

In the late '40s and early '50s, country musicians were beginning to add drummers to their bands—just not for the Opry stage. Pee Wee King hired "Sticks" McDonald. Paul Howard's Arkansas Cotton Pickers, a regular Western swing act at the Opry, used Joe Morello, who later became known for his work with Dave Brubeck. One of the first country drummers in Nashville was Farris Coursey, who played in Owen Bradley's dance band. You can hear Coursey slapping his thighs on Red Foley's 1950 hit recording of "Chattanooga Shoe Shine Boy." Even Hank Williams briefly used a drummer for his early work in Alabama—before he became a star.

Most of the percussion for early country recordings was provided by simple hand claps, thigh slaps, muted rhythm guitars, spoons, or other metal objects scraped over washboards. Most instruments in early country music, in fact, were used for providing background beat rather than melody. On those occasions when drummers were used, they often performed out of sight, off-stage.

As rock 'n' roll became popular and a form of music called "rockabilly" emerged, more and more country performers began adding drums to their bands and their recordings. In 1973 when the Grand Ole Opry moved to Opryland, the ban against full drum sets onstage—in sight of audience members—was finally lifted. Except for traditional bluegrass, drums have been routinely used in country music since.

Women in Country Music

The story of women in country music—in both song and on the stage—is as interesting a tale as that of the drum in this genre. While women have sung and played country music as long as it's been around, they were formerly subjected to an underlying male bias that promoted a one-dimensional perspective of their role.

As one country music historian wrote ("From Cowboys' Sweethearts to Redneck Women on the Pill"): "Men could be good-hearted but might be given to drinking, cheating, fighting, lying, and other complicated and questionable behaviors. They were free to be full, three-dimensional people endowed with a realistic spectrum of human emotions. Women, on the other hand, were just good-hearted, or they were cruel—typically one thing or another, rarely a human combination of both."

A dramatic change has occurred in the generations between the Carter Family's Sarah and Maybelle Carter reigning as country music's first ladies and the country superstars Dixie Chicks expounding on political issues of the day.

The Carter Family played traditional, mostly religious songs written by A.P. Carter, Sarah's husband. The Carter songs defined women as lovers, wives, and widows, stressing accepted ideas of family and gender. When A.P. and Sarah divorced, they did all they could to keep the news under wrap and continued to perform as "family" because that was the right and proper thing to do. It wasn't seemly for a God-fearing country woman—especially one in the public eye—to be a divorcee.

In 1935, Patsy Montana released a single, "I Want to be a Cowboy's Sweetheart," that became the first million-selling record by a female country singer. While the lyrics were written from a woman's perspective, that perspective didn't do much in terms of promoting a feminist viewpoint. In the early 1950s, Kitty Wells would record "It Wasn't God Who Made Honky-Tonk Angels." The irony was that the song was written by a man and recorded by a singer who was also a demure housewife—about as far away from a honky-tonk angel as you could get.

It wasn't until the brassy Patsy Cline came along that country women came out of hiding as sexy and confident individuals. Cline's candor laid the groundwork for other artists such as Loretta Lynn and Dolly Parton. In the 1970s when Tammy Wynette, the then reigning queen of country music, divorced her husband, the legendary country crooner George Jones, their breakup was an all-out public event, unlike the hushed Carter split. Wynette went on to remarry several times. Country women were finally allowed to be brash, intelligent, complicated, sexy, and as flawed as their male counterparts.

While women vocalists are still making their mark on the country music scene and are more popular than ever, women instrumentalists—especially women drummers—continue to be a rarity. Research turns up only a handful of names of those who have reached national or international stature.

Irlene Mandrell

One of the first women drummers to make it in country music was Irlene Mandrell, younger sister of country singers Barbara Mandrell and Louise Mandrell. Born in Corpus Christi, Texas, Irlene grew up in a music-oriented family. Her parents owned a music store, and her father Irby Mandrell was the family's musical mentor. He encouraged his daughters at early ages to master multiple instruments and was especially proud that his girls weren't afraid to take on instruments that were considered masculine. Irlene played drums, and Barbara played steel guitar, saxophone, dobro, and banjo. Louise played drums, accordion, fiddle, and bass guitar.

As a young girl, Irlene performed with the Mandrell Family Band formed by her father. Later she would play drums as one of the first members of Barbara's band, The Do-Rites.

Irlene first rose to national prominence not as a musician but as a Cover Girl model in the 1970s. From 1980 to 1982, she performed with her sisters on the highly rated television variety show *Barbara Mandrell and the Mandrell Sisters*. The show at the peak of its popularity had more than forty million viewers weekly and was the last of the successful prime-time television shows of its kind. After that show went off the air, she joined the cast of *Hee Haw* from

1983 to 1991, did a couple of episodes of *The Love Boat*, appeared as a celebrity panelist on *Match Game*, and was commercial spokesperson for a number of products. Along with drumming, the versatile Irlene was an avid auto racer and accomplished hunter.

Nancy Given Prout

Drummer Nancy Given Prout, co-founder of the American country music band Wild Rose also achieved success in the country genre. The band, initially called Miss Behavin', was started in 1988 by Prout and four other women: Pamela Gadd, vocals and banjo; Kathy Mac, bass guitar and vocals; Pam Perry, vocals, guitar and mandolin; and Wanda Vick, guitar, madolin, fiddle, dobro, and steel guitar. In three years (1988–1991) they recorded three studio albums. Signed to Universal, their debut album, *Breakin' New Ground*, produced one hit single in its title track on the Billboard country charts. Shortly after the album was released, Universal closed shop. In 1990, Capitol Records reissued the band's debut album, which received a Grammy Award nomination and another nomination from the Academy of Country Music for the band. After issuing another album for Liberty Records, the group called it quits in 1991.

Prout later became a member of The Right Combination, another all-female country band that performed with country music legend Porter Waggoner until his death in 2007. Waggoner formed the all-girl group in the mid-1980s and named it after a hit record he made with Dolly Parton.

Lisa Romeo

Country drummer Lisa Romeo is best known as founder of Mustang Sally, a critically acclaimed all-female band that routinely performs over two hundred dates a year, touring all over the United States as well as Europe and Asia. Country DJ Hall of Fame inductee J.D. Cannon calls them a combination of Alabama, Lynyrd Skynyrd, Comedy Central, and Lady Gaga. Romeo and the band have performed with high profile country artists such as Blake Shelton, Gretchen Wilson, Big & Rich, and Montgomery Gentry.

Lisa Pankratz

When ranking top roots and country drummers today, Lisa Pankratz of Austin, Texas, is always close to the top of the list. Pankratz, who's comfortable playing rockabilly, R&B, swing, and honky tonk, began performing in high school with her father's reggae band I-Tex. She also performed with her uncle's band Greezy Wheels and was featured in a reunited version of that band on Austin City Limits while still in high school.

Born in Austin and raised in Dripping Springs in the Texas Hill Country, Pankratz says she was like any kid who bangs on pots and pans, and because her father was a drummer, drums were always around the house. "I was about twelve years old when I got on fire with the drums," she said.

At age fifteen or sixteen, she joined her first band with some guys she met through an ad in the *Austin Chronicle*. "We played '60s favorites, and they laughed at me because I had never heard 'Secret Agent Man.' I mean, I knew a lot of songs from before my time at fifteen, but just not that one, yet."

She said from the start she was drawn to roots and country music. Her grandfather played country, her dad had a varied taste in LPs, and there was a great collection of rock and roll 45s she found in the closet. She grew up hearing her father play blues and R&B, and she was often with him at Austin's then mecca of the hippie country/rock scene, the Armadillo World Headquarters. "There was a guy at the Armadillo World Headquarters who handed my father a tape and said, 'I think your daughter will like this.' It was Elvis and the Johnny Burnett Trio on one side, and I listened to it over and over. After a few years, I heard the other side. It was Hank Williams, and I liked that, too."

"I thought at the time, I'm a country girl and I like rock 'n' roll, so I guess I'm a rockabilly. Plus, it was a way to rebel getting into the guys with shorter, greasy hair when it was the height of the long hair scene! I used to practice brushes to Bill Monroe records because there were no drums on them. When I discovered Buck Owens and Johnny Bush style country, I felt like I found a calling."

As a teen in the '80s, Pankratz began playing at clubs with her dad's reggae band. She also started getting together with friends who shared her tastes in roots music. "We'd go to places and try to get in well before I was legally allowed, but I never cared about getting a drink. I just wanted to hear the music."

Pankratz went to Rice University where she earned a BA degree in English literature. She returned to Austin and went to work as a full-time musician. She established a national reputation for herself as a powerful and exciting drummer when she went on tour in the early 1990s with rockabilly artist Ronnie Dawson, known as the "Blond Bomber."

She said playing with Dawson and High Noon on the *Conan O'Brien Show* was not only a personal highlight for her—"he was a fantastic musician and performer!"—but a victory for infiltrating "roots into the mainstream."

Pankratz became sought after by acts who wanted their country "to shuffle with soul" and their rock to have "some swing in the beat." For several years, she was flying the flag of traditional roots and country with bands such as Dawson, Deke Dickerson, the original Derailers, Marti Brom, Billy Joe Shaver, and Roger Wallace and others. In 2006, she began drumming for Grammy Award winner Dave Alvin, first with his band the Guilty Women and currently with the Guilty Ones.

Pankratz said that in 2008 Alvin wanted to do something different for his set at the Hardly Strictly Bluegrass Festival. "He called on a lot of the best female musician friends he knew, including me. So we all flew to San Francisco, rehearsed for an hour in a tent behind the stage, and then backed up Dave in front of thousands of people! It was fun and we ended up making a record called Dave Alvin and the Guilty Women for Yep Roc records and toured it for two years." Pankratz said the name was a nod to Alvin's regular band the Guilty Men. After that when Alvin put together a new band for touring, he asked Pankratz to play along with her husband bassist Brad Fordham and former Guilty Men member Chris Miller. They became the Guilty Ones.

Pankratz has also worked with the all-star blues rock group Texas Guitar Women, featuring Sarah Brown, Shelley King, Carolyn Wonderland, and Grammy winner Cindy Cashdollar. She's also worked with the all-female southern rock band Sis Deville and great country writers and singers Brennen Leigh and Noel McKay. Other artists include Rosie Flores, Robbie Fulkes, Jimmy Vaughn, Bill Kirchen, Marshall Crenshaw, and Hayes Carll. In addition to touring and her *Austin City Limits* and *Conan O'Brien Show* appearances, Pankratz also performed at the Grand Ole Opry and Carnegie Hall. In a city full of musicians, she is one of Austin's busiest.

"I consider it a compliment when normally drummer-less bands such as High Noon, Wayne Hancock, and the Carper Family ask me to play as I take it they trust me to add to their feel without ruining it," Pankratz said. She said she also loved performing with great bandleaders such as Ronnie Dawson and Dave Alvin who "appreciate musical sparring and going to new places in songs."

Her drumming influences have included her dad, Jerry Allison, Buddy Harmon, DJ Fontana, Earl Palmer, Dickie Harrell, Willie Cantu, Papa Jo Jones, Gene Krupa, Ed Thigpen, Hal Blaine, Mel Taylor, and Ringo, plus many more—in her words, anyone who "put the beat on the many 45s, CDs, under and overground radio hits from the '20s to the 2000s."

HYPHENS IN—FUSIONS OUT

As for her musical tastes, she says she likes "things that lend themselves more to hyphens [i.e., country-rock, punk-rock, surf-rock, garage-rock, funky-country, western-swing, swamp-pop, etc.]. But please," she adds, tongue in cheek, "no jazz fusion, or other fusions. I also don't really care for that Tuvan throat singing or anything involving didgeridoos."

For Pankratz, the dance hall is home. For her, playing and hearing the music are equally important, and she's most inspired by those moments of improvisation "where the music explodes in a whole new direction—inspired mayhem." She feels the role of a musician is to "be there to serve the song. I don't feel we ever put on a bad show, but there are some that are better than others—some where you're on a cloud for days after."

As a female musician, Pankratz said she has rarely experienced gender bias because she's always played with friends who were "just on a mission to play music." She said being a "girl drummer" when she was younger "was the 'elephant in the room'—I didn't want to acknowledge it or talk about it except to brush it off as quickly as possible. But over the years I have come to appreciate that as long as it is not the only focus it is fine to acknowledge that there are not that many in relative terms and that people are sometimes pleasantly surprised just because it has been such a traditionally 'male instrument.'"

"I've been very lucky," she said. "Oh sure, I've heard, 'She's so good for a girl,' and 'You're the prettiest drummer I've ever seen,' but I haven't had to deal with that issue the way some women have. The people who had a problem just didn't call me. I'm grateful to the many musicians who have gone through so much and paved the way for people like me."

She said she gets an idea from hearing people's comments whether "they just want to say something so badly that it comes out wrong or if they are really kind of patronizing. I think sometimes, weirdly, people will ask you odd questions or think it's OK to touch you or grab you in ways they would never even think about if it was a guy musician."

As a drummer, Pankratz says she embraces the "element of surprise"—the "musical explosion that happens with certain acts." She's also surprised by the number of women who have come up to her after shows and said that she was living their fantasy or that they wanted to play drums but were not allowed to by their family, school, or circumstances.

"I came to realize I had a little more privileged situation because I was never discouraged and the opportunities to play were there. Some say, 'I want my daughter to see you' or 'My boyfriend is a drummer but you kick his ass!' I am happy if I am any kind of inspiration to anyone."

As for lessons she's learned as a musician, Pankratz says it's important to "do your own thing—don't just be an imitator. Serve the song and the situation. Sometimes you need to be the bedrock and almost invisible, and sometimes you need to be able to turn up the juice and shine, add a musical idea, or kick something into a new gear."

Jyn Yates

Kentucky-born and -raised Jyn Yates went on to become a multi-versed drummer but her roots were country. Yates sat behind her first drum kit at the age of three and learned to play on her father's Ludwig Silver Sparkle with its two twenty-six inch bass drums. According to Yates in her biography on her official webpage, the drum set was an exact replica of the drum kit Ginger Baker played when he was with Cream.

Coming from a musical family that leaned toward bluegrass and gospel, Yates recalled holiday gatherings where everyone played and sang. Her grandmother played the organ, dulcimer, banjo, and guitar, and her father was an accomplished drummer who had played professionally with The Sterlings and The Dawnbreakers.

Even though Yates started playing with bands at age twelve, a school band director discouraged her drum playing. To appease her teacher, Yates agreed to play clarinet. That didn't keep her, however, from going home after school, locking herself up in her father's drum room, and practicing for hours on end. Lucky for Yates, her teacher caught her jamming on a drum kit at school and immediately moved her to drums.

Along with her experience in the multi-award winning Adair County Marching Band and drum line, which was never defeated during her stint with them from 1991 to 1995, Yates was opening for major label artists such as Tim McGraw, The Kentucky Headhunters, Tiffany, The Gin Blossoms, Jason & the Scorchers, and Drivin' n' Cryin'.

She played with sax player Bobby Keyes who toured with the Rolling Stones and who had played with John Lennon, Ronnie Wood, and Ringo Starr. She also did gigs with a number of bands, including White Horse, Crash Henry, The Dolly Crisis, Troubadours of Divine Bliss, She Groove, and The Synchopaths, a Japanese Taiko group that played huge drums made out of recycled whiskey barrels. She also played with the popular all-female band Most Wanted and was a session musician as well as drummer for the off-Broadway production of the musical *Rent* and the Alvin Ailey American Dance Theatre of New York, further showing off her versatility to tackle any kind of music.

Yates now teaches in Louisville at Mom's Music and continues her work with musicals and playing live.

For her, a career highlight was playing live on Bourbon Street in New Orleans in 2012. As a tribute to New Orleans Second Lines, she formed the Mighty Kind Second Line with the Troubadours of Divine Bliss and her percussion students. Another highlight was getting to play drums at the famed Michigan Womyn's Music Festival.

Yates says she's always felt like she had to work harder as a female drummer. "I struggled early on trying to get a snare roll for my local marching band, but I'm thankful for the direction that my life led me at the same time, though. It challenged me to be better and to study harder, which lead me to be a better player."

She says basically everything she's learned as a drummer has carried over to life. "Mastering the art of timing is a historic saying that definitely helps in all aspects of life. Muscle memory is another one. Focus, determination, and never giving up because you are a woman are big life lessons that I have learned both through life and drumming."

Yates says she doesn't remember a time when she wasn't playing or drumming. "I'm born and bred to music and sound via vibrations. In life, it's all connected. Playing can clear energy and can be very powerful craft. I look forward to learning everything I can about my gift and for everything coming up in the future!"

Karen Biller

Karen Biller says she's played so many Texas dance halls over the years that she's lost count. "Country has deep roots here in Texas," she said.

The popular Austin-based drummer grew up in Indiana and started played drums in high school—"mainly heavy metal." She was also in the marching band and later went to Indiana University where she received a degree in classical percussion. She also did freelance club gigs in jazz and R&B groups. While her parents were supportive of her musical inclinations, she said others tried to discourage her, telling her she couldn't play drums because she was a girl.

"I always wanted to play the drums," she said. "I feel an affinity with rhythm whether it be music, dancing, etc. Nature is based on rhythm and rhythmic cycles. It feels very natural to be connected to those rhythms, and drumming is an expression of that."

After her move to Austin, Biller found herself in a completely different scene. "I immersed myself in many different genres, including country, rockabilly, surf, blues, etc. The beauty about Austin is that as a developing drummer, I had access to listen to many genres and also play all of these styles live."

Breaking into the country genre and being taken seriously as a woman drummer can be difficult at first, she said, because country bands traditionally employ male musicians. "Female musicians (except singers) are the exception, not the norm. These days it has become more and more acceptable for female musicians to play any instrument in country music. Once it's become known that you can really play, it becomes much easier."

She said the role of a country drummer was much different from that in a rock or jazz setting. "The country drummer's job is to keep time, know how to play a killer country shuffle, have a great groove and make people dance. The groove and tempo are what matter here. There are not many, if any, extraneous fills and solos. The dance halls and country bands want a solid, no frills, groovin' drummer who will keep the dancers on the dance floor."

As a female drummer, Biller said she had often encountered challenges. "I have found that people, including other musicians, may judge female drummers differently than male drummers before even hearing them play first. Some people are very positive and enthusiastic about a woman playing drums. Others think that female drummers won't be able to play 'hard,' loud, [insert your adjective], here. Generally, once they realize you can really play and you have proven yourself, you are more accepted as a peer."

Biller has proven herself may times over, playing with some top artists such as Johnny Bush, Doug Sahm, Erik Hokkanen, Van Wilks, Teisco Del Rey, Rosie Flores, Amber Digby, Cornell Hurd, Frenchie Burke, Tony Booth, Louise Rowe (Bob Wills), and Johnny Gimble (Bob Wills). Recently, she has played with the Tony Harrison Band, a large nine- to eleven-piece "cocktail country" band with a horn section and a crooner in the rat pack (Frank Sinatra, Dean Martin) style. "We play a variety of country western swing, jazz, Latin, and pop." She's also the drummer for the Hot Texas Swing Band, a band "a la Bob Wills" that also branches out into jazz, Cajun, pop, blues, Latin, and country. Along with country, she continues to freelance in other genres as well, mostly blues, jazz, punk, rock, and surf.

She said over the years many women have come up to her and told her they had always wanted to play the drums. "When I asked why they didn't, they said that their parents, band director, boyfriend, et al, wouldn't let them and/or told them no. So I would encourage those women and anyone else in this situation, that regardless of age, the time to change that is now. Give yourself permission to experience the love of rhythm and drums or any other pursuit that you are passionate about. I have tried so many new things and had many great experiences because I didn't let someone tell me I couldn't do it because I was a woman."

Teri Cote

Drummer Teri Cote knew at age six what she wanted to be when she grew up. According to her artist biography on the Zildjian website, she began working toward that goal by fashioning her own drum kit with pots and pans from the kitchen. To that she added Tupperware filled with rice, beans, water, and coins in different containers to get different sounds. For sticks, she used wooden spoons, and for a drum stool, her "throne," a large Folgers can. Once all that was in place, she was ready to jam to the music of Earth, Wind & Fire.

Cote played in drum corps in junior high and high school. She got her first professional gig at age fourteen with The Marcy Brothers, a family band that opened for acts such as George Strait, Johnny Cash, Eddie Rabbitt, The Oak Ridge Boys, Roy Clark, and Alabama. That began a career that has spanned three decades and work with a virtual who's who of country artists, including Stephen Bruton, Freddie Powers, Asleep at the Wheel, Willie Nelson, Merle Haggard, Mel Tillis, Ray Price, The Glen Campbell Band, Gary P. Nunn, Rusty Wier, and Ray Wiley Hubbard.

Most recently Cote has played with David Cassidy—a gig she's had more than eight years. She formed the Teri Cote Band in 2013, specializing in "funky pop" and "Americana."

Michelle Josef

Undoubtedly, one of the most fascinating lady drummers in the country arena is Michelle Josef, who was named Canadian Country Music Association's Drummer of the Year in 1997.

Josef keeps busy as the drummer for the Edmonton Folk Festival House Band with guitar legend Amos Garrett, a "sweet gig" she's had for almost three decades. She also plays in a group called Sunbear led by singer songwriter Kate Boothman, performs regularly with the eclectic bluegrass band Whiskey Jack, and occasionally tours with "ferocious guitar players" Bill Bourne and Madagascar Slim.

Bazil Donovan, bass player with Blue Rodeo, called on her to play on his solo record, and recently, she's also recorded with Suzanne Doyle and Whitney Rose, who she describes as a "brilliant new talent, steeped in old school country, leaning towards the torchy side of Patsy Cline." Over her illustrious career, Josef has played on over 150 records, including hits with The Wild Strawberries and Good Brothers.

A past nominee for a Maple Blues award, Josef has played with some of the greatest in that genre, as well, including Etta James, Solomon Burke, Taj Mahal, Blind John Davis, Johnnie Johnson, Mick Taylor, and Mel Brown.

After a recent performance in an all-star tribute to the late Canadian folksinger Kate McGarrigle in a band that backed up Rufus and Martha Wainwright, Emmylou Harris, Bruce Cockburn, Broken Social Scene among others, one of the performers Robert Charlebois said to her: "You're not one drummer, you're five drummers—a folk drummer, a rock drummer, a jazz drummer, etc."

Josef is not your average female country drummer. Her history is unique in that she underwent gender transition in 1997, the same year she was named the Canadian Drummer of the Year. Ironically, the same day the courier brought the award to her door, she received a phone call from her band Prairie Oyster, telling her they were letting her go because her gender change was too much of an issue for them.

Josef was born Bohdan Hluszko of Ukranian descent. Hluszko was one of Canada's leading session drummers and appeared on numerous albums. He played with over fifty bands as well as the Detroit Symphony.

As a child, Josef became fascinated with drumming. She recalls going to Ukrainian weddings where there was always a live polka band. "While the other kids were running around, I would sit at the side of the stage and watch the drummer. I counted what the drummer was doing with each limb and started hearing patterns—eight hits on the hi-hat, a hit on the bass drum on the first, a snare on the second, etc. At the age of ten, I knew I wanted to be a drummer."

Josef was twelve when her hard-working parents, immigrants to Canada, scraped the money together to buy her first drum set. She began taking lessons in the local music store and in high school enrolled in the school band. "The music teacher lined us up in order of height," Josef said. "Since I was tall, I was given the string bass. The chubby kid played tuba, and the smaller girls played flutes and violins."

Josef said she really learned how to play drums by putting on headphones and "jamming along to Jimi Hendrix records. I was a total Mitch Mitchell freak." She recalls the first two records she bought were Hendrix's *Are You Experienced* and Aretha Franklin's *Aretha's Gold.*

By listening to drummers such as Roger Hawkins, Al Jackson, Jr., Bernard Purdie, and Harvey Mason, Josef learned that "you don't have to play a lot of fills to be a great drummer." As a student at Ontario College of Arts, she discovered Weather Report. "Psychedelic music and soul music were my first loves, although I have gone on to play a lot of 'roots' styles—country, reggae, blues, swing, etc." She says her favorite band is Massive Attack, and they've got two drummers.

When she was in her early twenties, she started playing with Canadian guitarist David (Karl) Wilcox, who she considers her musical mentor. "On and off stage he taught me how to be a musician." Recordings she made with him are now considered Canadian rock classics.

She says she was able to up her game touring with the Canadian trio Sharon, Lois and Bram for a couple of years, playing to thousands of people in concert halls. "When you play concert halls, you don't have the luxury of a first set to warm up. You've got to hit the stage running and deliver a consistent show from beginning to end."

All About the Song

Drummers who effectively play country and folk music have got to love the songs, she says. "Country and folk music are all about the voice and the song. The drummer's role is to be supportive. I am a singer's drummer. I look upon what I do as supplying the pulse and the rhythmic tonal spectrum of the song I'm playing. I do drum seminars and I tell the students that there's a time to pay the drums and a time to play the song. Ninety-nine percent of the time you are hired to play the song."

She says some musicians look upon country as simplistic. "There's not a lot of tight syncopation with wacky accents or odd time signatures. Still, there's a lot of skill required to play with dynamics, sensitivity, a deep groove with great tone at quiet volumes. Infinity runs in all directions, including simplicity. It's often what you don't play that counts. It's impressive to have the chops when you need them, but this kind of music rarely calls for elaborate or fast fills."

"Too many drummers think you really have to whack a drum to make it sound good. They confuse energy with tone. I love to play loud when appropriate. Music is a conversation. We punctuate certain words and phrases."

Josef said she learned to play quietly from Etta James. "She demanded that you play from a roar to a whisper, and slowly, too." She also made it clear, Josef said, that she "would punch your face if you didn't deliver." Josef said James had "incredible ears. She was aware of every note that every person on stage played. Etta could feel the slightest fluctuation in concentration. She demanded that you be totally in the moment. This is the greatest skill to be learned on the drums. Total commitment to the note you are about to play."

Her advice to others who aspire to be professional drummers in the country music world is to find a mentor, watch videos, read books, and learn how to read music.

"If you're determined to pursue drums professionally, then work your ass off. You will be up against someone else who is working their ass off. Country music is about big hair and tight jeans, but it's also about musicianship. Women musicians are slowly making inroads, although there aren't many well-known female country drummers."

"In country music as in all music, learn to sing the melody. It will influence how you play the song. Listen to master drummers such as Buddy Harmon, Larrie Londin and Kenny Buttrey. Listen to Hank Williams, George Jones, Merle Haggard, Patsy Cline, Tammy Wynette. If you're going to authentically play this music, you have to know where it comes from. Country waltzes and country shuffles have their own pocket. It's harder than you think to really lay it down."

As a person with the unique perspective of having been a drummer as both male and female, Josef is keenly aware that a music career is not just about ability or creativity. "It's about charisma, image, personality, networking, luck, zeitgeist, mentors, favors, serendipity, hair, clothes, and sex appeal," she said. "Did I mention luck? Popular music is about boys and girls. It's what the industry knows how to sell. The industry wants clearly defined gender lines."

She says the "tyranny of image" is much more severe for women than men. "The music industry is incredibly competitive and ego driven. You use what you have. Attractiveness can be a great advantage. Men like having attractive women around them. Women like having attractive men around them. But sometimes men resent women in their zone, and women definitely can resent men in their space. Being in a band requires a comfort level with the other band members. As a transgendered person, I know that my presence makes some people uncomfortable. I want to be accepted on the merits of my personality and my playing ability, but sometimes I am prejudged by what I am and what I look like by both women and men."

Josef says she has no desire to be in an all-gay or all-trans band. She says the "all-girl" group seems to be "the flavor of the month, although that's as old and tired as it gets. Prince has one. Beyoncé has one. Marketing gimmick. When's the last time you heard someone trying to sell an all-male group? I regularly play with men and women. I like it that way. The gender of a musician is not relevant to me."

She says she realizes her competitive advantage has to be her musicianship. To hone her skills, she went back to school, enrolling full-time in the jazz program at Humber College in Toronto. She says she watches videos of drummers such as Antonio Sanchez and works at the drums, running rudiments and exercises. "It's a wonderful challenge. I'm a better drummer right now than I have ever been. I no longer expend as much psychic energy internally fighting what I am. The energy I used to channel into suppressing my gender identity I can now put into drumming."

Josef's passion for drumming is obvious. "In the words of John Lee Hooker, 'it's in me and it's got to come out.' I simply love to play the drums," she said. "Whenever I sit down at the drums, I am a kid again."

Of her stint with Prairie Oyster, Josef says it's ancient history and she's moved on. "It was a great gig and I loved playing with them. After the soup hit the fan about my gender transition and I was let go, I didn't work for a year. It was not only financially challenging but spiritually and emotionally challenging. I always wonder how different it could have been if they had kept me in the band. They could have made this world a slightly more accepting place for transgendered people—but I guess they weren't up to the challenge. It was a different time then. I never wanted to be an 'issue.' I still don't. I just want to rock the joint and turn the audience's crank."

For Josef, her musical identity is as important as her gender identity. "I want to be known as a great drummer, not primarily as a transgendered person, although I am aware that the two cannot be separated." She says many of the younger people with whom she plays "are half my age and they don't care that I'm transgendered. They respect my musicianship. I feel good in that scene."

"Good things in life are usually the result of sacrifice, determination, and hard work. Discipline and dedication need to be worked just like a muscle to get strong. When I play the drums I feel complete. I feel in touch with my purpose in life. Some people may call this a state of grace or being in 'the zone.' I believe it's what most of us are looking for. I realize how lucky I am to be able to experience that. Music has been a beacon of life for me, giving me a sense of direction at times in my life when I have felt overwhelmed and lost. I count my blessings every day," Josef said.

"There have been some great times and tough times but I'm still here, still rockin', still learning and still looking for good days ahead."

CHAPTER 18

Lady Drum the Blues

> When I first started playing in Chicago, in the '40s, people said ugly things about a woman who plays the blues. They said, "She must not be a woman if she plays the drums."
>
> —Johnnie Mae Dunson

Blues music, like jazz, has deep roots in African American history, and the first blues musicians were slaves and their descendants who lived on the Mississippi Delta, upriver from the birthplace of jazz, New Orleans.

Working the fields of the plantations, slaves used "call and response" songs known as "field hollers" to help ease the drudgery of their labor. These work songs, along with spirituals, chants, and African country dance music, provided the basis for all blues music that followed.

Early blues musicians performed mostly solo with a guitar and used their feet to establish the beat. When they teamed up with other musicians, it might be in a jug band, which used washboards and other makeshift crude percussion instruments made from household items.

It wasn't until the late '30s and '40s that drum sets were added to bands. During the Great Depression, many Black blues musicians migrated to Chicago, and the nightclubs there readily adopted the new sound. To compensate for the noise and rowdiness of the nightspots, some performers begin adding electric guitars and drums. Muddy Waters, Howlin' Wolf, and John Lee Hooker were among the first to "electrify" and add drums to their bands.

Early blues instrumentalists were overwhelmingly male. One of the few women who sang and was as well known for her guitar skills was Memphis Minnie McCoy, who began performing in the 1930s. As blues transformed into popular music and evolved into the form known as rhythm and blues, more and more women entered the genre, mostly as vocalists. Among those achieving celebrity status were Gertrude "Ma" Rainey, one of the earliest known professional blues singers and the first woman to record the blues, and Bessie Smith, nicknamed the "Empress of the Blues" and considered one of the greatest singers of her era. Both made their musical mark during the 1920s.

Willie Mae "Big Mama" Thornton

The first known woman blues singer to combine her vocal and songwriting talent with drumming skills was Willie Mae Thornton, whose career spanned from the 1940s to the 1980s. She was affectionately known as "Big Mama" because of her physical size and powerful voice.Thornton was born December 11, 1926, in a rural area outside Montgomery, Alabama. With a father who was a Baptist minister, she grew up singing in a church choir with her mother and six siblings. She learned to play harmonica, some say with the help of her brother, "Harp" Thornton, who was an accomplished player. She also taught herself to play drums. Later both the harmonica and drums would become regular parts of her onstage performances.

After her mother died, the fourteen-year-old Thornton left home and got a job cleaning at a local club. Someone there was aware of her vocal skills, and she was soon substituting for the regular singer. It wasn't long before her talent attracted the attention of Sammy Green, an Atlanta music promoter.

In her biographical entry in the *Encyclopedia of Alabama*, two versions of her first encounter with Green are given. In one, he heard her when she won first prize in a local amateur contest. In another, she helped some musicians working with Green move a piano upstairs at a club where they were playing. Impressed by her physical strength, he was willing to see if she had the vocal ability to match.

In 1941, Thornton joined the Hot Harlem Review, Green's Georgia-based show, which she stayed with for seven years. In 1948, she moved to Houston where she became a major contributor to the Texas blues movement. While playing at the El Dorado Ballroom, the flamboyant Black producer Don Robey heard her and was impressed that she could not only sing but play other instruments, including drums. Realizing she was a rarity among other female vocal artists, Robey signed her to a five-year contract with his label, Peacock Records.

Thornton was a lesbian and while that caused some tension with Robey, he nevertheless decided to produce her recordings and use her as a regular performer in his Houston club, The Bronze Peacock. She also toured the South on what was then known as the "Chitlin' Circuit," the string of clubs and venues where it was considered safe for African Americans to perform in the days of segregation.

In 1952, she found herself playing the Apollo Theatre with the Johnny Otis Show and earning the nickname "Big Mama." Later that year at a Los Angeles recording session with Otis, the then young songwriters Jerry Leiber and Mike Stoller approached her and offered her a vocal they had entitled "Hound Dog." The record, released in 1953, went to number one on the R&B chart. Even though it sold more than two million copies, Thornton received only five hundred dollars. Elvis Presley would release his version in 1956 and receive not only the fame associated with that record, but significantly greater financial reward. Historians have noted this as one of the most notorious examples of the inequity that existed between Black and White artists at the time.

In the mid-1950s, rhythm and blues fell out of favor as rock 'n' roll took over, and Thornton's career felt the effects. She moved to San Francisco but had no contract or regular gig and struggled to earn whatever living she could, playing local blues clubs.

Blues Revival

Artists such as Bob Dylan, Eric Clapton, and the Rolling Stones came along in the mid-'60s, and traditional blues saw a revival. In 1965, Thornton toured Europe with the American Folk Blues Festival—a rare honor for a female artist.

During the blues revival, the Bay Area notably became a focal point for the genre. Thornton was invited to perform at the Monterey Jazz Festival in 1966 and 1968. She was recording again in the late 1960s, and many of the albums released during that time are considered some of her best: *Big Mama Thornton in Europe* (1966) with Buddy Guy, Walter Horton, and Freddie Below; *Big Mama Thornton with the Chicago Blues Band* (1976) with Muddy Waters, Sam "Lightnin'" Hopkins, and Otis Spawn; and *Ball & Chain* (1968), a compilation of original work by Thornton, Hopkins, and Larry Williams. Janis Joplin, one of Thornton's biggest fans, took the title song of the last album and made it her signature.

In September 1968, Thornton performed at the Sky River Rock Festival with the Grateful Dead, James Cotton, and Santana. After making more recordings in the 1970s, heavy drinking began to take a toll on Thornton's health. At the 1979 San Francisco Blues Festival, she had to be led to the bandstand, but still gave what was called a "stunning" performance. In 1983, she was in a serious automobile accident but survived and went on to perform at the Newport Jazz Festival that year. She died of a heart attack in Los Angeles on July 25, 1984, at the age of fifty-seven.

Johnnie Mae Dunson

When Johnnie Mae Dunson was ten years old, she overheard a doctor tell her mother, "She won't live to be fourteen years old." Dunson, a singing drummer who would become a Chicago blues legend, had contracted rheumatic fever when she was two years old, and the illness had left her with a weak heart. She believed, like everyone else, that she would die young. But fate decided otherwise, and Dunson was still drumming and singing the blues until her death in 2007 at the age of eighty-six.

Born in Alabama, Dunson's childhood was mostly bed confinement with minimum activity. Then as a teenager she began to get stronger. To earn a few extra dollars, she taught herself to do hair. She had grown up singing gospel songs and listening to the blues tunes of Bessie Smith, Memphis Minnie, and Ma Rainey on her mom's Victrola, so music was a constant presence.

In the early 1940s, a group of Chicago church women visiting Alabama heard Dunson sing and urged her to take her talents north. Dunson didn't need much convincing. She moved to Chicago in 1943 and to pay bills did hair in her apartment kitchen. Within a year, she was playing and singing on Maxwell Street, the celebrated birthplace of Chicago blues. An old vaudevillian, Eddie "Pork Chop" Hines, gave her drum lessons, and she formed a trio called the Globe Trotters that became a regular fixture in the rough, rowdy dives of Madison Street on Chicago's West End.

Dunson's drumming technique was described as "free bashing," based mostly on childhood memories of beating sticks against her mother's tin water buckets. An article by music critic Howard Reich ("Mother of the Blues") says Dunson as a drummer/bandleader was an anomaly for her time, but those who saw her thought she "looked and sounded magisterial."

Jazz harmonica virtuoso Charlie Musselwhite is quoted in the Reich article: "She could hold her own with anybody—nobody gave Johnnie Mae a hard time. People just looked at her, and they would think, 'This is somebody I'm not going to mess with.' She wasn't what you would call a shrinking flower."

But making it in the music business—despite her imposing demeanor—was a struggle for the young blues woman. In Reich's article, which appeared in the *Chicago Tribune*, she was quoted as saying: "When I first started playing in Chicago, in the '40s, people said ugly things about a woman who plays the blues. They said, 'She must not be a woman if she plays the drums.' They'd call me names. If they hit on me and I wouldn't respond, they said I must be a lesbian."

Dunson didn't let any of this deter her. She felt the reason she had been spared from an early death was because "God gifted me with the music I have . . . He knew I wouldn't be able to do any other kind of work," she said. She was also determined to prove her detractors wrong in their admonitions that she would never make it and that there was no place for her in music.

Not only recognized for her singing and drumming, Dunson was also a prolific songwriter, credited with writing over six hundred blues tunes in her over sixty-year career. She reputedly carried around huge ledger books filled with her original songs. She wrote for other blues artists as well. Muddy Waters recorded her song "Evil," and Jimmy Reed recorded her "Going Upside Your Head," "If You Want It Done Right," and "Life Won't Last Me Long." Yet she was never paid more than fifty dollars for any song; in many cases, she was paid nothing.

To supplement the limited income she was making as a musician, Dunson started buying buildings as "fix up" projects. According to her son, jazz guitarist Jimi Smith, she wasn't afraid of a sledgehammer and could take down any wall by herself. She also ran a diner off Madison Street where Buddy Guy and other jazzmen would hang out.

Her first solo recording *Big Boss Lady* was released in 2000, when Dunson was in her eighties. The lyrics of the title song weren't just talk, her son said. His mother was indeed one tough cookie.

Della Griffin

Jazz/blues drummer/vocalist Della Griffin knew music was her destiny after her brother-in-law trumpet player gifted her with a Billie Holiday recording. She was eleven years old at the time. Until then, the pre-teen Griffin had spent her allowance on movies. But after hearing Holiday sing, Griffin gave up the movies and started purchasing every record she could find by Holiday as well as Count Basie, Charlie Barnet, and other big bands of the day. Her passion for music would eventually lead her to become part of two of the first all-female R&B groups in the 1950s, The Enchanters and The Dell-Tones.

Griffin was the nineteenth of twenty children. She was born in Newberry, South Carolina, but grew up in Queens, New York. At age twelve, she began singing and became proficient on drums, alto saxophone, and piano. It was just a few years after graduating from high school in 1943 that she began performing professionally.

In 1950, Griffin was working in a factory that manufactured shoulder pads. It was there that she met Frances Kelly, and the two decided to form a singing group. A mutual friend and pianist, Chris Towns, one of Della's childhood friends, Pearl Brice, and a Harlem club vocalist, Rachel Gist, joined the group, and they named themselves The Enchanters. For about a year, the group played gigs in small clubs, mostly singing doo wop. At Griffin's invitation, Jerry Blaine, owner of Jubilee Records, heard the group perform and signed them.

The Enchanters' first and second recordings were released in 1952. They began touring the country and were featured at New York's Apollo Theatre, The Howard in Washington, DC, and The Royal in Baltimore, Maryland, becoming one of the most popular acts on the "Chitlin' Circuit."

After the successful tour, Griffin and The Enchanters appeared with Milton Berle, Ella Fitzgerald, Red Buttons, Duke Ellington, Arnett Cobb, Billy Eckstine, and Vic Damone in a special benefit for the *Amsterdam News* charitable fund in December 1952.

But despite their success, The Enchanters never felt Jubilee gave them the attention that it afforded to male groups such as The Orioles and Marylanders. They left the label and, shortly after, Gist and Brice left the group. Griffin and Kelley replaced them with Gloria Alleyne and Sherry Gary from the Dorsey Sisters. They took on a new name, the Dell-Tones, named after Della Griffin because she was the group's lead singer and drummer.

Griffin's husband at the time, Jimmy Simpson, was the band's manager and got them a recording contract with a Brunswick subsidiary. The group then went on tour with Jimmy Forrest's Night Train. Kelly, Alleyne, and Gary left the Dell-Tones shortly after. Griffin with new members Algie Willie, Shirley "Bunny" Foy, and Renee Stewart then signed with Baton Records. The group made more recordings, did a tour of Canada, and went through more personnel changes. Finally the Dell-Tones merged with Sonny Til and The Orioles. The ten-member group performed in clubs in New York and in 1957 made two recordings. Griffin eventually left to perform on her own.

When she left the Dell-Tones, Griffin's husband at that time, Paul Griffin, who had been the Dell-Tones pianist, urged her to leave the business and focus on their family. When they divorced, Griffin again began performing in New York City at some of its best known music venues, including the Apollo Theatre and the Blue Note. In 1973, she opened at Harlem's Blue Book, which turned into a fourteen-year steady gig. Over her career, the drummer/vocalist performed with Count Basie, Etta Jones, and Irene Reid, and became friends with her idol Billie Holiday. After Billie died, her husband would stop by Griffin's house regularly to hear Griffin sing because it reminded him of his late wife. According to some accounts, her vocal similarity to Holiday was often frustrating to the artist, because audiences were more interested in hearing Griffin sing Holiday's songs than her own work.

After suffering serious injuries in a car accident in 1984, Griffin took time off to recover and when she returned to performing, it was mostly as a singer rather than a drummer. She made her first album, *The Very Thought of You*, in 1998 at the age of seventy-three. That same year she was invited to perform overseas at one of Finland's major jazz festivals.

Although she had no children of her own, she was a foster parent to more than forty children over the years. When her house burned in 2005, Aunt Della had nine persons, including three great-foster kids, staying with her. The house fire may have been a setback, but it didn't keep her from making a regular gig at a Yonkers jazz club. After the fire, she was quoted in a December 26, 2004, article in the *New York Daily News*: "Music brings me great joy. It always makes me smile."

Carol Dierking

When she was performing, Carol Dierking was often compared to Janis Joplin for her powerhouse intensity behind the drum kit. Nicknamed the "Little Texas Drummer Girl," she collected a slew of honors over the years, including "Best in Texas" by the National Association of Jazz Educators in 1979.

Carol was born in Arkansas City, Kansas, and was adopted by her paternal grandparents as an infant. She moved to Wylie, Texas, when she was four and started studying piano at age five and classical guitar at age eight. She was ten years old when her babysitter introduced her to her first snare drum. She says it was "love at first sight." Throughout high school and college, she played in concert and marching band, along with several other ensembles.

She went to college at Stephen F. Austin State University in Nacogdoches with a full music scholarship, but after three years and feeling like a "super-star in town—playing with some East Texas blues veterans," she decided to quit school and pursue her dreams in Dallas.

"I had been teaching others for six years and was convinced that my degree would mean nothing more than a certificate to teach at a school, which was not my vision," she said. "Years later someone mentioned to me that I could have made a whole lot more money had I gotten my degree. Well noted."

Over the years she has played in a variety of musical genres, but she's best known as a "true blues powerhouse" who plays Texas blues and Chicago style, too—"old and new, groovin', roadhouse, outlaw, and gospel blues." The versatile drummer is equally comfortable doing country, funk, or original improvisation—or as she says, "no genre left behind."

A few of the groups she's played with include The Smokin' Joe Kubek Band featuring Bnois King, Intodown, Jimmy Thackery and The Drivers, The Dunn Deal, Texas Slim, Highway Rockers, Baloney Moon, Leo Hull and the Texas Blues Machine, The Jeff Stone Band, Voodoo Highway, The Outlaw River Band, and The Leon Street Blues Band with Stevie Ray Vaughan occasionally sitting in.

Carol gave up the drums when she became a parent of a baby girl. In an article, "Syncopated Acts of Accomplishment," she wrote: "In the beginning it was not that difficult to let the music be silenced because my days were consumed with overtime, housekeeping, and parental duties. My drums collected dust, went into storage, and then eventually were sold when times were rough."

She said as her daughter became more independent, she began to mourn the loss of her instruments. "I cried because I could no longer express myself with music. I could not release the notes that had been storing up inside me, screaming to be set free. I was compelled to come up with a plan to find the passage back."

"As long as I did something—anything—each day, having to do with drumming or being a drummer, the vision became more striking and vivid."

Carol said her new routine included practice, losing weight and gaining muscle, and modifying behavior. In 1999, she underwent gastric bypass surgery. At the time she was five feet tall and weighed 316 pounds. In 2003, she was once again poised for a career as a professional musician.

In 2013, Carol participated in the acclaimed Blues Women International Recording Project. Carol said in her early years as a student she never experienced gender discrimination. "Under the veil of written scores and daily challenges in performance, it was not questioned," she said. As a "band kid," her mentor was the late Dr. Judy Mathis, a world-renowned percussionist, whose circle of friends included Buddy Rich and Ed Shaugnessy. She was a ghost writer for much of the pop music of the '70s and a judge for the National Association of Rudimental Drummers.

"Mama Mathis taught us not only about music, but also about how to operate as a family, a band, onstage and off. We were all very competitive, and there were many more girl drummers in the band than boys. I developed the nickname 'Little Mathis' because I was her shadow. We were kindred spirits and I was her protégé. I don't pick up a stick without feeling her presence and greatly attribute who I have become as a player to her. I will never forget the day she looked at me square in the eye and said, 'Quit playing like a girl!!' I found my voice on the kit that day."

She said as a full music scholarship student at Stephen F. Austin University, she had more opportunities, thanks to Dr. Melvin Montgomery, the director of bands there and a master percussionist himself. "He took me under his wing and opened up the entire music department for my studies. I played for everyone, theatre productions, orchestra, drum line—then I would go play with the locals—everything from heavy metal to blues. The late great Stevie Ray Vaughan did come jam with my band The Leon Street Blues Band—at a big ole house on Leon Street where we used to play and have parties. At that point in my career, I have to admit that I was the one discriminating. I didn't really pay too much attention to the young guitar slinger, as I believed they were a dime a dozen. Everyone has to take a turn around and my groupies were surrounding me and the music was good—real good. I didn't remember that guy's name. My college cronies were like, 'Ca-rol!! That was Stevie Ray Vaughan!!!'"

Reality Check

Carol said her "dreams of grandeur screeched to a halt" when she returned home from school. "My support team and all my friends had moved on, and suddenly I had to start tooting my own horn. I sure wasn't used to that at all. Everyone had already known about me before I met them . . . or there was somebody there spouting off how great I was. Stick pin firmly into ego bubble and release."

She said what she found "were multitudes of garage bands scheduling practice around day jobs and/or raising kids—lots of excuses, no shows, and half-hearted progress. I heard horror stories about road life and crooked record companies—the guys would talk to each other and act as though I didn't know a lick of what they were saying."

"There were very few successful female drummers in the limelight, and the role models we did have wore high heels and played basic grooves that didn't require anywhere near the mastery I had trained so many years to achieve. I quickly found myself playing cover tunes by ear at endless rehearsals with few shows and working a day job to survive."

Carol said "being a little girl with a baby face who simply did not look like a drummer" didn't help. "People had to witness greatness when I played or be willing to listen to my list of awards and accomplishments while giving me that stare of disbelief."

She said once she was out of school she "left it all behind—no more tympani, xylophone, chimes, marimba—sheet music, etc. Somehow I believed that just in having studied it for so long and knowing how to play was going to get me into the studio and writing my own percussion pieces—creating original music all day and playing concerts on TV—drum solos like all my favorite players were doing. Instead I landed a job as a bartender, and the owner built me a stage. Paying my dues as they say."

Carol says few women are known for their master skills in drumming. She says when someone asks her what she plays, she shrugs it off and says, "Drums!" with a big smile. "Some people question to the point of interrogation, like a pop quiz to test my knowledge of music and players they know about. One poor guy just popped off the top of his head, 'so . . . what kind of drums do you play?' I immediately snipped, 'Bar-bie!'"

She says the majority of bands that she attempted to join over the years dissolved due to wives and girlfriends of the other players in the band. "Jealousy in the music business is epic—players' egos, insecurities about who is driving the bus (onstage and off), then most commonly, who is trusted to be faithful."

She says becoming a mother changed everything. "Being a freelance or contract musician, it is very common to get under-cut, under-paid, and hazed. There are no job descriptions, health care, retirement plans, guarantees. Simply to be in rotation with bands for gigs was an honor because there were so many other drummers waiting in line."

She said she chose a stage name, Ms. "Gypsy" Morgan, to protect her identity as a single mom with a teenage daughter at home. "I've had guys fall to their knees and follow me around, wedding proposals, flowers, notes on stage, numerous fanatic events. Using a stage name was a safety measure."

Carol said sub-work and freelance contracting were often "mandatory to survive." "Bandleaders cannot afford to hire a drummer who needs their own hotel room because of gender. Most bandleaders would just avoid the issue and hire a guy instead. There is that comfort level and ego—please don't let the drummer steal the show. The audience has no idea and mean no harm in doing it, but nine times out of ten, it means that the star of the show is now in the market for a 'regular' drummer—not one that everyone points at and says, 'Wow, that's a girl!' then rushes past them for autographs. Sometimes, you just have to close your eyes and play!"

She said over the years as her online presence has grown, she has periodically used the screen name "Little Drummer Girl," because "many have called me that, not knowing my name and I am little." Later, it became "Texas Drummer Girl" and evolved into "Little Texas Bad Ass Drummer Girl" by fans. When Carol's parents died and her daughter was grown, she left the stage name Ms. "Gypsy" Morgan in Las Vegas and began using her given name Carol Dierking in their honor.

She likens her journey to "one continuous drum solo."

"Staying focused on realistic, stepping-stone goals allowed me to hear my inner drummer. Though times have been challenging and sometimes a struggle, I am here to tell you that if you hear the beat of a different drummer—look around—it might be me."

CHAPTER 19

Jazz Chicks with Chops

> I instantly loved jazz from the moment I heard it—as most jazz musicians would say—it is a passion that finds you. Of course, I dealt with various gender-related issues, but it never stopped me for a second. When you are passionate about something and pursue it with your heart, you can't go wrong.
>
> —Sherrie Maricle

Jazz—both the art form and the subculture—has remained mostly a fraternity of male musicians. In 1973, an anonymous male pianist said, "Jazz is a male language. It's a matter of speaking that language, and women just can't do it" (Dahl 3).

While numerous women have made it as singers and pianists in the jazz world, as instrumentalists they have always been and continue to be at a considerable disadvantage. This likely goes back to the roots of the genre—blues, ragtime, and marching band traditions—all of which were historically male-oriented.

For many years, the unsavory and sometimes dangerous aspects of the jazz lifestyle also inhibited the participation of women in the genre. Liquor, drugs, vice, and the generally loose code of morality that prevailed in many early jazz clubs could be intimidating to women intent on keeping their respectability and reputations intact.

Two groups that did much to advance the status of women as jazz musicians were The Melodears, formed in 1934 and led by singer Ina Ray Hutton, and The International Sweethearts of Rhythm, formed in 1939 in Piney Woods, Mississippi. Members of The Melodears were highly proficient musicians with chops to play arrangements comparable to those of any male band. The International Sweethearts of Rhythm were respected not only as the best female band of the time but as a first-rate musical ensemble. Their drummers played key roles in building those groups' critical esteem.

Bridget O'Flynn

Bridget O'Flynn was one of the first drummers to break through the male jazz ceiling. Born in Berkeley, California, in 1923, O'Flynn began a lifelong love affair with jazz at age thirteen after hearing Fats Waller on the radio. She grabbed a couple of whiskbrooms and started playing. "I couldn't stand that marvelous beat without trying to play with it," she told Sally Placksin in an interview for *American Women in Jazz.*

Her mother, a classical pianist, wasn't happy with her daughter's new obsession. "What the hell's the matter with you?" she asked. Years later, her mother finally understood and told her, "Had I known, I would have sent you to school. I would have given you lessons. It never occurred to me that a woman would play a rhythm."

O'Flynn confesses in the interview that she was an "incorrigible" teenager and as a result wound up at a training school for girls where she formed her first jazz band, Doc Jazz and the Pills. "I played the drums, not knowing anything—not a damn thing except a beat and rhythms. So that was the beginning of that." Although she initially played by ear, she later studied with percussionist Henry Adler, and along the way gathered tips from the likes of Lionel Hampton, Lee Young, Harry "Sweets" Edison, Dale Reed, and Lloyd Reese.

In 1939, O'Flynn landed her first job playing with an all-woman band led by Sally Banning in San Pedro, California. She then played with a big all-male band led by Sally and George Banning. In that group, she played drums and was also one of the featured chorus girls. Later with the help of her musician husband at the time, she formed her own all-male band.

Then World War II broke out and many of the band members, including O'Flynn's husband, went into service, causing the band to break up. O'Flynn went to New York to join the musicians' union there so that when her husband came back they could work on the East Coast. But when the war ended, so did her marriage. Also, seven of the men who had played in the band were killed overseas, so O'Flynn found herself working in New York on her own.

She was playing what she called "little dumb grooves" at different clubs when one night pianist Mary Lou Williams walked in and caught her act at the Club Boheme. O'Flynn became part of Williams' all-woman trio that recorded "Hesitation Boogie," "Humoresque," "Boogie Mysterioso," and "Waltz Boogie."

In a 1948 *Esquire* review, Herbert Kubly calls O'Flynn a "female Krupa," but except for that mention, she and June Rotenberg, the other member of the Williams' trio, were rarely given any credit or even named for their performances with the ensemble.

In the mid-'50s, O'Flynn did a short stint with a small group that had broken off from the International Sweethearts of Rhythm. She left after three weeks, disillusioned by the racism that made it impossible for women of both races to work openly together. In fact, she was ready to quit the business for good, when writer Henry Miller admonished her, "You don't put down your instrument. In my case it's a pen; in your case it's a drumstick. Don't put your instrument down" (Placksin 172).

O'Flynn stuck it out for a few more years, then quit drumming in the early '60s after the death of her son and over a growing distaste for the sexism, racism, and compromises of the music business in general and jazz world in particular. Although she doesn't play, she sometimes goes to hear the women who were fellow performers.

Today O'Flynn is still noted for being one of the outstanding supportive jazz drummers of her time.

Rose Gottesman

Drummer Rose Gottesman became enamored with jazz in the mid-1930s, watching performances at New York's Apollo Theatre with her brothers. Her passion for the drums came alive when one of her brothers came home with drumsticks and a practice pad. Gottesman picked up what she could from her brother and then from male classmates at James Monroe High School in the Bronx, where Gottesman played in the marching band.

She credits her brother with encouraging her to pursue drumming. In Placksin's *American Women in Jazz,* Gottesman is quoted: "He was the one who thought I had talent, and encouraged me, and would take me downtown to sit in or take me to Harlem to sit in. I never could have done that on my own, because this was the thirties and girls just didn't do things like that. He guided me and trained me like a prizefighter. He saw that I listened to the proper bands, and whatever he couldn't explain to me, he would take me to hear" (Placksin 174).

Even though encouragement was never lacking from her brother and others, finding work at the start was not easy. Jobs were scarce and the all-girl big bands, such as Phil Spitalny's Hour of Charm and Sweethearts of Rhythm, weren't her thing. Mostly influenced by black musicians and inspired by Jo Jones, Cliff Leeman, and Gene Krupa, she sat in with the Savoy Sultans, Lucky Millinder, and at various jam sessions on 52nd Street. On Apollo Amateur Night, she sat in with Jimmie Lunceford and won that night's competition.

She "poked around" doing club dates and other small gigs and then joined Estelle Slavin's Quintet, mostly playing the cocktail circuit. Slavin had also played trumpet with Ina Ray Hutton's Melodears. "I think we were a little ahead of our time," Gottesman said. "We would have done better if we had come along with TV and also if we had had the proper handling."

Gottesman played with Slavin's quintet until the summer of 1945. She married musician Irving Lang that year and gave up her musical career to raise two children. She said even though she had no intention of quitting permanently, she decided her children came first, and that the music business could get along fine without her.

She still picks up the drumsticks occasionally and says she has no problems keeping time, "but if they give me four bars, I'm terrified." She says when she was younger, she never knew how many bars she was supposed to play. "I always thought those things were spontaneous . . . I had the confidence of youth" (Placksin 174).

At the time Gottesman was playing with Slavin's group, she says there were "hundreds or thousands of female musicians scattered throughout the country." She said while a lot of these women "fooled with playing jazz," they really weren't serious about it or passionate about the music. "They thought because they filled a sweater, they could get away with less practicing than a guy."

In addition to stints with Slavin and Williams, Gottesman also played with the All-Stars and Hip-Chicks.

She's quoted in Placksin's book: "I was quite willing to be the kind of drummer in the band who wasn't a soloist but who could back the soloists so that they played better."

Jerrie Thill

Until her death in 2010 at age ninety-three, drummer Jerrie Thill had been entertaining audiences at El Cid Restaurant in Hollywood, California, every Sunday afternoon since 1984. Thill, born in Dubuque, Iowa, in 1917, began her professional career as a drummer/singer/bandleader in the Chicago area when she was eighteen years old.

Between 1935 and 1938, she led an eight-piece all-girl swing band that toured the Pantages and Gus Sun Times vaudeville circuits in the West and Midwest. Before World War II, she was drummer with the Hollywood Sweethearts and during the early war years part of the Villa Maree Trio in Dubuque. At the end of the war, she was back in Chicago as a vocalist with the Danny

Ferguson Society Orchestra and then relocated to Southern California in 1945 where she became house drummer at the Flamingo Night Club until 1952. In 1953, she joined the Ada Leonard All-Girl Orchestra for their 1953–1954 West Coast tours. The mid-1950s found Thill on the road with the Biltmore Girls.

She became a sought-after drummer and vocalist for small jazz ensembles and in 1974 joined Peggy Gilbert's Dixie Belles, performing with that group for twenty years with appearances on the *Johnny Carson Show* and television shows such as *Golden Girls, Married with Children*, and *Trapper John*. The popular YouTube video, "Hey Jerrie," which was produced by Allee Willis, composer of the *Friends* theme, tells her life story in song and photo clips, and provides a sample of her skill beating the skins.

Dottie Dodgion

Of the female jazz drummers who emerged during the 1950s, Dottie Dodgion was one of the most successful. She was born in Brea, California, in 1929 and began her musical career as a vocalist. As a young girl, she also had a passion for dancing, but at age fifteen was stricken with polio. Her father was a professional drummer, and while he didn't discourage her interest in drumming, he never spent time teaching her to play. He did, however, give her a drum set and encouraged her to listen, "really listen" when he played recordings of his favorite artists. It was good advice, which would serve her well later.

As a teenager, Dodgion studied vocalese or scatting with Charles Mingus. She also performed with other jazz groups active in the Bay Area in the late 1940s. In an interview with Linda Dahl, which appears in the book *Stormy Weather*, she recalls tapping rhythm on magazines to fill in for a drummer who was late for a gig. "That's really how it started with the drums. And I thought that really it isn't so hard. If I'd known it was going to be as hard as it is, I don't know whether I would have continued or not!"

She tells a story in Dahl's book of being stranded in Omaha, Nebraska, after a singing gig. To get back home, she went to work playing "cocktail drums." Following that incident, she said she didn't even think about drums for many years. "I'd play a little brushes maybe, on a magazine or something to keep time. If I'd go to a session and there wasn't a drummer there but a snare or some drums were set up, I'd sit in and play a little bit."

That didn't please her first husband, bass player Monty Budwig, who was adamantly opposed to her drumming because he thought it was "unladylike." She said he loved her singing, but the thought of her being a lady drummer made him furious. Her second husband, alto sax player Jerry Dodgion, took a different view. "He said I should either sing or play," Dodgion said. "Otherwise I was going to end up known as a singer who sometimes played drums or a drummer who also sang."

Jerry Dodgion saw his wife's potential as drummer and did all he could to encourage her in that direction. "Jerry really wanted me to play. He didn't want me around the house doing wifely duties," Dodgion said. Jerry was behind her all the way and proved it—carrying her drums many times up the 156 stairs to their apartment in Larkspur, located in Marin County just over the Golden Gate Bridge from San Francisco, where they lived at the time she started playing.

Because of her second husband's gender blindness, Dodgion found herself practicing and playing with the pros. But even her husband's attitude didn't stop her from encountering prejudice in her ongoing search for gigs, especially after she moved to New York in 1959. In Placksin's *American Jazz Women*, she recalls her frustration: "I was at least accepted by the guys, even though they didn't hire me for those jobs; many a time a drummer who couldn't swing half as well as I would be hired."

In another interview with Linda Dahl, which appears in *Stormy Weather*, Dodgion says as a woman drummer, she had to "be better than better. . . . All the instruments are male-dominated. The way it's looked at, the drums are—pardon the expression—the balls of the band. When a guy turns around and sees a lady sitting there, it threatens his manhood in some way."

She recalls a time when a friend tried to get her a gig with Billy Butterfield, and the manager said, "A chick on drums? Are you kidding? Forget it!" Dodgion points out that was the prevailing attitude of the time, but that things seem to be changing a bit, and "guys are [finally] coming around." She acknowledges, however, there's still a long way to go.

Despite the gender bias she encountered, Dodgion performed with jazz greats such as Benny Goodman, Billy Mitchell, Al Grey, Wild Bill Davison, Ruby Braff, Al Cohn, Zoot Sims, Phil Woods, Hank Jones, Milt Hinton, and George "Jiri" Mraz.

Playing with Goodman

Her experience playing with Goodman was particularly memorable and one that she said came about by accident. "We had just come to New York. Benny had been trying out drummers, and he wasn't happy with them. . . . I went out to buy myself a coat, I remember, and then I came back and looked up the band, which was at Basin Street East. And Benny told me, 'Come up and play.'" Goodman had some familiarity with Dodgion's abilities because her husband Jerry had played with his band in Las Vegas and they had played in a session where Goodman sat in.

Dodgion who had, thanks to her father, been listening—really listening—to Goodman's music since she was nine years old, had no problem with the charts, and Goodman was so impressed he said, "Fine, you start tonight." She says she was so nervous that Zoot Sims who was the tenor player in the band took her to an Irish bar around the corner where they "threw down a few scotches" until she couldn't feel a thing.

The gig lasted ten days. She said everything was going fine until one night Goodman forgot to introduce her. She was the only woman in the band, and the audience was yelling, "The drummer, the drummer!" He introduced her with a less than enthusiastic "Huh? Oh, yeah, Dottie Dodgion." That brought the house down, Dottie said, much to Goodman's chagrin. The next night she got her notice. "Nobody gets a bigger hand than the 'King'!" Dottie says with a smile.

Dodgion kept busy through the '60s and '70s but still felt the sexism so rampant against women drummers. To blend in and meet others' perceptions of a true jazz person, she kept her hair short and would wear clothes that were "unfeminine" and black. Her goal was to not look glamorous or "cutesey." She also had to learn how not to smile when she was playing. "If you smiled, you weren't jazz."

Another protocol she practiced for a while was not singing. The serious hard core jazz musicians—people like Miles Davis and John Coltrane—didn't sing. Singing jazz players were considered "commercial," she said.

Dodgion was never uncomfortable being the sole female in a band, because she actually preferred performing with men. There weren't many women to follow so all her role models were men. While she considered Kenny Clarke her major influence, other favorites were Billy Higgins, Al "Tootie" Heath, Mickey Roker, and Grady Tate. When one interviewer asked her about Buddy Rich, her reply was, "He plays good for a man."

She felt many women who entered the music business were not entirely serious about it. Despite reservations based on a belief that "nobody likes to be sold because of their gender," Dodgion joined an all-female group in the late 1970s. She especially disliked the fact that many considered instruments gender-specific.

She also found that as she aged, it became harder and harder to acquire gigs. She said after turning fifty, she thought, "Oh my God, nobody will hire an old drummer. There is no gimmick for selling an old lady," she said. "If you're a young woman and have a decent figure, they can sell you like mad."

She said life for a jazz musician is always uncertain from gig to gig—"but the older you get, the longer the periods are . . . in between."

September 2013 marked Dottie's eighty-fourth birthday. She plays weekly with her trio at the Spanish Bay Inn in Pebble Beach, located on the Monterey Peninsula on the California Central Coast.

Terri Lyne Carrington

Terri Lyne Carrington was born in Medford, Massachusetts, on August 4, 1965, into a musical and jazz-loving family. Her mother played piano and her father played saxophone and was president of the Boston Jazz Society. Her grandfather, Matt Carrington, had played drums with Fats Waller and Chu Berry. By the time she was five years old, Terri was playing drums much to the delight of her father who decided she had a natural talent. The Carrington house was full of musical instruments, but a drum set that had belonged to her grandfather was the instrument to which Terri was drawn.

Her father taught her a few things and then sent her to a teacher. His love for jazz inspired the same in her. Her rise to success was immediate.

A child prodigy, at age ten she played for Buddy Rich and then played her first major performance at the Wichita Jazz Festival with Clark Terry. At age eleven, she was the youngest student ever to receive a full scholarship to the Berklee College of Music, and at age twelve, she was profiled on the PBS kid's biography program *Rebop* and became the youngest musician to endorse Slingerland Drums and Zildjian Cymbals.

At Berklee, she studied with master drum instructor Alan Dawson and played with Kevin Eubanks, Donald Harrison, Greg Osby, among others. Before turning seventeen, she made a recording entitled *TLC and Friends*, with Kenny Barron, Buster Williams, George Coleman, and her father. As a high school student, she traveled across the country doing clinics at schools and colleges.

But for being as sought after as she was at such a young age, Carrington also felt isolated as a female drummer. In an article she wrote for *Percussive Notes* on her life as a woman drummer, Carrington said, "I got very excited when I saw people like Karen Carpenter on television. At least I was seeing someone who was in some ways like me, which made it feel not quite so strange."

"For many years I felt like I was in a club by myself. If I met other young girls that played drums, chances are they lived in other cities, making it difficult to develop camaraderie."

In 1983, Carrington moved to New York on the encouragement of her mentor Jack DeJohnette. There she found work with Stan Getz, James Moody, Lester Bowie, Pharoah Sanders, Cassandra Wilson, David Sanborn, and others. In the late 1980s, she relocated to Los Angeles where she gained national recognition as the house drummer for the *Arsenio Hall Show*, then again in the late 1990s as the drummer on the late night TV show *VIBE*, hosted by Sinbad. In 1996, she collaborated with Peabo Bryson on "Always Reach for Your Dreams," a song commissioned for the 1996 Olympic Games.

As a woman, Carrington still feels underrepresented and outnumbered in the drumming world. She blames gender stereotyping and cultural norms set by American society for the sad lack of female drummers. Drums are considered an aggressive, dominant instrument, and "women have been socialized not to do things that seem aggressive or male."

In another interview with jazz historians Wayne Enstice and Janis Stockhouse, Carrington admits the obstacles that women drummers encountered in the past are still around today. She also finds it unfortunate that many women, "in the attempt to be viewed as equals, have taken on the personas and developed the attitudes of their male counterparts."

In her words: "It is precisely the feminine aesthetic that will make our contributions different and bring another perspective to the industry—a perspective needed for balance."

Marilyn Mazur

Marilyn Mazur, born January 18, 1955, has demonstrated her jazz chops with some of the best—Miles Davis, Wayne Shorter, and Gil Evans among them. Of Polish and African American descent, Mazur was born in New York and has lived in Denmark since age six. As a child and teenager, Mazur studied ballet and piano.

As a drummer, she was mostly self-taught but eventually went on to get a degree in percussion from the Royal Danish Academy of Music. In 1973, she formed her first band Zirene, and two years later she was regularly performing as a percussionist, drummer, and vocalist with various groups. Her rise to fame began when she played with the fusion band Six Winds with noted Danish jazzman and drummer Alex Riel and became leader of the all-female Primi Band.

In 1983, she formed the jazz quartet MM4 and received the Ben Webster Award, an annual prize presented to outstanding American and Danish jazz musicians. In 1985, she was asked to take part in a recording paying tribute to Miles Davis. Davis was at the recording sessions and was so impressed with Mazur he asked her to join his band. She toured all over the world with the jazz legend and then did tours with the Gil Evans Orchestra and Wayne Shorter Quartet. By 1988, she was back playing with the Miles Davis Band.

She left the Miles Davis Band in 1989 to concentrate on her own music and to form the seven-piece orchestra Future Song. Future Song was active for more than a decade.

Mazur joined the Jan Garbarek Group in 1991 and toured with them until 2005. Since then she has spent most of her time composing, working on creative music projects, and touring the world with various bands, including Celestial Circle, Mystic Family, and her own band, the Marilyn Mazur Group.

She continues to receive accolades for her accomplishments, including the Jazzpar Prize in 2001, and Percussionist of the Year finalist by the Jazz Journalists Association. For seven years (1989, 1990, 1995, 1997, 1998, 2002, 2008), *Down Beat* magazine has selected Mazur as "talent deserving wider recognition" in the percussion category of its annual critics' poll.

Lucia Martinez

Lucia Martinez is one of the new generation of young percussionists making a name for herself in the European jazz world. Born in Vigo, Spain, in 1982, she began studying percussion and hurdy-gurdy at La Universidad Popular de Vigo at the age of nine. By the eighth grade, she was in London studying percussion at the Guildhall School of Music. In 2006, she received a degree in classical percussion from the Conservatorio Superior de Musica de Vigo, and the next year a degree in jazz from the School of Music and Performing Arts in Porto, Portugal.

As a multi-instrumentalist and composer, Martinez says her style is influenced by Spanish folk music, flamenco and Mediterranean, and the new avant-garde. Along with her own projects, Martinez is popularly sought after by some of the top jazz groups in Europe as a vibraphonist, percussionist, and drummer.

In Berlin, her current residence, she completed the master's program in jazz at the University of the Arts (Universität der Künste) in 2009 and is now working on a master's degree in film and television music at the School of Film and Television in Potsdam.

Allison Miller

New York City–based drummer Allison Miller has become a familiar name in contemporary jazz circles. Miller grew up in the Washington, DC, area and started playing drums at age ten.

"I always wanted to drum," Miller said. "My mom is a choir director, and she says I would kick to the rhythm of the choir in her belly when she was pregnant with me. So I guess my earliest influence was my mom's choir."

Walter Salb was Miller's first drum teacher and later became one of her best friends. "He introduced me to jazz, and he taught me four-way independence. He also taught me how to 'hit' the drums, providing propulsion for the band while still pulling a warm and full sound out of the drums. Oh, and he taught me the rudiments! He also taught me about life, culture, politics, and the music business. Not a day went by that Walter didn't read every page of *The New York Times.* He stayed present until the day he died. I admire this insatiable curiosity. He also started sending me out to play his gigs a soon as I got my driver's license. This was probably the biggest lesson of all!"

Miller said she was determined to have a professional career as a musician and set out for it at a young age. "I started gigging at the age of fourteen and had a lot of support from my mentors, colleagues, and parents." In 1991, at age sixteen, she was featured as an "Up and Coming" artist in *Down Beat* magazine.

At the age of twenty-one, she moved to New York after graduating from West Virginia University in 1996 with a music performance degree to study with Michael Carvin and Lenny White and pursue a career as a freelance drummer, composer, producer, and teacher.

"Luckily I knew a few great musicians living in NYC, so I started making money on gigs quickly. I also had a ton of energy, was completely fine with humiliating myself at as many jam sessions as possible, and had no problem living off bagels and falafels. This was the mid-'90s and the jazz scene was really hopping. I could go to two or three sessions a night meeting so many great musicians. The scene felt like a real community back then. Also, rent was still fairly cheap so, with some mindfulness, I was able to get by on little money. I pieced my living together with subway gigs, club gigs, and the occasional wedding gig. Eventually I started getting called for better gigs, tours, and recording. My career has slowly built from there and is still building I still love practicing and improving my musicianship so I hope my career just keeps following along."

Miller has led or co-led several bands, including Emma with singer/songwriter Erin McKeown; Tilt with pianist Taylor Eigsti and bassist Jon Evans; and Agrazing Maze with trumpeter Ingrid Jensen, pianist Enrique Haneine, and bassist Carlo DeRosa. Miller's music was also featured in the Showtime network series *The L Word.* The U.S. State Department chose her to tour East Africa, Eurasia, and Southeast Asia as a Jazz Ambassador.

As a Jazz Ambassador, she said her most memorable experiences revolved around collaborating with professional musicians from each culture. "I love the sound of mixing jazz with other genres from around the world. Music is truly a universal language and we were able to communicate with each other even though we did not speak the same language."

Her second solo album *Boom Tic Boom* was released by Foxhaven Records in March 2010. The album pays homage to and is inspired by all the important women in Miller's life.

Miller also produced the critically acclaimed children's album *Ask the Planet* in 2009. The album uses song to educate children about respecting the environment and learning from nature's plan.

Recently she has toured with her band Boom Tic Boom and also with Dr. Lonnie Smith, Ben Allison, Todd Sickafoose, and her collective trio Honey Ear. She has also recorded and toured with mainstream artists such as Brandi Carlile, Ani DiFranco, Norah Jones, and Natalie Merchant.

Miller founded the Walter Salb Memorial Musical Scholarship Foundation in 2008 to honor her former teacher and mentor. The foundation provides promising young musicians monetary awards to further their study in music. She is also active as a teacher and holds an adjunct position at Kutztown University as well as giving lessons and master classes at schools throughout the United States.

"I'd like to say that putting music into the world is my greatest contribution," she said, "but my gut tells me that teaching is actually my greatest contribution."

She says she takes her teaching very seriously and is committed to passing on the tradition of jazz.

Miller and her drumming skills have been featured in a number of publications, including *Down Beat*, *Jazz Times*, *Modern Drummer*, *Tom Tom*, and *Female Musician*.

She says as a female drummer, she's experienced many of the same challenges that many women pursuing careers face. "There is a general misconception that during the feminist movement women yesterday paved the way for women today and that we are now navigating the world with quality. It is true that they did good work, but that work is unfortunately not finished and that fight is still alive and well—just more hidden and harder to tackle because the feminist movement is a thing of the past." An avowed feminist, she says she is always fighting for equality. "Equality for all. I am pro-choice and an environmentalist."

Miller says she loves improvising and playing with other musicians. "Enthusiastic audiences inspire me and give me energy. I love it when a bunch of people are packed into a small room to hear live music. It doesn't get any better. I am also addicted to endorphins that get released when I play music."

Her advice to young aspiring female drummers: "Practice hard and love what you do. Stay true to yourself. Stay curious and open to new influences."

And from her own musical experiences, she's learned these lessons: "Listen to others. Simplicity is best. Space is the place."

Susie Ibarra

Suzie Ibarra is considered a leader for her work in free jazz, avant-garde, world, and new music. She's known for her collaborations and recordings with classical, world, and indigenous musicians. She is also active as a composer, educator, and documentary filmmaker in the United States, Philippines, and internationally.

Born in Anaheim, California, and raised in Houston, Texas, Ibarra was the daughter of physicians who emigrated from the Philippines. The youngest of five children, she began playing piano at age four and in grade school sang in school and church choirs. In high school, she joined a punk rock band. She became interested in jazz while a student at Sarah Lawrence College in the late 1980s. According to a biographical sketch by Joslyn Lane, a performance by Sun Ra kindled that spark.

She received a degree from New York City's Mannes College of Music and then continued studies at Goddard College. Teachers who influenced her included jazz drummers Vernel Fournier, Earl Buster Smith, Milford Graves, and Denis Charles who had weekly duo sessions with Ibarra for the few years before his death in 1998. A live recording of the duo, *Drum Talk*, was released that year on the Wobbly Rail label. Ibarra also studied and performed in Balinese and Javanese gamelan and Philippine kulintang ensembles.

She began establishing a reputation as a leading free jazz drummer when she moved to New York City in the early '90s and joined the Little Huey Creative Music Orchestra led by William Parker. She and her trap kit were also part of Parker's In Order to Survive quartet group. On Parker's recommendation, she took the drum chair in David S. Ware's Quartet in 1996, replacing Whit Dickey who went on to form his own trio. She performed and toured in the United States and Europe with the Ware quartet and was the featured drummer on three of their critically acclaimed albums. She also played with the Matthew Shipp Trio, which included the same lineup as the Ware quartet, minus Ware.

In 1998, Ibarra was named Best New Talent of the Year by *Jazziz Magazine*. The next year she started her own label, Hopscotch, with her husband, saxophonist Assif Tsahar. The duo toured to support Hopscotch's first release *Home Cookin'*. In 1999, Ibarra started her own trio with pianist Cooper Moore and violinist Charles Burnham. Their first recording *Radiance* was released that same year.

She was named Best Percussionist in the 2010 *Down Beat* International Readers Poll and Best Percussionist, Rising Star in the 2009 *Down Beat* Critics Poll. She has made the cover of *Tom Tom* and *Modern Drummer* magazines and continues to win widespread acclaim for her groundbreaking work.

Sherrie Maricle

No wonder Sherrie Maricle has been called "the miracle worker of music." In between performing, composing, and teaching, Maricle also finds time to lead the fifteen-piece Diva Jazz Orchestra, Diva Jazz Trio, and her quintet Five Play. Not only has she mastered the art of multi-tasking, her ability behind a drum set has been described as "contained fury of the power plant of a nuclear submarine" (divajazz.com).

Maricle and her three bands have performed throughout the United States and abroad in diverse venues: Carnegie Hall, the Hollywood Bowl, Playboy Jazz Festival, and on S.S. Norway and QE2 jazz cruises. She has performed at jazz festivals throughout Europe and has toured overseas annually with the New York Pops in countries such as Japan and Korea. She has toured Europe with the Oliver Jones Trio, Japan and Vietnam with Five Play, and Switzerland with The Diva Jazz Trio.

The Diva Jazz Orchestra, which celebrated its twentieth year in 2013, has been featured on *CBS Sunday Morning* with Charles Osgood and was part of the Kennedy Center Twenty-Fifth Anniversary Celebration in Washington, DC. In 2009, the Diva Jazz Trio was on Marian McPartland's NPR show, *Piano Jazz*, and recently the Diva Jazz Orchestra was prominently featured in the documentary, *The Girls in the Band.* The renowned jazz group has also performed with top artists such as Nancy Wilson, Diane Schuur, Maurice Hines, Marlena Shaw, and Carmen Bradford.

In between Diva, Five Play, and trio gigs, Maricle is also music director and drummer for Maurice Hines and the director of education and drummer for The New York Pops. She also composes and arranges in both classical and jazz mediums, is a sought-after clinician, operates a private drum set and percussion studio, and keeps busy as a freelance performer.

A native of Buffalo, New York, Maricle took up drums in sixth grade after trying two other instruments. In fourth grade, she really wanted to play the trumpet, but her music teacher told her "girls don't play trumpets" and gave her a clarinet instead. That didn't suit the young musician, so she switched to cello. When she discovered the school band needed someone to play the bass drum, she volunteered.

"When I was eleven, I saw Buddy Rich and his Killer Force Orchestra and immediately KNEW that I was going to be a drummer for the rest of my life," she said. "I instantly loved jazz from the moment I heard it—as most jazz musicians would say—it is a passion that finds you. Of course, I dealt with various gender-related issues, but it never stopped me for a second. When you are passionate about something and pursue it with your heart, you can't go wrong."

When Maricle was sixteen, she got to play with Slam Stewart and made her first professional recording with Slam in 1986. She worked her way through college, playing drums for choirs, musical theatre, jazz bands, the Ice Capades, the circus, etc. She also performed in local wedding bands and during the summers played with local jazz groups in parks in upstate New York.

After earning a bachelor's degree in 1985 from Binghamton University, she moved to New York City where she completed her master's and doctorate at New York University. During that time she formed another wedding band with her boyfriend to pay the bills.

In a 2004 *New York Times* interview with Chris Hedges, she tells how the song "The Bride Cuts the Cake," played to the tune of "The Farmer in the Dell," finally broke her. After pounding it out for fifteen minutes at a wedding, she threw her sticks down in disgust and walked to the bar, thinking, "Why am I doing this?"

Fortunately, she didn't give up drums altogether, much to the benefit of the jazz world and music, in general. In particular, she has been an inspiration and role model for young girls, many of whom have gone up to her after performances and told her she's changed their lives.

Maricle has received numerous awards for her achievements such as the Mary Lou Williams Lifetime Achievement Award from The Kennedy Center in 2009, a tour grant from Arts International, The Kennedy Center Alliance Award for Outstanding Achievements in the Arts, and being named New York University Music "Teacher of the Year" in 1997 and 2000. However, among all her accomplishments she is particularly proud of the formation of The DIVA Jazz Orchestra and being the first woman drummer-leader of an internationally acclaimed concert jazz orchestra.

Her inspiration for an all-female jazz band came from her manager Stanley Kay, a former drummer who managed Buddy Rich and a person she considers a mentor. At first she was wary of Kay's idea. As quoted in the *Times* interview, "I was not going to form a band where we all wore miniskirts and showed our cleavage—especially since mine is not impressive to begin with. The few women swing bands in the past had to do this, performing in long strapless evening gowns. I knew a lot of serious women jazz musicians who wanted a chance to play. This was the only thing that interested me."

In another interview with Eric Harabadian in *Jazz Inside Magazine*, Maricle addressed the female aspect of her band. "In general, it's a cliché, but people listen with their eyes first. And yes, we still have crazy experiences of people being skeptical, perhaps disrespectful, until they hear the band play. . . . One of my favorite reviews we ever got was from the late '90s. The headline was 'The last thing I wanted to do on a Saturday night was go and hear a bunch of girls play a watered down version of "In the Mood."' That was the headline and then underneath it, it said 'Boy, was I wrong!'"

Maricle is also known for her longtime association with The New York Pops, which started in May 1990 when she was working as a pickup drummer for the twenty-fifth anniversary of the Schubert Theatre in New Haven, Connecticut. "Skitch Henderson was the conductor. At the end of the show I thanked him for the experience, and he asked if I would come play/audition for The New York Pops. I was so thrilled and, of course, said, yes. I've been there ever since."

As a teacher, Maricle said her major goal was to "make sure my students are equipped to make a living in music." She also wants her students to benefit from her "passion for teaching and sharing American music and straight ahead jazz—to share and make listeners and students walk away with an excellent musical experience."

On the DIVA Jazz Orchestra website, Maricle's bio states that her "drum set is a real-life metaphor for her career." To quote the bio: "Just as playing the drums requires coordinating four limbs at the same time, Maricle's career coordinates successes as a jazz artist, composer, teacher, and music director." As a musician, she has played the balancing act well and has won the respect and admiration of peers and fans worldwide.

"If you are fortunate enough to make music (or whatever you do) for a living," she said, "go into each situation with the desire to give your very best for the benefit of everyone involved—aka 'play well with others.' The music is bigger than the individuals in a group . . . serve the music."

CHAPTER 20

Drummers of a Different Beat

> To play an instrument is one thing. To function as a musician is something else.
>
> —Dame Evelyn Glennie

While previous chapters have focused on women notable for their mastery of the drum set in popular music idioms, a few drummers known for their work mostly outside that realm are worthy of note. They are respected worldwide for their musicianship and are role models for female drummers and percussionists, no matter the genre.

Dame Evelyn Glennie

Certainly in this category is Dame Evelyn Glennie, the first person—male or female—in musical history to successfully create and sustain a full-time career as a solo percussionist. As a world-class performer and teacher, she has inspired millions with her extraordinary contributions to the percussive arts.

Glennie presents more than one hundred performances annually and has worked with some of the world's greatest orchestras and conductors in more than forty countries on five continents. She has demonstrated her versatility in collaborations with diverse artists such as Bjork, Bela Fleck, Bobby McFerrin, Sting, Emmanuel Ax, DJ Yoda, beat boxer Schlomo, and the Mormon Tabernacle Choir. She was a featured solo performer at the 2002 Winter Olympics in Salt Lake City and in July 2012 took a starring role in the Opening Ceremony for the London Olympics. Her performance there with one thousand drummers performing an original composition with Underworld was the musical climax of that event. It also provided the opportunity for her to debut a new instrument, the aluphone, described as a cross between a vibraphone, gamelan, and tubular bells.

Glennie is a double Grammy award winner and composes and records music for film and television. She is also the leading commissioner of over 170 new works for solo percussion.

The fact that she is profoundly deaf and has never viewed her hearing impairment as an obstacle makes this all the more amazing. In her Hearing Essay, which appears on her website, she states: "My hearing is something that bothers other people far more than it bothers me. . . . For me my deafness is no more important than the fact I am female with brown eyes."

Glennie was born July 19, 1965, in Aberdeen, Scotland. She is the youngest of three children and the only daughter. As a child raised in a rural farming community, she enjoyed Scottish country dancing. Her father played accordion in a Scottish country dance band, and music was part of the family's social life. There was no music store, so repertoire, she said, was rather limited to compositions mostly for violin and piano.

Introduced to music at age five, her first instruments were the mouth organ, piano, and clarinet. At the age of twelve, she heard the school orchestra play, was fascinated by the percussion section, and began playing tympani. At age sixteen, she was accepted into the Royal Academy of Music in London from which she graduated at age nineteen. Her family was supportive, although, like most parents of children bent on pursuing careers in music, they told her, "You might want to consider another profession." She said they also realized they were dealing with "a very stubborn individual."

At the Royal Academy, she studied with Nicholas Cole, the principal percussionist for the Royal Philharmonic Orchestra. She also met distinguished percussionist the late James Blades, who became a mentor, encouraged her to explore new ideas, and convinced her that she could become a solo percussionist. Among the numerous honors she's received over the years, she said being awarded the James Blades Prize twice and being the first percussionist to receive that honor is high on that list.

She is also quick to point out that every honor bestowed on her was significant at the time she received it. "When you're a youngster and get an award, it's an amazing thing," she said. "Every accomplishment is a building block. It's important to realize an award is by no means an end."

Unlike the case for many women drummers and percussionists, gender has never been a problem for Glennie. "Since I am a solo player and playing in an orchestra wasn't my main intent, being a woman has never been an issue. If there was an issue, it was being accepted as a solo percussionist."

Considering the scope of her work—and in a relatively short timeframe—she's obviously met that challenge. Not only is she the first full-time solo percussionist in the world, her eclectic and innovative approaches have redefined the world of percussive performance.

In 2007, Glennie became the first percussionist to be awarded the Dame Commander of the British Empire. She is also the youngest person ever elected to the Percussive Arts Society Hall of Fame. She was named Scotswoman of the Decade in 1990 and Musical America's Instrumentalist of the Year in 2003. She is the recipient of more than twenty honorary doctorates and close to ninety international awards.

IMPORTANCE OF BALANCE

Balance is important in Glennie's life as a musician. She says just as one doesn't eat twenty-four hours a day, a musician also has to take a break. Just as important as listening to the music is "listening to yourself, to find out what your own voice is saying."

She stresses the importance of learning how to allocate time to have energy to do other things. Glennie says she's also learned from her experience as a musician that it's important to be organized, reliable, and to aim at certain standards. "It gives you a sense of confidence that when something doesn't work, you've done all you could, and the situation is simply beyond your control."

As part of keeping balance in her own life, Glennie is involved in a number of activities both in and outside music. She has her own jewelry line now, inspired by percussion and her childhood love of trinkets. She is a sought after motivational speaker. According to the "Facts" section of her website, she has taken flying lessons and rides a motorbike. In 2010, she reached the summit of Mount Kilimanjaro in Tanzania to support a charity, Able Child Africa. She's an avid collector not only of percussion instruments (over 1,800) but modes of transport such as unicycles and electric scooters, bells, music boxes, masks, incense holders, to name a few. She's an avid gardener and enjoys exploring antique fairs. She plays the bagpipes. Her list of future things to do includes learning to dance the mambo and doing a rap concerto with Eminem. Another interesting fact, gleaned from Glennie's website, is that as a teen, she wanted to be a hairdresser. Fortunately for all who have experienced her extraordinary talent, the beauty industry's loss was the music world's gain.

Glennie is also an enthusiastic and active advocate for music education and deplores the fact that many schools no longer have orchestras and that in many cases parents have to pay for their children's instruments and lessons. She believes every child should be given the opportunity in school to learn at least one instrument free of charge. She spearheaded a consortium with James Galway,

Andrew Lloyd Webber, and the late Michael Kamen to raise 332 million pounds for music education in the United Kingdom.

Her advice for young women who aspire to be professional drummers or percussionists is to "Go after your dream. Get your head down and focus. Make sure you practice the art of creating your own opportunities. No one else will do it for you. Get yourself out there. Work hard. To play an instrument is one thing. To function as a musician is something else."

Ikue Mori

Electronic percussionist Ikue Mori is considered a pioneer in creating radical rhythms and dissonant sounds that have played a major role in altering the face of rock music. Mori was born in Tokyo and moved to New York in 1977. At the time she had no musical experience or interest other than listening to punk rock.

Her first attempt at playing drums came when she joined guitarist Arto Lindsay and bassist Tim Wright in the seminal no wave band DNA. DNA enjoyed legendary cult status for its radical rhythms and dissonant sounds. As drummer for the group, Mori quickly won critical praise for her distinctive style and was lauded for being a master of asymmetrical rhythm and one of the best free jazz drummers of that time.

DNA disbanded in 1982 and Mori became part of New York's experimental music scene, abandoning her drum set for drum machines. Again critics praised her creativity, and one, Adam Strohm, wrote in a 2004 review that she "founded a new world for the instrument, taking it far beyond backing rhythms and robotic fills." The '90s found her collaborating with improvisers throughout the United States, Europe, and Asia to produce and record her own music.

In 1995, she and Japanese guitarist Kata Hideki from Ground Zero and Fred Frith from Henry Cow formed the experimental music trio Death Ambient. Death Ambient recorded three albums, the last *Drunken Forest* in 2007.

In 2000, Mori replaced the drum machines with her laptop computer to further expand her experiments in musical expression. She has won numerous awards and grants for her innovative works and bases many of her compositions on inspiration from the visual arts.

In addition to her solo recordings, she has recorded and performed with Dave Douglas, Butch Morris, Kim Gordon, Thurston Moore, Hemophiliac, and John Zorn's Electric Masada. Mori has also recorded and toured as part of the duo Phantom Orchard with rock harpist Zeena Parkins.

Vera Figueiredo

Vera Figueiredo has been called the drumming Queen of Samba. Indeed, she is one of Brazil's most active ambassadors for its culture and music. She has toured in Scotland, Northern Ireland, England, Wales, Mexico, Chile, Italy, Luxemburg, Spain, Portugal, Sweden, Argentina, Australia, Canada, and the United States, performing in concerts and festivals and leading workshops and master classes. T. Bruce Wittet wrote in *Modern Drummer* of her performance at the Montreal Drum Fest: "From behind the drum set, Vera Figueiredo took the audience from the Brazilian rainforest into the clubs and concert halls of the world. Jaws dropped at her unique presence, approach, and distinctive licks" (verafigueiredo.com).

In 1990, she founded the Instituto de Bateria Vera Figueiredo, a much respected drum set institute located in Sao Paulo and the host of the annual Batuka! Brazil International Drum Festival.

Her discography includes three solo records, including the critically acclaimed *Vera Cruz Island* (Rainbow Records).

She has released a DVD with instructional videos on Afro-Brazilian and Afro-Cuban drumming and also appears in *The Ultimate Drummers Weekend 11th Birthday* DVD, playing with Thomas Lang, John Blackwell, Jr., Jimmy DeGrasso, Andrew Gander, Gustavo Meli, and other world class drummers.

Figueiredo has her own band and also plays with The Banda Altas Horas, featured on the *Altas Horas* television show on the Globo Brazilian television network.

Caroline Corr

Caroline Corr is the Irish drummer and singer for the popular Celtic folk rock band The Corrs. The group consists of Caroline and her siblings Andrea, Sharon, and Jim. In addition to drums, Caroline also plays the bodhran and piano.

Music was very much a part of the Corr household as both parents were musicians and had their own band. Caroline and her siblings were all taught piano by their father and grew up traveling to gigs on weekends with their parents along Ireland's east coast.

When the Corrs formed in 1990, Caroline played piano for the group. She didn't start playing drums until she was seventeen. In a May 2005 *Modern Drummer* interview with Billy Amendola, she said, "I had a boyfriend who played drums, and he had a band room next door to where we were making our music at the time. He was a big U2 fan and he loved Larry Mullen. He showed me a few beats, and I just kind of got into it and started playing. The next thing I knew I was on tour playing drums and going, 'Oh my God!'"

The Corrs had never used a drummer, but because Caroline took to it so naturally, they decided it would be a good thing for the group. "I was kind of thrown in the deep end. But that wasn't a bad thing when I look back at it."

The Corrs first performed as a band when they auditioned to play in the musical film *The Commitments* in 1991. The film's musical director liked the group and became their manager. In 1994, the band signed with Atlantic Records. To date, they have sold over thirty million albums. They have performed on *Saturday Night Live* and *The Tonight Show* and have made an MTV "Unplugged" video. They have performed on tour with U2, Celine Dion, and the Rolling Stones. Mick Jagger commented, "They blew us, the Stones, off our own stage."

Caroline said she'd like to see more girls playing drums, but she also believes the number is increasing. In the Amendola interview, she said, "There's really no reason why there shouldn't be more. I think the more women you see playing drums, the more women will think, 'Oh, that's not just a male thing to do.' Sometimes parents want them to play the violin or piano because it's more feminine, and they have this idea that drums are noisy, and 'Let's not have them in the house.' I don't like that attitude," she said. "Male or female—if you want to play drums, go for it!"

Layne Redmond

Layne Redmond was never in a commercially successful pop, rock, or jazz band, but that didn't keep *DRUM!* magazine from naming her one of the fifty-three "Heavyweight Drummers Who Made a Difference in the '90s." She was the only woman on a list that included Tony Williams, Roy Haynes, Zakir Hussain, Elvin Jones, and Mickey Hart.

Redmond, who died from cancer in October 2013, created a niche for herself as one of the world's foremost authorities on the small hand-held frame drum played primarily by women in the ancient Mediterranean world. She was a known scholar on the subject, and her book *When the Drummers Were Women* is considered the definitive history of the frame drum in religious and cultural rituals.

She performed and was a master clinician and lecturer at percussion festivals around the world. Her numerous accolades include being named *DRUM!* magazine's Percussionist of the Year in their 2002 Readers' Poll. In that same poll her recording *Trance Union* was named in best percussion album of the year and her video *Rhythmic Wisdom* was named percussion video of the year. In 2003, *Trance*

Union was once again recognized as best percussion recording, and in 2005 her album *Invoking the Muse* took that honor.

Julie Hill

Percussionist and teacher Dr. Julie Hill is a firm believer in the transforming power of music. She's seen firsthand how through music one can do anything.

Dr. Hill is considered one of the world's foremost experts in Brazilian percussion. As a member of the renowned Caixa Percussion Trio, she has performed in France, Brazil, Korea, Mexico, and Puerto Rico.

She is an associate professor of percussion at the University of Tennessee-Martin and a sought after lecturer and clinician. She is one of the few women to ever serve on the executive board of the Percussive Arts Society. She also serves on the international advisory board for Escola Dida, a project in Salvador de Bahia, Brazil, dedicated to social transformation for Black women and at-risk children through music.

Hill said her musical journey started at about age four when she went to hear her older brother playing clarinet in a sixth grade concert. She recalls two things from that experience: "One, I couldn't hear my brother playing anything by himself as part of the clarinet section; and two, when the high school band played their part of the concert, the sound of the chimes was glorious, and I could certainly see who was playing them."

She said by the time she was in sixth grade and had been taking piano lessons, she knew she wanted something that was a little more "special." In her mind that was "one person on a part, playing a variety of things, and, of course, being the only girl in the section." Naturally, that attracted her to playing percussion.

Her mom, however, wanted her to play the piccolo or flute. "I remember her saying, "Honey, you can put that flute in your purse," and I said, "But, Mom, then I would have to PLAY the flute." Hill already had an inkling then that she was "good at this rhythmic stuff" after she was picked out of the entire fourth grade to play the tambourine in a school musical. "Positive reinforcement at a young age and done publically is very powerful," she said. "We were always struggling for money as a family, but I remember my mom and Grandma took me out to buy some fancy knickers at the nice store in town for that performance so I would feel as proud of my clothes as my playing for my big debut. That was special for me."

After her "big debut," Hill eventually went on to study percussion and earn her bachelor's, master's, and doctoral degrees in music.

Along the way she became fascinated with Brazilian percussion. "A Brazilian presence came into my life multiple times, and I eventually decided to pay attention," she said. "I was always the kind of kid that befriended the exchange students in school. A Brazilian named Jorge was her first junior high boyfriend. She said after completing her undergraduate degree in 1994, she went to graduate school at Arizona State University. "I was only twenty-two and didn't know a soul anywhere in the state. This was before cell phones and Internet, and, frankly, I was a little scared and perhaps a bit homesick." She said Caio Pagano, a Brazilian, was teaching piano at Arizona State University, and he had brought many of his students with him from Sao Paulo. One of those students befriended Julie and pretty soon, she was listening to Brazilian music, learning Portuguese phrases, and hanging out with the Brazilians.

"I really started to expand my curiosity and knowledge of all Afro-Cuban, Afro-Caribbean, and Afro-Brazilian music styles as I had little training in non–classical-based percussion as an undergraduate. This really was where I began to get very hungry about world music styles, and it turned out to be the start of a lifelong pursuit in the migration of rhythm."

Hill said when she finished the master of music program at Arizona State University, she moved back to rural West Tennessee. Her mother was seriously ill, so Hill got a job as a band director to be close to her. "Here I was in a mostly agrarian region with lots of 'rednecks,' but there were all sorts of wonderfully hungry percussion students." She said one of her star students, a seventh grader named Davy Anderson, to her surprise turned out to be half Brazilian. His mother, Josephina, chaperoned a trip to the Percussive Arts Society International Conference in Orlando, and Hill and she became "instant best friends." Hill started learning the language and was invited to tag along on the Andersons' annual family trip to Brazil.

It was then she realized this was too much good luck to be coincidence so she started listening and began to focus on Northeastern Brazilian music. She recalls on her first trip to Brazil, they went to Salvador da Bahia where she hoped to see and hear the noted samba percussion group Olodum. "They were not in town the week that we were there," Hill said, "but I had the good luck of following my ears and came across Banda Dida, an all-female bloco Afro. This was one of the biggest 'pay attention' moments of my life. I just remember seeing beautiful women playing the grooviest, most infectious patterns I could imagine and dancing on cobblestone streets in the rain for hours until they stopped." She said that motivated her to move forward researching music from Bahia, Brazil, while also exploring the transformative power of music, which was "present, it seemed, everywhere I turned in Salvador."

As for her involvement with the Caixa Percussion Trio, Hill said it started when she moved to Nashville to "make it big" with the band 27 B Stroke 6. "We had some big shows, but all of us had to have day jobs to make ends meet," Hill said. For Hill that included band directing at a middle school in Murfreesboro and teaching high school percussion. Her friend and fellow percussionist Julie Davila was working in the same area. Hill said the two were commiserating on a long bus trip together how much they missed playing. Another percussionist Amy Smith happened to be living in Murfreesboro because her husband was in a graduate program at Middle Tennessee State University studying with Davila's husband, Lalo.

She said "it was easy and a no-brainer" that the three women got together even though in the beginning it was difficult to find time to practice. The trio started rehearsing after drum line rehearsals on Monday evening. "We would start late and get up early for our jobs the next day, but we loved it. We were hooked and decided to make it official. We are musically 'married,' and will be a trio as long as we can. Those girls are my sisters in so many ways."

As a teacher, Hill says her major goal is to inspire her students to be "life learners, ones that are open and not afraid of anything new that comes their way." After all, she said, "music helps make the world a little less scary, and it is so powerful and important. It has integrated societies and transformed generations with the ability to bring people together. If a little of my spirit with regard to music and social transformation has rubbed off on them, that would make me happy, too. I might teach a few hundred students in my career, but if they, in turn, take this same spirit with them in their own teaching and it is passed down, exponentially, we can really make a difference."

As for the transforming power of music in her own life, she said: "I am a girl from a rural town in West Tennessee from a family of little means. How did I end up having the confidence to explore a career in music at all, much less, become someone who would travel to Brazil alone multiple times and study music in a culture very foreign to my own in another language? This is the power of music, too. Hard work practice, discipline, and integrity are always recognized and it doesn't matter the background if you have the perseverance. Through music we can do anything."

Alessandra Belloni

Tambourine virtuoso Alessandra Belloni has been lauded as one of the world's best percussionists by *The New York Times*, *Los Angeles Times*, and *DRUM!* magazine. She is the artistic director, founder, and lead performer of "I Guillari di Piazza," an Italian music, theatre, and dance ensemble, and has been artist-in-residence at the Cathedral of St. John the Divine in New York City since 1993.

Belloni is the only woman in the United States and Italy who specializes in traditional Southern Italian folk dances and percussion.

A singer, dancer, and actress, Belloni has devoted her career to preserving her Italian cultural heritage. Belloni, a native of Rome, Italy, grew up listening to her grandfather playing the snare drum, mandolin, and tambourine. However, it wasn't until she was in her early twenties and was living in the United States that she became interested in the music that was so much a part of her childhood. "In the late '70s I met a group of talented Italian musicians and an amazing tambourine player from Sicily, Alfio Antico."

She said that inspired her to form a company specializing in Southern Italian folk music and dance, and she went back to Italy to do research, mostly learning "from the old people in the fields." She said her parents loved rock 'n' roll and she herself was into rock 'n' roll "big time," so they were a little surprised at this new musical interest.

The noted percussionist started out as a singer and actress. She said that experience taught her the value of incorporating theatre and "show" in every performance. "There must be a sequence and choreography in every performance. You must tell a story to the audience."

She said living in New York and being surrounded by people of different ethnic backgrounds also influenced her as an artist, as evidenced in her work, which combines Southern Italian, Native American, African, and Brazilian percussive styles along with a drum set here and there.

Over more than three decades, Belloni has established her reputation as one of the top performers in world music. Her recordings have been universally lauded. *DRUM!* magazine named her 2003 recording *Tarantelle & Canti D'amore* the second best percussion CD of the year. *Tarantata: The Dance of Ancient Spider* won that magazine's Best World Percussion CD of the Year in 2002. It was also nominated as one of the best CDs of the year by Jon Parales from *The New York Times* and Dan Hackman from the *Los Angeles Times*.

DRUM! named her one of three runners-up with Babatunde Olatunji and Mickey Hart to Arthur Hull in the New Age/Worldbeat Percussionist category in their 1998 awards.

She has performed with master drummer Glen Velez and was invited by Nana Vasconcelos and Gilberto Gil to perform in PERC PAN '98 in Brazil. She's also collaborated with Rick Allen, drummer for Def Leppard, and other world famous percussionists such as Gordon Gottlieb at Julliard.

A performance at Peter Gabriel's WOMAD festival in Seattle in 2001 was particularly memorable. "I led the jam and couldn't stop." Fortunately, the audience loved every minute, she said.

She also recalls a performance at a festival in Brazil where she had to be literally "pushed onstage because I was so nervous. It was the hardest thing I've ever done—complete improvisation, and I didn't have a clue what to do." She said she then remembered the advice of a mentor, "Relax, close your eyes, and listen to your heart."

"I started playing the samba, which I had never done before and it really worked. I got a standing ovation. Now every time I get nervous, I go back to that moment."

Belloni also leads workshops, which focus on the healing power of rhythm and dance. She says she has seen firsthand the healing power of the drum especially with young women who have been abused.

"I feel like I am tapping into something in our collective memory," she said, "back to the ancient tradition of women priestesses in different cultures. Whenever I perform, I try to make a connection to the divine."

Conclusion: Not by a Long Shot!

The battle is still on.

—Carla DeSantis Black

A website that will go unnamed posts numerous sexy photos of women drummers with the caption: "One of the great mysteries of life is why chick drummers are so cool." The implication, of course, is that they're cool because they're sexy. The drummers are not given the respect of being identified by name, and nothing is noted of their musical skill.

For all the progress they've made over more than a century and especially over the last three decades, women drummers are still fighting for deserved recognition. In the ever-changing world of popular music where females often dominate as vocalists, women drummers are still considered a novelty. Despite the many contributions they've made to music and their proven ability to match the chops of their male counterparts, the female drummer is still too often a victim of sexism in the music industry. To paraphrase one female drummer, in the corporate world, employers can be legally forced to hire the most qualified—not so in music where personal preference still rules.

Even Phil Hood, publisher of *DRUM!* magazine admits that even though it's been talked about more lately, the amount of coverage given to women drummers in his publication over the last few years hasn't increased substantially. He did say the magazine had covered a "decent number of women who were highly visible drummers such as Sheila E., Cindy Blackman, Samantha Maloney, and Stephanie Eulinberg."

"I think there are just a lot of great male drummers in the history of the instrument," Hood said. "Women drummers were so rare as to be considered unusual up until the '80s and '90s. What I see changing now is that the overall percentage of young women drummers is rising. And students, too. Guitar Center says that 23 percent of all their students are women. I think it's higher for a lot of teachers of drums and other instruments."

A Drumming Sisterhood

Hood said male responses to and opinions about women drummers ran the gamut from supportive to stupid. "Drummers have always been a brotherhood, and I think drumming can be a sisterhood, too. A lot of people think drumming is masculine-oriented, because it's physical. But I've never seen a situation where a woman didn't have enough strength to drum. It's really about technique. And I see a lot of women who have a sort of feminine techniques on drums—they can be loud if they want or soft and sensitive, which is really more difficult in a lot of ways. That's a great skill," Hood said.

Heather Smith, managing editor of *Drumhead* magazine, said her publication doesn't specialize in women drummers, "but we do cover them—as we cover all drummers." She said the magazine's coverage of women drummers has not increased or decreased over time. "We are a bi-monthly publication and cover great drummers who are brought to our attention and who our writers choose to feature, without bias."

Smith said her magazine has featured Cindy Blackman (before Santana), Stella Mozgawa from Mink, and Skillet's Jen Ledger. "Top on my list," she said, "is Kid Rock's Stefanie Eulinberg; she's a force to be reckoned with who has one of the fattest grooves in rock today. Young Hannah Ford is sure moving and shaking as well."

Mike Dawson, managing editor of *Modern Drummer*, said: "While there has been a noticeable increase in female drummers in all areas of music, we feature artists in our products solely based on playing and career achievements. That said, we've had several female drummers on the cover of our magazine over the years: Sheila E., Terri Lyne Carrington, Nikki Glaspie, Kim Thompson, and Cindy Blackman."

Changing Attitudes or Status Quo

Numerous women drummers who were interviewed for this book are optimistic that attitudes toward the female drummer are changing, especially among the younger generation. There's more acceptance, simply based on the fact that more and more females are visible now as drummers, thanks not only to live performance but social media, YouTube, and other Internet sources. There's no doubt that since the female band explosion of the 1970s, people have grown more accustomed to seeing a woman behind a drum kit.

Renee Solano, a drummer in the Boston band Sans Nomenclature, in a July 2011 interview with music journalist Bill Copeland, said discrimination still happens all the time. "To your face they're really nice and polite, and they'll go behind your back and hire somebody who's not half as good as you." Solano, who also teaches, says some parents won't let their children study with her because she's a female. On the other hand, she says with all the students she's taught, it will "reach a point that when a girl drums they won't even blink."

Numerous female drummers cited discrimination in being chosen as road musicians. They said that most male bands find having a woman around is awkward, especially if she might report certain incidents of indiscriminate behavior to wives and girlfriends at home.

Others said being a female sometimes gave them an edge in being chosen for gigs. They cited female drummers such Sheila E. and Cindy Blackman who paved the way by drumming for big stars such as Prince and Lenny Kravitz. Beyoncé, too, deserves credit for using female drummers in her bands.

Dawn Richardson, who played with 4 Non Blondes, said it was hard to know if it would have been easier if she had been male. "I feel that our culture does have certain expectations of us in regards to male/female roles, and playing the drums is still a male-dominated field. So there are times when the concept of having a woman on the kit is just not in the spectrum. I think that we are in the midst of changing times, though. There are so many women doing things that were once traditionally reserved for men. I have hope for more equality in every facet of our society."

Rock Camps

Every summer, thousands of girls, aged ten to sixteen, enroll in rock 'n' roll camps, where they not only learn about music but also about female empowerment, including self-defense. Most of these camps grew out of a 2000 project by Misty McElroy, a women's studies major at Portland State University. As a musician, McElroy had experienced gender discrimination and wanted to encourage girls to start their own bands. The first camp was held in Portland in August 2001. Girls Rock camps are now held at over forty sites in North America and seven European countries.

An alliance of Girls Rock camp leaders has been organized, and a documentary about the camps called *Girls Rock* was released in 2008, along with a book by that same name. At the camps, girls get to pick their instruments, learn basic chords and drum beats, and put on a concert. All the instructors are women.

Terri Lord, Austin drummer and former volunteer for the Girls Rock camp in Austin who now runs the Terri Lord Badass School of Rock, says she thinks an important aspect of such camps is teaching collaboration as part of the musical experience. "Everyone works together. Everyone has to share in the writing of a song." She said this all-inclusive participation of every band member in the creative process also helped to destroy the prevailing "caveman mentality" prejudice against drummers in general—male and female.

Rock camps are also sprouting up for the "older" woman. Sara McCabe shares her experience of taking the proverbial plunge and enrolling in Ladies Rock Camp in Boston. "I've wanted to play drums since I was a kid," McCabe said, "but always talked myself out of it because it was too loud, too masculine, too juvenile, too embarrassing to start as an adult, or too whatever-was-my-hangup-at-the-time. So I played a variety of other instruments that were more socially acceptable. Then at age forty-seven, I went to Ladies Rock Camp Boston, and the 'socially acceptable' voices in my head were replaced in a matter of hours with the voices of dozens of women shouting 'I rock!'—the unofficial camp motto."

McCabe says she now has her own electronic drum kit. "OK," she confesses, "I'm still worried a little about too loud." Her goal is to lead a band as the drummer by the time she turns fifty. "We may play nothing but free gigs at senior centers, but I'll still be rocking my way into the sunset with no regrets!"

YouTube is also doing its part to inspire women of all ages to become part of the drumming sisterhood. For instance, sixty-three-year-old Mary Hvizda, who was known for a time as the "mystery grandma drummer," became a YouTube sensation in July 2013 when a music store in LaCross, Wisconsin, caught her on video, twirling her sticks and putting on a show that got 3.5 million views in less than a week. Later, it was learned Hvizda had honed her drumming skills in her own rock band, the Chantelles, in the '60s.

Tom Tom

At least one publication is doing all it can to promote the cause for females and their drum kits: *Tom Tom* magazine, a publication exclusively devoted to women drummers. Founded by Mindy Seegal Abovitz in 2009, the inspiration for the magazine was to "effectively change Google search results when searching the terms, 'woman drummer,' 'girl drummer,' or 'female drummer' to relevant and non-demeaning data and articles."

Abovitz, herself an accomplished drummer, was drawn to the drum set in her early twenties and says she "slowly became obsessed with drums and expressing my feminism through music." After being involved in Rock Camp for Girls and Vibe Songmakers and "setting up tons of shows at my loft in Brooklyn, The Woodser, I decided to try and affect the media in regards to its representation of girl and women drummers. I felt and still feel that the existing media was doing a poor job of accurately representing us."

She said the first issue came together very naturally. "We already had an overwhelming amount of content and photographs. It was just a few of us, and that crew included our original and brilliant designer Candice Ralph."

Abovitz said for the first few years, the writers were almost exclusively female drummers. "This was an attempt at giving as many women drummers as possible exposure. Nowadays we are hiring more and more trained music writers and journalists to tell the stories of the drummers we cover."

Each issue has a theme, and recent ones have included Metal, Orchestra, Drum Corps, and Glamour. Abovitz says the magazine has been its "own hype machine" since day one. "We promote via social media, our own website, events, and word-of-mouth. Occasionally we trade ads with other media sources as well."

Readers of the publication—in both its print and web formats—are from around the world. "Our print readership is distinguished from our web readership essentially by its physical reach. We ship *Tom Tom* to stores and to our subscribers, and that is seeming to be an increasingly archaic process. Yet, we love it," Abovitz says. The only difference in the print and web publications is accessibility. "One is free to the reader with Internet access, and one costs money."

Abovitz said she's learned from experience that the prejudice against women drummers runs deep. "We have a LOT of work to do if we are going to make any changes for the generations to come."

Hit Like a Girl

The Hit Like a Girl Contest, sponsored by *DRUM!* magazine, working with *Tom Tom* and TRX Cymbals, is evidence of positive results of some of the work being done. The contest was conceived in 2011 and launched the first time in 2012 with the aim "to promote, support, and highlight women drummers around the world."

DRUM! publisher Phil Hood said the competition had received "an incredible outpouring of support from the musical products industry and from girls and women of all ages who love to see females succeeding at what has traditionally been an art form associated mostly with males."

Nearly three hundred girls from thirty-five countries participated in the competition in 2013. Entrants were divided into Over 18 and Under 18 categories to provide a better competitive environment for younger girls. "During that time we logged more than 370,000 visitors and 1.9 million impressions," Hood said.

Celebrity judges took over and evaluated twenty popular vote and wild card finalists chosen by sponsors in each category. Judging was based on a combination of technique, style, and personality. "In the end we had three Under 18 winners from the U.S. The Over 18 winner was from Chile, while the runners-up were from Austria and the United States," Hood said.

Judges for the competition have included some of rock's biggest names: Gina Schock (The Go-Go's), Meytal Cohen (independent), Dawn Richardson (4 Non Blondes, Tracy Chapman), Kimberly Thompson (Wallace Roney, Mike Stern), Elaine Bradley (Neon Trees), Jess Bowen (The Summer Set), Hannah Ford (Prince, Bellevue Suite), and Shauney "Baby" Recke (Pussy Cat Dolls, will.i.am).

"We're involved to promote and publicize female drummers worldwide," Hood said. "This drumming contest really celebrates female drummers and also is intended to recognize their contributions to the drumming arts."

MEOW

Carla DeSantis Black has also been a strong advocate for women drummers—in fact, all female musicians—as founder of MEOW (Musicians for Equal Opportunities for Women). Black, a musician, said she "couldn't help notice the stupid comments women got on a regular basis. I knew I couldn't be the only one whose morale was completely shot down because of it. Turns out the 'pretty good for a girl' thing is still alive and well."

In response to the stupid comments, Black started *ROCKRGRL* magazine, the first national publication for female musicians in 1994. Black also organized two *ROCKRGRL* Music Conferences in Seattle in 2000 and 2005 to give women in the music industry a chance to network and show off their talent in music showcases.

"After *ROCKGRL* ended in 2005 I was done," Black said. "Unfortunately the sexism in print only grew online. It was depressing to read comments about female artists from anonymous knuckleheads. Also I moved from Seattle to Austin and thought that continuing on with conferences was a good idea." That led to the founding of MEOW.

"I truly believe that if women are in a room together and see how much we are all having the same discussion in our own genres of music, we can make change happen—in the way STEM programs got women more involved in science, technology, engineering, and math. United, we stand—divided, we fall."

Black said the gender imbalance for women drummers will continue to exist as long as they are a minority and men think it's "cute" to see a female drum. "The more drummers we see and the more they are successful, the less of a novelty it will be."

"I did an issue about women drummers back when I had *ROCKRGRL* magazine and just include them routinely like everyone else in *MEOWgazine*—www.meowonline.org."

"The battle is still on," Black said. "When you see how few women have top slots at music festivals—how radio ghettoizes women as singer/songwriters or 'angry chicks'—lists of hottest chick singers, etc.—it is obvious that the ONLY way this will change is if we work together across all instruments, musical genres, etc., to ensure our survival and economic health."

More Female Students

Julie Hill, associate professor of percussion at the University of Tennessee-Martin, says over the years she's been teaching, she's definitely seen an increase in the number of female students. Her studio is now one-fourth female.

Hill, who is one of the few women to serve on the executive board of the Percussive Arts Society, believes the lack of recognition for female drummers is simply because there are fewer women in the business overall. "You wouldn't want to be singled out as Hall of Fame worthy just because you were a woman. That would really be degrading," Hill said.

"If I was nominated to be on the docket for the Percussive Arts Society executive committee because I was a woman, I think I would quit. I hope that I was chosen because I am good at what I do and dedicated to serving the Percussive Arts Society. I will do so as long as I am needed. I certainly think there will be a natural evolution of incorporating more women in to leadership and distinguished awards in the society as the numbers of females increase as a whole. That's just logic!"

Sherrie Maricle, director of education for the New York Pops, notes there have always been more women studying percussion than drum set. "I primarily teach drum set and I haven't really noticed an increase in the numbers, but I have met a few recent college grads on drums, so maybe there are a few more."

She said the lack of women studying drum set as well as their absence on so many lists of top drummers was a sociological issue. "Those ideals and conventions take ages to change," she said. "As more women continue to do extraordinary things on drums, they will rise to the top—can't be ignored!"

Breakthroughs

As *DRUM!* magazine writer Kristin Bartus said in a 2012 article titled, "A Look at Drumming's Leading Ladies," "It remains to be seen whether the day will come when female musicians will become known simply as musicians, but at the very least the new millennium seems to have brought women more diverse career opportunities."

For example, women are finally breaking into the once all-male and still predominantly male professional steel drum community. Austin's Carolyn Trowbridge shines in gigs as an outstanding pan soloist. She's equally skillful as the standout percussionist and vibes player for the Latin/jazz/funk group KP and the Boom Boom.

Lisa Rogers, the only female to ever serve as president of the Percussive Arts Society, heads the Percussion Studies program at Texas Tech University with Alan Shinn. In addition to being known for her solo work on vibraphone, Rogers also directs the steel band ensemble Apocalypso Now.

Mia Gormandy, who started playing pan in her native Trinidad at age five, teaches steel band at Florida State University. At the time this book went to press, Gormandy, aged twenty-four, was a doctoral student in ethnomusicology but firmly resolved to make steel pan an integral part of her career path.

Still others have carved unique niches for themselves, such as virtuoso Alessandra Belloni, who's become a world authority on Southern Italian folk percussion, and the late Layne Redmond, a specialist on the hand-held frame drum played by women in the ancient Mediterranean world. Redmond's book *When the Drummers Were Women* and her many writings on the subject have established her as a foremost scholar on this topic.

Linda McDonald of Phantom Blue and Iron Maidens says the attitudes toward female drummers today, especially in hard rock and metal genres, are far more accepting and embracing. "Hell, yeah!" she says, There are some girls out there just tearing that stuff up!!"

She points to all the educational avenues available instantly online these days. "With any style of music accessible, the learning curve has just gone off the hook, and girls as well as guys are just advancing at an incredible pace with their drumming in all styles."

Janet Weiss, formerly of Sleater-Kinney, now with Wild Flag, said in *Tom Tom* magazine that she felt non-corporate media such as weeklies, zines, and blogs have definitely helped the way female drummers are perceived. "The more images the mainstream sees of women at drum kits, the less threatening they will be."

She said society traditionally doesn't encourage women to be loud, primitive, or aggressive. "These properties are crucial in the drummer's world—they cannot and should not be avoided."

In *Tom Tom*, she recalled the extensive media coverage given Sleater-Kinney. "We were very careful about how we were photographed—we made sure we weren't portrayed as weak or helpless because we weren't. We never liked sitting down in photos or looking passive. Photographers often wanted us to be playful and sweet and to style us in clothes that weren't ours like we were dolls. I'm not sure guy bands get that same kind of treatment. We wanted to look like the Stones, to be cool, to be tough, to be heroes. Why don't women get to be heroes?"

Drummers such as Weiss, Karen Carpenter, Sheila E., Cindy Blackman, Terri Lyne Carrington, Gina Schock, Dottie Dodgion, Pauline Braddy, and countless others have earned their hero status. They are role models for a younger generation, which someday may prove Kurt Cobain's prophecy true: "The future of rock belongs to women." To that add women drummers. They've already proven what pioneer drummer Viola Smith so eloquently stated in that *Down Beat* editorial many years ago: "Hep girls can sit in any jam session and hold their own!"

Appendix

SELECTED DISCOGRAPHY, VIDEO LINKS, AND ONLINE RESOURCES

The following lists are not in any way meant to be complete or comprehensive. They are also not to be construed as "best of the best." They are provided only as a starting point for the reader's further exploration.

Recordings

Bobbye Hall, *Body Language for Lovers*
20th Century Records, 1977
Many deplore the fact that this experimental foray into funk and jazz never made it to CD. Hall co-wrote all but two of the songs and shows off her drumming chops on every track.

Terri Lyne Carrington, *The Mosaic Project*
Concord Jazz, 2011
Carrington, in collaboration with some celebrated female artists, creates some imaginative improvisation on this risk-taking album that is sure to be loved by anyone who likes their jazz flavored with a big dose of R&B.

Sheila E., *The Glamorous Life*
Warner Brothers, 1984
This is the Prince-produced album that established Sheila E. as a legitimate artist in her own right. It is considered an essential recording of 1980s funk rock.

Cindy Blackman, *Music for the New Millennium*
Khepera, 2013
This double-disc collection is Blackman's first outing on her own and shows off her technical proficiency as one of the best female drummers today. Listeners will find it edgy but accessible.

Gina Schock, *House of Schock*
Capital, 1988
Schock was the last of the three Go-Go's to release a solo album, but she makes it clear here that she is definitely the top rocker in the group.

Liver Favela, *BIRTHA*
See for Miles UK, 1997
Critics still rave about this album by a band that many say was ahead of its time, and drummer/vocalist Favela shines as its bad-ass, hard rocking star.

Alice de Buhr, Fanny, *Charity Ball*
Reprise, 1971
De Buhr and her Fanny bandmates do their thing in this piece of rock 'n' roll history. The recording features great ensemble playing with de Buhr holding forth as anchor.

Allison Miller, *Boom Tic Boom No Morphine No Lilies*
The Royal Potato Family, 2013
Miller's drumming is the highlight of this adventuresome jazz recording—full of speed and energy.

Sherrie Maricle, Diva Jazz Orchestra, *Johnny Mandel: The Man and His Music*
Arbors Records, 2011
Maricle is a wonder not only as drummer but as an arranger and bandleader. Imagine what historic big bands of the past would be doing if they were performing today.

Nancy Given Prout, *Wild Rose: Breaking New Ground*
Prout demonstrates what a great country drummer can do in this recording, one of three made by the group, which, alas, no longer exists. Though critically acclaimed, they never sold many records.

Stefanie Eulinberg, Kid Rock, *Devil Without a Cause*
Lava, 1998
Eulinberg's considerable chops are much in evidence in this recording that's considered a rap-rock masterpiece.

Kopana Terry, *Stealin' Horses*
BMG Music, 1989
Terry's drumming and Kiya Heartwood's songwriting skills played major roles in making this a collector's item for those seeking musical gems from the '80s.

Video Links

Viola Smith/Frances Carroll and the Coquettes: http://www.youtube.com/watch?v=OW2S9gFOVV0

Honey Lantree/The Honeycombs "Have I the Right": http://www.youtube.com/watch?v=D3lbIpJxJS4

Gina Schock/The Go-Go's "We Got the Beat": http://www.youtube.com/watch?v=TiCwIPGkTy4

Ginger Bianco/Goldie and the Gingerbreads: http://www.youtube.com/watch?v=lsoXZMuoUp4

Karen Carpenter: http://www.youtube.com/watch?v=1f7qtpuMR5s

Cindy Blackman/Drummersfestival 2009: http://www.youtube.com/watch?v=uf-v5vT-UmE

Janet Weiss and Sara Lund Drum Battle/*Tom Tom* magazine: http://www.youtube.com/watch?v=7YkpRP3fCLU

Sherrie Maricle/The Diva Jazz Orchestra: http://www.youtube.com/watch?v=2QoEPTiKchg&feature=c4-overview-vl&list=PL1C516488940D4D69

Terri Lyne Carrington/Tribute to Roy Haynes Part 1: http://www.youtube.com/watch?v=JdD3Bqr8e78

Meg White/The White Stripes "Little Cream Soda": http://www.youtube.com/watch?v=SicUcvP_P7k

Emmanuelle Caplette Drum Solo: http://www.youtube.com/watch?v=U52ezW-E5p8

Hannah Ford Drum Solo: http://www.youtube.com/watch?v=WvdiJYGf2JU

Dottie Dodgion "This Is Always": http://www.youtube.com/watch?v=mQ0cBG9y_5g

Vera Figueiredo: http://www.youtube.com/watch?v=yRDQi-b5TqY

Online Resources

http://tomtommag.com/
http://femaledrummernewsletter.blogspot.com/
http://www.drummagazine.com/
http://drummerworld.com/
http://www.moderndrummer.com/
http://www.drummercafe.com/
http://drumchattr.com/

Bibliography

Abeles, Harold F., and Porter, Susan Yank. "The Sex-Stereotyping of Musical Instruments," *Journal of Research in Music Education*, Summer 1978.

"Alice de Buhr: Iowa Rock 'n' Roll Music Association 2005 Hall of Fame Inductee." https://www.iowarocknroll.com/inductees/105/alice-debuhr

Allen, Fred. *Much Ado about Me*. New York: Amereon, 1956.

Amar, Erin. "Gina Schock of The Go-Go's: Lips Unsealed." http://www.rockerzine.com/index.php/2011/11/gina-schock-of-the-go-gos-lips-unsealed/

Amendola, Billy. "Caroline Corr of the Corrs." *Modern Drummer*, May 19, 2005.

Appelstein, Mike. "Interview; Moe Tucker of the Velvet Underground Sets the Record Straight." *Riverfront Times*, Oct. 18, 2010.

Aube, Meghan Georgina. "Women in Percussion: The Emergence of Women as Professional Percussionists in the United States, 1930-Present." DMA dissertation, University of Iowa, 2011.

The Bangles. http://www.thebangles.com/

Barbieri, Nick Gio. "Punky, Poppy Brewster: An Interview with Imperial Teens' Lynn Truell." *Austinist*, Mar. 8, 2012.

Barton, Geoff. "Cult Heroes No 28: Rock Goddess." *Classic Rock* Magazine, Sept. 3, 2010.

Barker, Danny. *Bourbon Street Black: The New Orleans Black Jazzman*. London: Oxford University Press, 1973.

Belloni, Alessandra. http://www.alessandrabelloni.com/

Berger, Melody. "Ms. Bobbye Hall." *Tom Tom* magazine, July 2013.

Bartus, Kristin. "Drumming's Leading Ladies." *DRUM!* April 2012.

———. "Marcie Chapa: She's Got the Touch." *DRUM!* February 2009.

Basedow, Neph. "14 Notable Female Rock Drummers." *Houston Press*, Nov. 17, 2011.

"A Benefit for Della Griffin." All About Jazz Publicity, Jan. 14, 2005.

Benson, Ivy. http://www.ivybenson-online.co.uk/

Bianco, Ginger. "Walk with the Drum." http://dramarockproductions.com/

Birtha. http://www.birtharocks.com/

Black, Carla DeSantis. http://carladesantisblack.com

"Black Women Drummers of the 1940s." dogpossum.org, March 2012.

Blackman Santana, Cindy. http://www.cindyblackmansantana.com/

Blaster, Johnny. "Poni Silver of The Ettes." *Ghettoblaster Magazine*, June 8, 2012.

Bocciardi, Paula. "Female Drummers." Reprinted from *DRUM!* magazine. http://lusciousjackson.net/articles/femaledrummers.html

Bodkin, Bill. "Pop-Break Live: The Black Angels." *Pop-Break*, April 25, 2011.

Bolden, Tonya. *Take Off: American All-Girl Bands During WWII.* New York: Alfred A. Knopf.

Bonham, Mick. *John Bonham: The Powerhouse Behind Led Zeppelin.* London: Southbank Publishing, 2005.

Bradley, Elaine. "Elaine Bradley of Neon Trees." *Modern Drummer*, July 22, 2010.

Brennan, Sandra. "About Wild Rose." http://www.cmt.com/artists/wild-rose-00/biography/

"Bricktops Play for Dance Tonight." *Indianapolis Evening Gazette*, Jan. 29, 1932.

Brightwell, Eric. "All Female Bands of the Early 20th Century." http://www.amoeba.com/blog/2012/03/eric-s-blog/all-female-bands-of-the-early-20th-century-happy-women-s-history-month-.html

Brown, Robbie. "Rocking Out, No Boys Allowed." *The New York Times*, July 13, 2012.

Budofsky, Adam, editor. *The Drummer: 100 Years of Rhythmic Power and Invention.* Cedar Grove: Modern Drummer Publications, 2010.

Burke, Timothy, and Kevin Burke. *Saturday Morning Fever: Growing Up with Cartoon Culture.* New York: St. Martin's Press, 1999.

"Butthole Surfers." http://www.lyricsfreak.com/b/butthole+surfers/biography.html

"BYT Interview: Janet Weiss." *Brightest Young Things*, Mar. 28, 2008.

"Carla Azar of Autolux." *Tom Tom* magazine, April 15, 2011.

"Kay Carlson Obituary." *Los Angeles Times*, May 1, 2010.

Carlyon, David. *Dan Rice: The Most Famous Man You've Never Heard Of.* New York: Public Affairs, 2001.

Carpenter, Susan. "Beyond Beer and Boys." *Los Angeles Times*, Nov. 11, 2004.

Carrington, Terri Lyn. http://terrilynecarrington.com/

———. "A View from My Side of the Drumset." *Percussive Notes*, 41, 2003.

Cartwright, Garth. "Sandy West: Drummer in Teenage Girl Rock Group Who Overcame the 'Bimbo' Tag to Lasting Effect." *The Guardian*, Oct. 24, 2006.

Cliff, Nigel. *The Shakespeare Riots: Revenge, Drama, and Death in Nineteenth Century America.* New York: Random House, 2007.

Cody, B. "Women's Work Week—Goldie, Carol, Margo and Ginger." *Funk or Die.* http://codyb3.blogspot.com/2011/02/womens-work-week-goldiecarol-margo-and.html

Cohen, Barbara A. "The Psychology of Ideal Body Image as an Oppressive Force in the Lives of Women." Article originally published in 1984.

"Meytal Cohen Bio." http://www.meytalcohen.com/bio.html

Coleman-Dunham, Cora. Artist Page, Sabian Cymbals, http://www.sabian.com/en/artist/cora-coleman-dunham

Collins, Beverly C. "Viola Smith: High Heels & High Hats." *Not So Modern Drummer*, Summer 2002.

Copeland, Bill. "Chick Drummers: They Are Woman. Hear Them Pound." Bill Copeland Music News, July 18, 2011. http://www.billcopelandmusicnews.com/2011/07/chick-drummers-they-are-woman-hear-them-pound/

Corea, Juanita Parra. Mapex Drums Artist's Page. http://www.mapexdrums.com/artists/chile/bio_Correa.html

Cote, Teri. "Teri Cote Artist Biography." http://zildjian.com/Artists/C/Teri-Cote

Crawford, Sabrine. "Georgia Hubley is the Bashful Basher." *DRUM!* February 2001.

Dahl, Linda. *Stormy Weather: The Music and Lives of a Century of Jazzwomen*. New York: Pantheon Books, 1984.

Dale, Sharon. "The Kay Carlson Interview." http://www.noisytoys.com/interviews/Kay_sources/Kay_Carlson_01.html

"David Grohl Raves about Meg White's Drumming Style." *NME*, Jan. 28, 2013.

Dean, Matt. *The Drum: A History*. Lanham: The Scarecrow Press, Inc., 2012.

Dierking, Carol. "Music Bio." Facebook, Jan. 14, 2013.

———. "Syncopated Acts of Accomplishment." Facebook, Aug. 7, 2010.

"Estelle Mae Dilthy." http://familytreemaker.genealogy.com/users/s/i/m/Carol-Anne-Simmons/WEBSITE-0001/UHP-0002.html

Dolbear, Mike. "Female Drummers: Crissy Lee Interview." http://www.mikedolbear.com/story.asp?StoryID=2202

———. "Interview with Alicia Warrington." http://www.mikedolbear.com/story.asp?StoryID=2432

Doerschuk, Andy. "From the Archive: Dee Plakas of L7." *DRUM!*, March 1995.

———. "Meytal Cohen: Israeli Metalhead Invades Los Angeles, *DRUM!*, July 2011.

Dlugacz, Judy. "Olivia Back Then." olivia.com, Aug. 1, 2007.

Dougan, John. "The Clams: Artist Biography." http://www.allmusic.com/artist/the-clams-mn0001616296/biography

"Drummer Hits the Books." *Stanford Alumni Magazine*, March/April 2011.

"Drums in Country Music." http://www.thanksforthemusic.com/history/drums.html

"Johnnie Mae Dunson." Jazz Foundation of America. http://jazzfoundation.org/real-stories/johnnie-mae-dunson

"Earth's Drummer Adrienne Davies Interview on Tom Tom TV." Jan. 7, 2013. http://www.youtube.com/watch?v=HoaJVB0BsJI&feature=youtu.be

Eby, Margaret. "10 Badass Lady Drummers," Flavorwire.com, Feb. 15, 2011.

Edgeplay: A Film About the Runaways. DVD directed by Victory Tischler-Blue, 2004.

Elevate Hope Foundation. "Sheila's Story." http://www.elevatehope.org/sheilas-story/

"Ensembles." Women in Jazz. http://www.lib.odu.edu/exhibits/womenshistorymonth/2003/ensemble.htm

Enstice, Wayne, and Stockhouse, Janis. *Jazzwomen: Conversations with Twenty-One Musicians*. Bloomington: Indiana University Press, 2004.

Erlewine, Stephen Thomas. "The Go-Go's Biography." http://www.allmusic.com/artist/the-go-gos-mn0000766385

Eve, Deborah. "Lady Jazz! Drummer Jerrie Thill at Age 93." http://www.laterbloomer.com/jerrie-thill

"Ex Glamour Gal." *Down Beat*, May 1, 1940.

"Stefanie Eulinberg." http://www.geocities.ws/worlddrummers/stef.html

Eyler, David P. "Development of the Marimba Ensemble in North Amerca During the 30's." *Percussive Notes*, 34, 1996.

Falzerano, Chet. "Here's to Mary McClanahan." *DRUM!*, 2000.

"Fanny: The Godmothers of Chick Rock." http://fannyrocks.com/

"Fanny: Back to the Past." http://www.metalmaidens.com/fanny.htm

Figueiredo, Vera. http://www.verafigueiredo.com.br/

Fitzgerald, Britney. "Music Piracy: Moochers Are Also Big Spenders Within the Record Industry, Study Finds." *The Huffington Post*, Oct. 16, 2012.

Fogerty, Rod. "Karen Carpenter: A Drummer Who Sang." *Modern Drummer*, May 1983.

Foltz, Tanice G. "Contemporary Women Drummers and Social Action: Focus on Community Service." *The South Shore Journal*, 1, 2006: 56–68.

Ford, Hannah. http://www.hannahforddrums.com/biography.html

Fossum, Bob. "Girls Shouldn't Play Too much Jazz, Says Ada." *Down Beat*, Dec. 1, 1942.

Freedman, Marvin. *Down Beat*, Feb. 1, 1941.

"From Cowboys' Sweethearts to Redneck Women on the Pill: Gender in Country Music History." http://www.shmoop.com/country-music-history/gender.html

Fuhre, Rachel. "Rachel Fuhrer: Artist Profile." Gretsch Drums. http://www.gretsch-drums.com/?fa=artistdetail&id=1187

Gaar, Gillian. "Women's Rock Zine Marks 10th Year." *The Seattle Times*, Jan. 12, 2005.

Gallay, Caroline. "Houston-bred Psychedelic Rocker Goes Mainstream on *Twilight* Soundtrack." Culture Map Houston, June 16, 2011.

Gelt, Jason. "Rockin' Women of the '70s: 10 Songs to Belatedly Celebrate International Women's Day." Examiner.com, Mar. 10, 2009.

Gilbert, Peggy. "How Can You Blow a Horn With A Brassiere?" *Down Beat*, April 1938.

Gioia, Ted. *The History of Jazz*. New York: Oxford University Press, 2011.

Girls Rock! DVD directed by Arne Johnson, 2007.

Girls Rock Camp Alliance. http://girlsrockcampalliance.org/

Glaspie, Nikki. "Nikki Glaspie." *Drummerworld*. http://www.drummerworld.com/drummers/Nikki_Glaspie.html

———. http://www.nikkiglaspie.com

Glass, Daniel. *The Ultimate History of Rock 'n' Roll Drumming 1948–2000*. Los Angeles: Self-published, 2005.

Glennie, Evelyn. http://www.evelyn.co.uk/

"Go Betty Go: Interview." The Cover Zone. http://www.thecoverzone.com/RantsNRaves/GBG.html

Goodman, Abbey. "Luscious Jackson on Reuniting." CNN, Mar. 27, 2012.

The Go-Go's. http://www.gogos.com/

Gourley, Catherine. *Rosie and Mrs. America: Perceptions of Women in the 1930s and 1940s*. Minneapolis: Twenty-First Century Books, 2007.

Grierson, Tim. "What is Rock Music?" http://rock.about.com/od/rockmusic101/a/RockHistory.htm

Half Japanese: The Band That Would Be King. DVD directed by Jeff Feuerzieg, 1993.
Hall, Shaunna. "4 Non Blondes 1989–1992." Electrofunkadelica. http://www.shaunnahall.com/4nb.html
Handy, Antoinette. *Black Women in American Bands and Orchestras* (2nd ed). Lanham MD: The Scarecrow Press, 1999.
———. *The International Sweethearts of Rhythm: The Ladies Jazz Band from Piney Woods Country Life School* (2nd ed). Lanham, MD: The Scarecrow Press, 1998.
Harabadian, Eric. "Sherrie Maricle." *Jazz Inside* magazine, October 2012.
Hawley, David. "SPAM and Legs: Hormel Girls Danced, Sang, Sold." *Minnesota Post*, Nov. 13, 2007.
Hayden, Chance. "The Corrs Interviewed," *Steppin' Out* magazine, June 1999.
Hedges, Chris. "The Beat is From Mars and From Venus: Sherrie Maricle." *The New York Times*, Jan. 30, 2004.
Hit So Hard: The Life and Near Death Story of Patty Schemel. DVD directed by David Ebersole, 2011.
The Honeycombs Biography. http://www.allmusic.com/artist/the-honeycombs
Honeycombs Fan Site. http://www.thehoneycombs.info/
Huet, Timothy. "Têtes Noires Will Turn Heads," *The Michigan Daily*, Sept. 30, 1987.
Hunt, Donna. "U.S. Army Honors Denison Women." *Denison Herald-Democrat*, Mar. 18, 2007.
Hyman, Dick. "A Long Way Baby!" Riverwalk Jazz. http://riverwalkjazz.org/a-long-way-baby-by-dick-hyman/
Ibarra, Suzie. http://www.susieibarra.com/
Iknadossian, Armine. "Leah Shapiro." *Modern Drummer*, June 1, 2013.
"Ina Ray Hutton." http://www.collateralworks.com/linernotes/inarayhutton.html
Infantry, Ashante. "Cindy Blackman's Got the Beat." *Toronto Star*, June 7, 2008.
"Interview with a Drummer: Stella Mozgawa." *Flab* magazine, April 15, 2013.
Invisible Oranges Editor. "Interview with Adrienne Davies," *Invisible Oranges*, April 29, 2011.
"It's a Lot of Noise Shippin Point Says: All Women Drum and Bugle Corps, Seeking Legion Title, Arouses Community Ire." *New York Times*, Aug. 24, 1947.
"The Jazz Age." http://www.historylearningsite.co.uk/1920s_America.htm
Jazz: A Film by Ken Burns. DVD Ken Burns, producer, 2001.
"Jazz and Gender Equality Trumpeting Women Instrumentalists." http://www.wikigender.org/index.php/Jazz_and_Gender_Equality:_Trumpeting_Women_Instrumentalists
Jelone, Jelone. "The Slits." http://www.punknews.org/review/11369/the-slits-cut
Jenson, Sally M. "Diana Rene/Shuffle Queen/Blues Drummer/Bio." ReverbNation. http://www.reverbnation.com/artist_1090097/bio
Jensen, Trevor. "Johnnie Mae Dunson: 1921-2007." *Chicago Tribune*, Oct. 7, 2007.
"Hilary Jones." drummercafe.com, March 25, 2013.
Jones, Jenny. http://www.jennyjones.com/
Jones, Mia. "Kate Schellenbach on the Return of Luscious Jackson, Working on 'The Ellen Show' and Being Out in the '90s." AfterEllen, Mar. 27, 2012.
Jones, Peter. "Of Course Honey Played On Our Disc." *Record Mirror*, Oct. 17, 1965.

"Josie and the Pussycats Biography." http://www.sing365.com/music/lyric.nsf/Josie-and-the-Pussycats-Biography/C93DD6F108224AC348256A2900062256

Kearns, Kevin. "Athena Kottak." *Modern Drummer*, Dec. 1, 2006.

Kenrick, John. "A History of the Musical Minstrel Shows." Musicals101.com, 2003.

Kid Rock. http://www.kidrock.com/forum/stefanie-eulinberg-0

Kindelan, Kate. "Grandma Drummer Drums Her Way Into Internet Stardom." ABC News, July 22, 2013.

Kissel, Bud "Ada Leonard: Variety Makes Good Stage Show at Palace." *Columbus Citizen*, Aug. 2, 1944.

"Klymaxx: Biography. http://www.lyricsfreak.com/k/klymaxx/biography.html

"Klymaxx Presents Bernadette Cooper." http://www.bbkingblues.com/bio.php?id=2718

Kopp, Ed. "A Brief History of the Blues," All About Jazz, Aug. 16, 2005.

"The Ladies of Jazz, Swing—And Beyond." http://www.ou.edu/cls/online/lstd4700jaz/pdf/ladies.pdf

Lander, Mercedes. http://zildjian.com/Artists/L/Mercedes-Lander

Lane, Joslyn. "Susie Ibarra: Biography." http://www.allmusic.com/artist/susie-ibarra-mn0000755956

Latrobe, Benjamin Henry. *The Journal of Latrobe*. New York: Appleton & Co., 1905.

"A Legend in the Making; Drummer Frankie Rose of Crystal Stilts." *Tom Tom* magazine, Aug. 3, 2009.

Ledger, Jen. http://www.skilletfan.com/biography/jen-ledger

Lee, Crissy. http://www.crissylee.co.uk/home/default.asp

Lemire, Jonathan. "Fire Leaves Jazz Great with a House of Blues," *New York Daily News*, Dec. 26, 2004.

Leonard, Ada. "Ada Leonard and Her All-American Girl Orchestra." Old Magazine Articles.com, *Yank Magazine*, 1943.

Losey, Stephen Douglas. "Jen Ledger," *Modern Drummer*, Dec. 1, 2011.

Long, Jen. "Four People, Playing Together, Simplicity: The Line of Best Fit Meets Wild Flag." *Best Fit*, Feb. 17, 2012.

Longrigg, Clare. "Not Bad—For A Girl." *The Guardian*, Jan. 29, 2004.

Lovell, Veronica. "Farsley Historian Launches Appeal About Pioneer of Girl Power," *Yorkshire Evening Post*, Nov. 4, 2008.

Lund, Sara. "The Corin Tucker Band's Sara Lund." *Modern Drummer*, Sept. 2010.

"Luscious Jackson's Kate Schellenbach." *DRUM!* June 1999.

Maloney, Samantha. http://www.samanthamaloney.com/

Mandrell, Irlene. http://irlenemandrell.com/

Maricle, Sherrie. http://www.divajazz.com/sherrie.html

Marcus, Sarah. *Girls to the Front: The True Story of the Riot Grrrl Revolution*. New York: Harper Perennial, 2010.

Mayhew Bergman, Megan. "The International Sweethearts of Rhythm." *Oxford American*, 75, Nov. 21, 2011.

Matzner, Franz A. "Allison Miller: Breaking Ground." All About Jazz, May 17, 2010.

Mazur, Marilyn. http://www.marilynmazur.com/

McCue, Radim. "Roxy Petrucci is Still Revvin' It Up." *DRUM!*, October 2009.

McDonald, Linda Bio. Phantom Blue. http://www.phantomblue.com/linda.htm

McEwen, Lauren. "Sheila E., An Inspiration to Drummers of All Ages and Genders." *Washington Post*, May 17, 2013.

McGee, Kristen A. *Some Liked It Hot: Jazz Women in Film and Television, 1928–1959*. Middletown: Wesleyan University Press, 2009.

MEOW. http://meowonline.org/about/

Messina, Jessica. "Three Minutes With . . . Athena Lee." TheyWillRockYou.com, Aug. 30, 2011.

Miller, Allison. http://www.allisonmiller.com

"Minstrel Show." http://www.britannica.com/EBchecked/topic/384587/minstrel-show

Mitchell, Claudia, and Reid-Walsh, Jacqueline, editors. *Girl Culture*. Santa Barbara: ABC-CLIO, 2008.

Moayeri, Lily. "On the Line with . . . Black Rebel Motorcycle Club's Leah Shapiro." Boxx News, March 22, 2013.

"Molly Neuman." http://www.punkrockacademy.com/stm/int/mn.html

Mori, Ikue. http://www.ikuemori.com/

Mozgowa, Stella. "Stella Mozgowa; Artist Biography." http://zildjian.com/Artists/M/Stella-Mozgawa

Mrs. Ahab. "Birtha." http://www.headheritage.co.uk/unsung/reviewer/4828

"MTV Launches." This Day in History, History.com. http://www.history.com/this-day-in-history/mtv-launches

Mudge, William. *The Tabernacle of Moses*. Whitefish, MT: Kessinger Publishing, 2010.

Mulholland, Liam. "Stephanie Eulinberg: Rockin' Kid Rock." *DRUM!*, September 1999.

"The Music Staff: Kopana Terry." Off the Shelf, University of Kentucky Libraries, Oct. 13, 2011.

New York Times staff, editors. *New York Times Television Reviews 2000*. Abingdon: Taylor and Francis, 2007.

"No Glamor in Soldier Shows." *Yank*, Sept. 10, 1943.

Norris, John. "Frankie Rose Is Center Stage." http://www.interviewmagazine.com/music/frankie-rose-and-the-outs#_

O'Brien, Lucy. *She Bop: The Definitive History of Women in Rock, Pop & Soul*. New York: Penguin, 1995.

"Pagan Religion: Drums in Pagan Worship." http://www.all-about-drum-set-drumming.com/pagan-religion.html

Palmolive. http://palmolive2day.com/index.html

Pandey, Swati. "The History Page: Spam, Spam, Spam, Spam: The Hormel Girls Sell America's Mystery Meat with a Smile." *The Daily*, Nov. 6, 2011.

Parks, John. "Athena (Lee) Author, Drummer of Krunk, and TV Star Talks About Her Show, Her Childhood and Her Family." Legendary Rock Interviews.com, Nov. 22, 2011.

Patterson, Sonja. "No Man's Band," *Bust*, April/May 2013.

Pearson, Sheelagh. "A Modernist at Heart." http://jazzpro.nationaljazzarchive.org.uk/profiles/SheelaghPearson.htm

Pendle, Karin, editor. *Women & Music: A History, Second Edition*. Bloomington: Indiana University Press, 2001.

Pendrak, Stephen B. "An Abridged History of Blues." http://morozshs11ap.weebly.com/uploads/1/0/5/5/10558090/blues.pdf

Peters, David. "Girl Drummers." *Long to Share*, August 2013.

"Peterson, Debbi Biography." imdb.com, http://www.imdb.com/name/nm0677106/bio

"Percussion Family." http://www.music.iastate.edu/antiqua/percuss.htm

Petrucci, Roxy. http://www.roxypetrucci.com/

Phillips, Edie. "The Women's Liberation Movement." http://ideaofdemocracy.homestead.com/20120501.html

Placksin, Sally. *American Women in Jazz: 1900 to the Present.* New York: Wideview Books, 1982.

———. "The Ladies of Jazz, Swing . . . and Beyond." http://www.ou.edu/cls/online/lstd4700jaz/pdf/ladies.pdf

Pleasure Seekers. http://www.60sgaragebands.com/pleasureseekers.html

"Poni of The Ettes," *Tom Tom* magazine, Feb. 10, 2012.

"Poni Silver of The Ettes." *Ghettoblaster*, June 2012.

Powell, Austin. "Out of the Mouths of Children: The Improbable Return of the Butthole Surfers." *Austin Chronicle*, Sept. 26, 2008.

"Precious Metal: Chasing That Rainbow." http://aordreamer.com/show_bios.php?artist_id=570

"Precious Metal." Metaladies—All Female Metal Bands. http://www.metaladies.com/bands/precious-metal/

Prince Vault. Prince Website. http://www.princevault.com

"PV Co-Eds Keep Music Alive While Boys Battle Axis." *Pittsburgh Courier*, Mar. 11, 1944.

Redmond, Layne. *When the Drummers Were Women: A Spiritual History of Rhythm.* New York: Three Rivers Press, 1997.

Reeves, James A. "Ragtime Terror," Big American Night. http://bigamericannight.com/ragtime-terror/

Reich, Howard. "Mother of the Blues." *Chicago Tribune*, June 10, 2005.

Richardson, Dawn. http://www.dawnrichardson.com/

———. "Dawn Richardson Artist Biography." Zildjian Artist Page, http://zildjian.com/Artists/R/Dawn-Richardson

Rivas, Jorge. "But What About Beyoncé's Band?" *Colorlines*, Feb. 4, 2013.

"Rock for Choice." http://www.feminist.org/rock4c/

Rock Czar. "Top 100 Female Sung Songs of the 90s." http://www.therockczar.com/by-year/blog/page-5

Roland Team. "Jody Linscott (The Who, Paul McCartney, Jay-Z, Santana)." Roland UK Blog, May 21, 2009.

Rose, Frankie Bio. http://www.last.fm/music/Frankie+Rose

Runaways. http://therunaways.com/

Sandlin, Michael. "Moe's Bio." http://archive.is/NaPHC

Santelli, Robert. *The Big Book of Blues*. New York; Penquin Books, 2001.

Scaruffi, Piero. *A History of Jazz Music 1900-2000.* Self-published, 2003.

———. A *History of Rock and Dance Music.* Self-published, 2005.

Schellenbach, Kate. http://www.beastiemania.com/whois/schellenbach_kate/

Schmidt, Randy L. *Little Girl Blue: The Life of Karen Carpenter*. Chicago: Chicago Review Press, 2010.

"Shauney Baby." TAMA Drums Artist Page. http://www.tamadrum.co.jp/artist/tama_interview.php?interview_id=2

Sheila E. http://www.sheilae.com/

"Sheila E. Bio." The E Family. http://the-e-family.com/mds/bios/sheila-e

Schonberg, Lisa. "One Drummer One Question: Janet Weiss." *Tom Tom* magazine, Nov. 2009.

"Shonen Knife—Bio." https://myspace.com/shonenknife/bio

Shuster, Fred. "How Jody Linscott Lucked Into Drumming." *Los Angeles Daily News*, Nov 24, 1994.

Signore, John Del. "Janet Weiss, Drummer." http://gothamist.com/2008/07/17/janet_weiss_drummer_jicks_quasi_sle.php

Simon, George T. *The Big Bands*. London: McMillan, 1967.

Sleater-Kinney. http://www.sleater-kinney.com/

Smith, Bill, editor. *The Vaudevillians*. New York: MacMillan Publishing, 1976.

Smith, Dinitia. "When Women Called the Tunes: Rediscovering the Players Who Kept Things Swinging After the Men Went to War." *The New York Times*, Aug. 10, 2000.

Smith, Viola. "Give Girl Musicians a Break," *Down Beat*, February 1942.

So, Adrienne. "Interview with Mindy Abovitz." *Culture*, Jan. 20, 2010.

Sobel, Bernard. *A Pictorial History of Burlesque*. New York: Putnam, 1956,

Sounes, Howard. *Down the Highway: The Life of Bob Dylan*. New York: Grove Press, 2011.

"SPIN Magazine: Imperial Teen's Lynn Perko-Truell Named Top 100 Greatest Drummers of Alternative Music," imperialteen.com

"Spotlight on Alicia Warrington." *Tom Tom* magazine, May 22, 2012.

Stanley, Bob. "Ina Ray Hutton: The Forgotten Female Star of 1930s Jazz." *The Guardian*, July 7, 2011.

Stapinski, Helene. *Baby Plays Around: A Love Affair with Music*. New York: Villard Books, 2004

Stermin,, Pamela. "Interview with Bikini Kill's Tobi Vail." *Seattle Passive Aggressive Magazine*, Nov. 8, 2012

Steven-Taylor, Allison, *Rock Chicks: The Hottest Female Rockers from the 1960s to Now*. Sydney: Rockpool Publishing, 2007.

Stone, George Lawrence. "For Ladies Only." *Jacobs Orchestra Monthly*, 8, 1923.

"The Story of Yo: The Oral History of the Beastie Boys." *Spin*, September 1998.

"The Storytelling Drum: Teaching a Brief History of the Drum in Judaeo-Christian Contexts." Feb. 24, 2009, accessed Oct. 8, 2012. http://drummingforpeace.blogspot.com/2009/02/storytelling-drum-teaching-brief.html

Strohm, Adam. "Zena Parkins and Ikue Mori: Phantom Orchard," *Dusted*, Oct. 20, 2004.

Sullivan, Jill and Keck, Daniel. "The Hormel Girls." http://www.public.asu.edu/~jmsulli/documents/FINAL_Hormel%20Girls.pdf

Sutherland, William. "Della Griffin: Jazz and R&B Pioneer." http://ezinearticles.com/?Della-Griffin:—Jazz-and-RandB-Pioneer-(Part- 1)&id=274148

Swensson, Andrea. "Meet Têtes Noires and the Clams, Two of Minneapolis's First All-Female Rock Bands." Minnesota Public Radio, Mar. 10, 2013.

Thill, Jerri. http://www.jerriethill.com/

Thompson, H.O. "Woman Who Was Drummer Boy in the Civil War Kept It Secret for Sixty-Three Years." *Mansfield News*, Aug. 19, 1922

Thompson, Kim. http://www.kimthompson.net/bio.html

Thornton, Willie Mae "Big Mama." Encyclopedia of Alabama, http://www.encyclopediaofalabama.org/face/Article.jsp?id=h-1573

Tillery, Linda. http://www.lindatillery.com/

Tiny and Ruby: Hell Divin' Women. DVD directed by Greta Schiller and Andrea Weiss. Jezebel Productions, 1989.

Toll, Robert C. *Blacking Up: The Minstrel Show in Nineteenth Century America*. New York: Oxford University Press, 1974.

"Top 7 Female Drummers of All Time." http://afunda.hubpages.com/hub/Top-10-female-drummers

Treppel, Jeff. "The Lazarus Pit; Rock Goddess's Rock Goddess," *Decibel*, Aug. 3, 2012.

Tucker, Maureen. Velvet Underground Official Site. http://www.thevelvetunderground.co.uk/

Tucker, Sherrie. *Swing Shift: "All-Girl" Bands of the 1940s*. Durham: Duke University Press, 2000.

———. "Rocking the Cradle of Jazz." Ms. Magazine, Winter 2004.

Vail, Tobi. *Jigsaw*, 2, 1990.

Van Poorten, Toine. "Back to the Past: Rock Goddess." metalmaidens.com. http://www.metalmaidens.com/rgoddess.htm

Vargas, Andrew. "Cindy Blackman: Jazz Backhand." *Drumhead*. http://www.drumheadmag.com/web/feature.php?id=6

Valentino, Bianca. "Molly Neuman—The Collapse Board Interview." July 7, 2011.

"Vaudeville: A History." http://xroads.virginia.edu/~ma02/easton/vaudeville/vaudevillemain.html

Warrington, Alicia. "Spotlight on Alicia Warrington." *Tom Tom*. http://tomtommag.com/tag/alicia-warrington/

Waldo the Squid. "Emmanuelle Caplette." *DRUM!*, September 2009.

———. "Rachel Fuhrer: A Combo of Bashing & Brains." *DRUM!*, January 2012.

Walsh, Jim. "R.I.P. Runaways Drummer Sandy West," *Minneapolis City Pages*, Oct. 22, 2006.

Ward, Geoffrey, and Ken Burns. *Jazz: A History of America's Music*. New York: Alfred A. Knopf, 2000.

"Wednesday Week." MTV.com. http://www.mtv.com/artists/wednesday-week/biography/

Weiss, Lauren Vogel. "Evelyn Glennie." Percussive Arts Society Hall of Fame. http://www.pas.org/experience/halloffame/GlennieEvelyn.aspx

White, Jack. "Jack White Interviews Carla Azar." *Tom Tom* magazine, Jan. 11, 2013.

White, Meg. http://megwhite.com/

White Stripes. http://www.whitestripes.net/band-info.php

"Why Women Musicians Are Inferior." *Down Beat,* February 1938.

Widner, Cindy. "Terri Lord: Austin Music Hall of Fame Drummer." *Tom Tom* magazine, February 20, 2010.

Wizard of Roz. "Classic Reviews." Female Drummer Newsletter. http://femaledrummernewsletter.blogspot.com/p/classic-review

"Women and Drumming." http://blog.x8drums.com/2011/02/women-and-drumming.htm

"Women Who Rock Resources." Rock and Roll Hall of Fame. http://rockhall.com/education/resources/women-rock-resources/

Worley, Gail. "She's Got the Beat: An Interview with Go-Go's Drummer Gina Schock." *Ink 19,* June 2002.

Yael. "Drum Addict," *Modern Drummer,* Dec. 7, 2009.

———. "The Love Project." Drum Addict. http://www.drumaddict.net/

Ya'el: Vic Firth Artist. http://www.vicfirth.com/artists/yael.php

Yates, Jyn. http://www.jynyates.com/

"Yo La Tengo's Georgia (Hubley) and Rachel (Blumberg) Drummer 2 Drummer." *Tom Tom* magazine, May 30, 2012.

Ziegler, Sonya. "Jyn Yates." http://www.jynyates.com/Biography.html.

Index

About the Author

Angela Smith is a freelance writer and executive director emeritus of the Writers' League of Texas. She is the author of the award-winning *Steel Drums and Steelbands: A History* (2012, Scarecrow Press). A former reporter for the Associated Press, she is also a working musician who plays cello, piano, and steel drum. This avid amateur astronomer and news junkie is also a political activist and advocate for women's rights.